Very Ordinary Officer

The social and naval story of a
Yorkshire-born Australian

called

Geoff Feasey

Very Ordinary Officer:
The social and naval story of a Yorkshire-born
Australian.

Published in Australia 1999 by Geoff Feasey
4 Yampi Place, Fisher, ACT 2611.

ISBN 0-646-36815-X

Copyright Geoff Feasey 1999.

The right of Geoff Feasey to be identified as the author of this work is asserted in accordance with the UK Copyright, Designs and Patents Act 1988.

All rights reserved. This book is sold subject to the condition that it shall not be lent, sold, hired out or otherwise circulated by way of trade or otherwise without the publisher's prior consent.

The author does not know who took some of the old black and white photographs and regrets he is therefore unable to acknowledge their work.

The 1967 oil painting reproduced on the cover shows the author much burnished by some months in the Caribbean. It was the work of Mrs Marian Melim whose talents were recognised by the Royal Society of Portrait Painters when she lived in London with her submariner husband Commander Bob Melim USN.

Contents

Chapter		Page
	Foreword	
	Author's Note	
1	Beginning and End	1
2	Early Years	6
3	Evacuation	24
4	In Time for the Bombing	31
5	Rites of Passage Years	49
6	I Joined the Navy	66
7	'Snottie'	82
8	College	93
9	Back to Sea	106
10	Getting Started	115
11	The Real Thing	129
12	One Job in a Submarine	143
13	A Soft Patch	163
14	Damn the Torpedoes	172
15	Some Real Work	188
16	Third Division North Again	206
17	'Greenie'	221
18	Training and Torpedoes	242
19	Bottom-up Study	255
20	Plans and Administration in Malta	261
21	Dead Centre and Dead End	280
22	A New Beginning	296
23	Sittin' and Thinkin'	317

Foreword

As the widow of a Royal Navy Officer who started his career as a Dartmouth Cadet at thirteen and finished as an Admiral of the Fleet and Chief of the Defence Staff, I was honoured to be asked by the author to write a foreword to his book. I served as a post-war WRNS officer, during which time I met my husband. Our long association with the Royal Navy ensured my considerable interest in this book, "Very Ordinary Officer".

I found it was a book of the "can't put it down" variety. I especially enjoyed the story of his early life in Hull, evacuation and the bombing. Determined to be classified as "working class", he wrote, "How little the officers who had taught me the ways of the Navy knew about working class life" and I realised how much the Navy has changed over the years to the present day when I honestly believe that class does not come into the equation. Also, the behaviour of senior officers and their wives towards junior officers and their wives has certainly changed today. When my husband was Chief of the Defence Staff and we lived in some grandeur in the RN College, Greenwich, we used to have supper in the pub with our retinue staff, which was hugely enjoyed by us all!

I was also interested, and surprised, to read of the training and experience in a wide range of disciplines, shore establishments and ships that junior officers underwent in the fifties and sixties. They worked enormously hard, but sadly, could not afford to play equally hard! Though having said that, the social life they all enjoyed seemed tremendous.

Of particular interest to me was the Geoff and Lise's sojourn in Faslane, the "Third Squadron North", as my husband *was the second Captain of HMS Dreadnought, and then Captain S/M 10 of the Polaris Squadron. So I know well the way of life there. I was struck by the number of moves and different accommodation they had, and the good tempered acceptance which they displayed. No "counselling for stress" in those days, just the desire and ability to get on with things.*

I wonder, when his old shipmates read this book, as I hope they will, if they will recognise themselves; the Chief Electrical Artificer called by Lt Cdr Feasey "a cantankerous old sod". That had obviously been the Chief's life's ambition.

The contrast between seagoing then and now were made clear when Geoff's ship, HMS Zest, was sent to do an eight-month commission, unaccompanied, in the West Indies. This rarely, if ever, happens today. Have we become softer in our approach? Today's wives expect to fly out to spend some time with their husbands if they are abroad for any time at all, and of course, pay is so much better, which makes it possible.

The stories of Malta, under the dreaded Dom Mintoff, and Geoff's subsequent approach to leave the RN and join the RAN were fascinating. I know that he made the same impact on the Royal Australian Navy that he did on the Royal Navy, and is now, of course, happily settled in Canberra with his lovely wife, Lise.

I believe that the Royal Navy that Geoff knew and so obviously loved is still the Royal Navy of today, warts and all. This book gives us a marvellous insight into the life of, in my opinion, a very "UN-ordinary officer", in the difficult and trying circumstances of the immediately post-war days. I enjoyed it enormously and I wish it, Geoff and Lise every success.

Midge Lady Fieldhouse

Author's Note

It was a long trail from boyhood as a tram conductor's son in the East Yorkshire city of Hull during the nineteen thirties to the life my wife Lise and I are lucky enough to enjoy in Canberra, the capital of our new country, Australia. Unlike J P W Mallalieu who served in the Royal Navy as a 'Very Ordinary Seaman' during World War 2 and became the First Lord of the Admiralty in a post war government, I began as a 'Very Ordinary Officer' in the post-war navy and remained very ordinary. Nevertheless, the current fashion in history encourages the recording of everyman's contributions to complement those of the good and the great. Hence this book, the story of my trail.

Leslie Thomas's Sergeant Morris defined being old as, 'When you can say what you mean. Do what you like'. It is true within limits but there is no point in saying things which offend people who, I hope, are still alive, so I have usually used full names only for public figures. Ordinary mortals are called by their first names, a familiar practice in the Australian way of life. I have used the Imperial measures which were in use during most of the period of the book. Initials are impossible to avoid in any book involving Service matters and I have followed the journalists' practice of using abbreviations and acronyms shortly after the words for which they stand have been written in full.

The heart of Sergeant Morris' definition is that 'old' is being able to record events without worrying about anyone's reactions. It no longer matters if anyone thinks I must be 'as wet as a scrubber' to write such drivel, nor whether they think my prose pedestrian. I haven't time to develop a better style. My approach has therefore been to write down what would normally be oral *history, imagining that I am trying to divert the members of the Probus Club of Canberra, keen students all of the trivia of history, by some talks. That I cannot reproduce the oral advantages of timing, tone and emphasis is a pity, but it cannot be helped. Except, that is, by punctuating the text to make it easy to read aloud, my favourite test of punctuation.*

I am grateful to all who have contributed to the book, refreshing my memories of past events, examining the drafts, writing the Foreword, advising on publication, and all the other things that had to be done. To my family whose recollections have supplemented my own, to so many friends old and new, to the kindly owners of places where Lise and I have lived, and to the many others who have helped and encouraged: thank you all.

And above all, thanks from Lise and I to all who have made the long trail of our forty six years together so enjoyable.

Geoff Feasey

Chapter 1

Beginning and End.

The Captain of the Royal Naval College Dartmouth inspected me, a nervous, newly joined, 17 year old 'Special Entry' cadet from a working class home, across what seemed a quarter of an acre of polished mahogany desk. He was a short man. This only enhanced his formidable presence for the four gold stripes stretched almost to his elbows. There were many reasons to be nervous. The naval world I had just entered was obviously very different to the one I had left. I had made a bad start, misunderstanding my joining instructions and arriving some days late wearing a uniform with the wrong colour of stripe indicating my membership, however junior, of the 'Purple Empire' of naval engineers. How was I or the merchant navy outfitters in my home town, Hull, to know that the Royal Navy meant mauve when they wrote purple?

The only part of that first interview that I remember is one question which puzzled and infuriated me: 'What does your father do?' The only part I enjoyed was observing a certain awkwardness on his part when I answered 'He's a tram conductor, Sir'. It seemed unlikely that he had ever met a tram conductor or the son of one before. In fact my father was now a trolley bus conductor, not a tram conductor but I knew that many people from other places didn't know what trolley buses were. I thought the Captain might be one of them.

Why was I puzzled and infuriated by the question? I knew little of the world outside working class circles in my home town, but I recognised a class-conscious question when I heard one. The year was 1948 and times were generally supposed to be changing. The people of Britain had made it very clear at the 1945 General Election that change was expected, and in the *intervening years the Daily Mirror had singled out the Royal Navy for special mention as a British institution that needed to ensure that its officer entrants were selected on merits other than birth and family influence.*

Even though some people still called the selection system through which I had joined the 'Public Schools' entry, I had survived odds of about fifty to one against success to get a cadetship and I therefore assumed the RN had changed its ways. So my immediate, angry reaction when asked about my father was to wonder what that had to do with my merits as a cadet. I should have known better, the Captain's question suggested that little had changed.

Had I possessed the self confidence of some of the public school entrants, I might have engaged the Captain in a discussion on the subject. But I remembered one of the many northcountry sayings, 'Least said, soonest mended'. I held my tongue. It had been my ambition to go to sea as an engineer since I was eleven or twelve. I lived in a Merchant Navy city. Since early childhood I had been conditioned to remember that Hull was then the third largest mercantile port in England. Yet some stubborn desire to swim against the stream made me want to join the Royal Navy. My education at the Riley High School, the secondary school component of the Hull Technical College, was well suited to a career in engineering but the teachers and headmaster regarded it as more suitable for entry at the artificer apprentice level. Pigheaded perhaps, I was determined to become an officer. I worked hard for my cadetship and I wasn't going to risk upsetting anyone by arguing at the first meeting with my first captain.

With hindsight, I should have been bolder, for I had unknowingly taken the first step towards allowing the navy to exert influence on me which stopped little short of brainwashing, and the confidence and determination which had enabled me to resist my headmaster's conviction that I would not get a cadetship began to be eroded. A process had begun. The Royal Navy, using the natural authority attributed to it by John Masters who, in 'Pilgrim Son', rated the navy as second only to the MCC in the hierarchy of British institutions qualified to confer the status of 'gentleman', was beginning to turn a narrowly educated tyke with a Yorkshire accent into a passable naval gentleman. The process made me feel an obligation to subordinate many of my own views to those of 'the Service' for many years.

It wasn't that the Royal Navy didn't have some excellent ways of doing things, ways based on sound principles of care and consideration, loyalty and responsibility. It did, and those teachings have been an enduring asset during a service career and were later proved to be equally applicable in civilian life in a completely different setting on the other side of the world. Rather, my concern is that we were taught that the navy way was the only correct way of doing anything, navy opinions and attitudes were the only ones worth having. That was not true and the narrowness of that thinking has played a large part in the genesis of this book in which I outline my reservations about and reactions to some of the navy's ways.

The most obvious example was the prejudice against the civilians who served the navy in the Admiralty and the Royal Dockyards. There was obviously much that was wrong with the organisation of the industrial staff in the dockyards, their adherence to outdated and restrictive work practices and lack of commitment have been well documented in fact and fiction from World War 2 onwards. But how could any civilians possibly match the dedication of officers who were taught to put the navy's priorities ahead of their families' concerns? Having had a provincial upbringing, a narrow technical education and having been taught to give unlimited loyalty to the navy, it took me some years to be comfortable with the other ways of doing things which I encountered, especially when working with civilian scientists and engineers on the navy's first nuclear submarine project, HMS Dreadnought.

It has long been understood that although every tale should have a beginning, a middle and an end, they need not necessarily be in that order. I'll take advantage of that freedom to jump the thirty one years that I served in the RN, the six in the Royal Australian Navy, and the seven as Chief Engineer at the Australian Commonwealth Government's Bureau of Mineral Resources, to quote from 'Vanguard to Trident, British Naval Policy since WW2' by Eric J Grove,

'(Secretary of State) Nott asked the three services for their ideas on their changing roles and functions so he could assign rational priorities between them. He found some difficulty, he said later, in getting satisfactory answers from the navy. As he put it on television in early 1986 ". . . and I tried and tried and tried to get rational analytical and coherent answers from the navy but normally failed to do so". To Nott it seemed that the navy itself was arguing more on grounds of sentiment than anything else, "The navy is the navy is the navy and you are a fool if you do not understand what it is for" '.

It seems to me that though the RN has changed in various ways since the late nineteen forties, the process continues to lag behind the changes in the political, social, technical, and economic realities. At the time of writing thirty six 'admirals various' are listed in 'The Broadsheet', the navy's publication for its retired officers. Given the nature of humankind, most are probably 'empire builders' by nature and thus unlikely to wish to expose the shortcomings of the Service's ways to scrutiny.

Experience suggests, though it does not seem to have been discussed in the textbooks, that although most managerial types, in the Services or elsewhere, are empire builders, about five percent are by nature, nurture or both, 'hatchet men', iconoclasts who feel compelled to analyse, criticise, and ever seek the shortcomings in the organisations they serve. I feel like that. It always seems more important to be worrying about what is wrong, to be identifying and sorting out the problems, than to be uncritically loyal, supportive and a subscriber to the trendy view that 'there are no problems, only opportunities'. I hope that while setting out my formation and experience for the benefit of my family and friends I can cast some light on the ways of the Navy as I perceived them from the late forties to the seventies..

Chapter 2

Early Years

Anyone with a British working class background is at a disadvantage when they attempt to describe their childhood and early years. When middle and upper class people are drafting the 'early years' sections of their biographies, they rely heavily on the relics stored in their family homes for the raw material from which their childhoods can be reconstructed. Attics yield clothes, schoolbooks, long forgotten toys, examination papers, early drawings and letters to stimulate the memory. Better still, parents may have had the resources, leisure, energy and desire to keep journals and diaries recording those early years.

The working class child had no such advantage in my early days. The houses were, and many still are, simply too small to store much. And in the case of the working class children of the 1930s, even if their parents had the will and sense of continuity which might have motivated them to keep records, few had pennies to spare for paper and pencils, few had time and energy to spare for writing. So for better or worse, memories, with all their defects, must serve to supplement the facts available from public records.

One of my greatest regrets is that I failed to get my father to talk about his early years before, during and immediately after the First World War. That is partly my motivation for attempting this record. Fortunately, one of my half-brothers, Clifford, seven years older, was able to fill some of the gaps. And thanks to the researches of Donald Ward Feesey, we know that my father, Edward, was the eleventh child of Thomas Feasey, a cabinet maker, and his wife Millicent Edgill. My parents' marriage certificate described my mother as Gladys Gwendoline Lockwood, 29, spinster daughter of John Lockwood, a watchman, when my parents married on 18 April 1927. And although they did not keep copies of their birth certificates, we know they were born on 23 March 1894 and 4 July 1896.

Work could rarely be found for so many children in the area where they were brought up, so my father emigrated, while still a teenager, to Canada. He worked as a lumberjack and on the Canadian Pacific Railway. His wonder at the size of Canada, seven days coast to coast by train in those days he used to tell us, never left him.

Apparently my father earned and saved enough money and satisfied some entry requirement for medical school, dubious though that may sound, given that there is no evidence of his having received much education in England. Be that as it may, several medical text books survived later adventures and, though hidden in a cupboard in my parents' bedroom, provided an illicit and very explicit contribution to my education.

During world war I, my father had to decide between joining the Canadian and the British forces. If he joined the Canadians he might not be sent to England and might not see his family again. So he enlisted in the British army and served as a private in the RAMC. At some stage he was gassed but recovered and became one of the many unemployed of the post war years. None of us learned more than that bare outline. My father shared in good measure the unwillingness of many of his contemporaries to talk about the war.

To return to Canada after leaving the British army was not a practical option. In 1917 father had married 17 year old Olive Hayton and my elder half-brother was born in 1918. His names were registered as Robert Raymond Ivan but he sometimes called himself Raymond Ivan Robert or Robert Ivan Raymond, another of life's little mysteries. Had my father joined the Canadian forces, he could have returned to Canada with his wife and would have been eligible for a grant of land. He was never a bitter man and I heard no word of regret for the choice he made but the possession of a small parcel of land became one of his *enduring ambitions. He achieved it and hoped to build the traditional 'cottage in the country' for his retirement. He didn't achieve that one. He sold his little block of land between Hull and Beverly to pay for my uniforms and other expenses when I joined the navy.*

He had an unusual approach to unemployment. He drew his dole and having equipped himself somehow with a bicycle with a big carrier basket at the front, bought fish at Hull's St Andrew's fish dock. He had an eye for a business opportunity. He might have made a few shillings profit hawking the fresh fish around the suburbs of Hull but instead he pedalled out to the farms in the Cottingham and Beverly areas. To use the modern expression, he had sussed out that the farmers and their wives liked fresh fish. But they had a problem. Farmers commissioned by their wives to buy fish when they went to market did tend to have a jar of ale or three before they remembered to buy fish and they were then an easy prey for traders wishing to dispose of their fastest decaying stock. My father found a ready market for his wares.

Eventually he had earned enough to buy a corner shop at 192 Thoresby Street in Hull, the sort made famous by Ronnie Barker and the team in the BBC television series 'Open All Hours'. The eye for a business opportunity was at work again. As the number indicates, Thoresby is a very long street, not a matter of great importance now that most people have cars, but when walking was the usual way of getting about it virtually conferred monopoly status on the corner shop at the bottom of the street. Furthermore, Thoresby Street led to other streets even further from the Beverly Road, and as gilding on the gingerbread of opportunity there was a large school just across the street and a laundry at the end.

Opportunity it certainly was but the living it brought was earned by very strenuous effort. Not only was the shop 'open all hours', but some stock had to be hauled from the suppliers on a hand cart. No vans, not even a horse and cart for small shopkeepers in those days. But that gave father another idea. He had a big box fitted to his handcart. This not only sheltered stock from the rain when delivering it to the shop, but it provided a hygienic means of hawking goods around the streets, thereby increasing sales. It was a hard life for all concerned. My elder half brother Raymond, though only 7 or 8 when his mother died in 1926, always believed that overwork associated with the shop was a major factor in her death. He was probably right.

Left with two young sons, my father sought a housekeeper. That's where my mother came in. She was older that father's first wife, one of nine Lockwood children who lived in one of the little terraces off Cave Street. When my father's first wife died my mother was 'in service' looking after the children of some well-to-do family. Whether she was recognised as a proper governess is uncertain but she had certainly developed a very cold 'governessy' disposition. There can be few children who have no recollection of ever receiving a loving hug, kiss or term of endearment from their mother! From earliest childhood, the formal peck was the only intimacy, exchanged only on parting or reunion.

Closeness to the family was very important in those days and when my mother's family heard that father wanted a housekeeper, they saw it as an opportunity for Gladys to return from her remote life somewhere in Cheshire to Hull. The thought that this might also be a heaven sent opportunity to get a 30 year old spinster daughter married off probably crossed the minds of her parents who had six daughters at a time when so many of the men they should have married had been killed in the war. Be that as it may, family hearsay has it that my father soon recognised how much money could be saved if he didn't have to pay my mother's wages. They were married in 1927. Hard times, hard people.

I know nothing more about my mother's background other than that she had had a double mastoid operation in 1918. This left her hard of hearing, a fact which she would never acknowledge, just as John Mortimer's father would not admit to blindness, suggesting perhaps that human nature varies little with social class. She compensated for her deafness by some lip-reading, and offering, in later, more affluent years, notes to pay the bill in shops when she could not hear the amount requested or see the cash register's total. The possibility of hearing aids did not arise in the pre-welfare state days of the 1930s but that did not matter. When aids became available after World War 2, she refused to use one because they made everything 'too loud'. Human nature is never satisfied!

However hard the life, it seems my mother and father prospered because in 1927, after they married, father bought a house. He found a hard pressed speculative builder, placed a ten pound deposit on the fifty pound deposit on a five hundred pound house at 161 Lee Street, off the Holderness Road, paid off the remainder of the deposit during the next few months, and got a mortgage for the reminder. It's not clear why he should have made the purchase when he was so obviously short of money. Perhaps it was just his small scale version of the form of entrepreneurship practiced in Australia in the 1980s. Whatever the reason, he couldn't live in it because it was too far from the shop but he let it and presumably the rent paid the mortgage.

The depression came and in 1930 so did I. Life must have continued much the same at the shop for it is the scene of my two earliest memories. The first is of being disgruntled. Despite the depression, sales of sweets must have been good and my mother had to fetch two more large glass jars from a supplier. I have no idea how far she had to walk. I was too busy hating having to sit with my legs spread annoyingly wide apart because the jars, empty or full, had to ride on the footrest of my pushchair. The other memory is a much happier one of my first 'work *experience'*, unpacking cartons of soap powder, and stacking them on the shelves so that I could play in the empty boxes. Early memories indeed for my father sold the shop in 1933 and we went to live in Lee Street.

It's not at all clear why my father sold the shop. He was not bankrupt and he seems to have had little difficulty getting a job as a tram conductor. My guess is that he judged that the tough times were going to get harder still for small businesses and that a steady wage for a limited number of hours would be better than the uncertainties and open ended commitment of keeping a shop. It cannot have been an easy decision because he had been elected to represent the South Newington Ward on the Hull City Council in 1931. Councillors had to live in their wards. The move to East Hull forced him to resign his seat and he never served on the Council again. There is no evidence of any significant achievements during his brief term in office, but credit where it's due, he tried.

The expression working class is sometimes used as if it were a precise descriptor. Lee Street and the streets around it in East Hull exemplified the fallacy of that belief. The street divided into old and new parts each about a quarter of a mile long The terraced houses of the old half had a life of their own and I knew little of them. The new was the domain of those who considered themselves fairly well up in the ranks of the working class. The houses were in blocks of four, two semi-detached and two terraced. They had front gardens about five feet wide and bay windows instead of 'Coronation Street' style flat fronts like the old houses. And even the terraced houses had a narrow passage between them on the ground floor to allow dustbins to be brought to the front and coal carried to the rear without going through the house. Luxury indeed!

Lee Street may have been 'looked down on' by some of the people in the next street, Summergangs Road, for there was a strict hierarchy, but it attracted 'respectable' families. They had jobs even during the depression, worked hard, lived frugally to pay their mortgages, never bought anything unless they could pay cash for it, and, most important in their scheme of things, they 'kept themselves to themselves'. Neighbourly chats occurred but only at the gate or over the garden fence. They lived for decades without ever entering each other's houses.

Even within our end of Lee Street there was a hierarchy of status. At the highest level were those spoken of with great respect, 'He has a trade'. Others, like my father, though having no trade, could be trusted by their employers to handle money. By contrast, some of the rather self-righteous Lee Streeters looked down on what they regarded as the 'common' streets less than half a mile away, where other workers lived, they believed, in rented houses, furnished on the 'never-never' as hire purchase was known, often jobless, given to spendthrift ways when they had money and gossiping on their doorsteps when they hadn't. And, I later found, often being much kinder and having much more fun than the Lee Street lot!

The Lee Street house was quite a refined design by the standards of the day. In a plan covering 392 square feet, there was a living room, kitchen and bathroom downstairs and three bedrooms, one with a small storage cupboard, upstairs. A 9 feet by 8 feet extension of the kitchen, known as 'the verandah', housed the larder, coal store and lavatory. Quite an achievement for the price! Restriction of the plumbing to the ground floor was one of the measures adopted to achieve savings. A 'back-boiler' behind the living room fireplace was the only means of heating water and we were lucky enough to be able to afford the coal. Not lucky enough though to be able to afford coal for the fireplace in the main bedroom. That was only ever lit when someone was ill.

The expression 'Jerry built' was common in the 1930s as speculative builders competed to stay in business. It implied poor standards of work with the threat of consequential maintenance problems over the years. *Brewer's Dictionary of Phrase and Fable* suggests that Jerry was probably a corruption of Jury as in jury mast, signifying temporary or makeshift. Be that as it may, it's a pleasure to record that the unknown builder of 161 Lee Street did a good job. The house, much modified after sixty four years, has never given cause for serious concern and the present owners June and Roy say they love living there.

My memories of the early years at Lee Street reflect the life of the times. Shortage of money was the key to everything. Without money, life and living were monotonous. But being poor instilled habits of frugality some of which, once learned, remain throughout life. The switching off of electric lights when leaving a room is the most obvious example. Less obvious was growing up without realising that 'posh' households actually had a special kind of paper to use in the loo! Needless to say, the use of old newspaper did not become a lifelong habit!

The ultimate example was revealed one day at school when a group of girls were talking of womens' mysteries. Those working class girls of Yorkshire had much in common with the aborigines of Australia in their segregation of knowledge on a sexual basis but we boys persuaded them to reveal that they had been talking about 'rags', which, they told us, were to be used by girls from the age of 14 for 'the rest of their lives'. The age of menarche may have changed and the girls had not found out about the menopause, but they were wiser than we were. We boys had not hitherto realised the significance of the stained cloths mixed with the rest of the washing on clothes lines.

Fortunately, being poor was not a matter of hunger for those of us with abstemious parents in the 'respectable' levels of the working class, but the food was dull and frugality was all. A common expression described the reigning philosophy 'bread and scrat'. This phrase recognised that bread and something, usually jam or dripping, was a major part of our diet and the 'scrat' part was a form of shorthand for 'spread it on and scratch it off *again'.* In my case there was also deliberate confusion in the matter of meat. My father said he disliked pork. My mother dealt with this by serving pork when she felt like it and telling him it was either beef or lamb. Why he didn't know the difference I have no idea but I am now well aware that my early difficulties in differentiating between the tastes of the various joints were a direct result of my mother's deviousness.

Tastes aside, the shortage of money for food sometimes provided a treat. I loved the occasional tram rides to the Hull meat market, known as the Shambles, a place of barrows and stalls, with fresh meat dripping blood on the sawdusted cobbles. There, on Saturday nights, we could buy joints which were auctioned off cheaply for there was no refrigeration to keep them fresh during the weekend. It was a place full of life and excitement for children, sliding on the sawdust and creeping under the carts and stalls. Life was different for those whose fathers were by that time in the pubs drinking a large part of the family's weekly income.

Other memories of the earliest days at Lee Street are of walks in the East Park and visits to my maternal grandmother. The park seems to have been underrated by the Hull Daily Mail. Referring to Hull's preparations for Queen Victoria's Golden Jubilee it commented, 'Beyond the opening of the Market Hall and the East Park, which are after all the veriest formalities, nothing in the shape of sight seeing has been provided to relieve the monotony of daily life'. The opening might have been a formality but the provision of the 52 acre East Park and the other parks of Hull was of immense benefit to the people and especially the young people of the heavily polluted city. Without those parks we would have seen little green. And I have to confess that when taken, after my normal bedtime, to see some of the park's flower gardens and grottoes, illuminated for a special occasion, I was half convinced this was fairy land.

My maternal grandmother was the only grandparent who survived long enough to play a part in my memories. In those days there was no question of granny pulling out Lego or another toy for her grandson to play with during visits. So the memory is of the trivia important to a child of three or four, such as sitting, bored, at a scrubbed wooden table in the 'living' room of her tiny house off Cave Street and being told off for picking out the greasy residues which lay in the gaps between the rough boards. My grandmother died before I was five, long before I was old enough to ask her about my mother's early life.

One memory of a visit to my grandmother's house is still vivid. After that visit, my mother and an aunt began to walk the mile to the city centre to reduce the tram fares home from two to one. Following a well established routine, after turning from Cave Street into Beverly Road I raced ahead to look into my favourite toyshop window. Even then I was mesmerised by the methylated spirit powered steam boilers and miniature engines. Eventually, assuming that mother and aunt had overtaken me, I rushed to follow them. I never caught up with them and, wondering what had happened, made my way to Lee Street, over 3 miles away. Finding no one at home I went to our neighbour Mrs Last and, according to her account of the incident, told her that my mother was lost. Factually reasonable, for I was certainly not lost: I was at home. But was it sturdy self reliance? Or precocious arrogance?

Even though times were hard, occasionally there was some money for a visit to the cinema. The earliest visits were obviously for my mother's benefit rather than mine for I was young enough to misunderstand and be profoundly upset by one scene in, if I remember correctly, a Gracie Fields film 'Sing As We Go'. A race number was being pinned to a runner's vest. I was convinced that the pin was being pushed into the runner's back and howled a protest at such barbarity. One lesson of that incident is that not all protests are justified. More importantly, memory of the incident reminds me how vulnerable the young are to what they see in films and other media.

By the age of five or six I was seeing and enjoying films appropriate to my years. The first screening of Snow White remains a vivid memory as a masterpiece of colour, drama and, it must be admitted, sentimental appeal. But the sentimental appeal of Snow White was as nothing compared to the attraction of the Shirley Temple films. Documentary programmes have been made about the life and varied career of Shirley Temple Black but I have never seen one so I do not know whether she winces when she sees her early work. I certainly do when I recall how attracted I was to the curly haired star of those saccharine productions.

When, at the age of eight or so, I was old enough to go with friends, unaccompanied by any adult, to spend, literally, my Saturday penny at the matinees at the Savoy cinema, Snow White and Shirley had given way to Flash Gordon, a fearless spaceman who battled strange life forms such as the Clay Men, creatures who could merge into the walls of the subterranean world to evade our hero, and emerge again to threaten him. When, half a century later, some of those primitive science fiction films were screened on Australian television, I could understand why, despite the crudity of the effects and models, the themes were far more attractive to me than cowboys and Indians.

Films obviously provided the background for much of our play. But not all. I have memories of playing Lawrence of Arabia and it was only many years later that I realised the motivation for those games was probably the increased publicity following his death in 1936. Something of that interest in Lawrence has stayed with me and though I have not been keen enough to plough through The Pillars of Wisdom, I was pleased to learn from one of the many books about him that papers which may throw further light on the complexities of his character are to be released by the Bodleian Library at the turn of the century. Something to look forward to.

Life was enlivened too, by the presence of books in the house. I have my father to thank for early awareness that reading is the key to so much knowledge. There were only about ten books on the shelf reserved for the ones we owned, a shelf to be replaced in the more affluent years after the war by an actual bookcase, but they seemed a treasure trove. There were a dictionary and an encyclopedia. Apart from these, my choice was limited to gardening, woodwork and general knowledge. The books didn't do my father much good. His general knowledge was not remarkable. He was a hopeless gardener and though he liked woodwork, his few tools were abused and blunt. The books scored better with me. They failed on gardening but did well on general knowledge and woodwork. Much more importantly, they gave me a lifelong love of books.

There were a few other books in the house. In an old tin trunk in the cupboard in my parents' bedroom, there were medical books complete with beautiful diagrams of human anatomy, male and female. I'm not sure at what age I discovered them and I was very anxious not to be caught reading them but they obviously held my attention and were studied in some detail. How else would I know that at the time of publication of the books, the youngest mother to give birth to a live child was an Indian girl thirteen years old?

My love of reading found a broader fulfilment through the books I borrowed from the local library and I shall always be grateful to the city fathers of Hull for ensuring that even in the hard times of the thirties, escape and enlightenment were always plentifully available. The library enabled my friends and I to enjoy Wind in the Willows and Alice in Wonderland even though for some reason we remained ignorant of Winnie the Pooh.

Some families owned a radio, others, like my parents, subscribed to Radio Rediffusion, a cheaper option which did not *require the purchase of a receiver. Instead, the house was connected to cables which had been laid along the street. These powered a loudspeaker and offered a choice of two programmes called National and Regional. My infant years were cheered by the voices of Larry the Lamb, Mr Mayor and the other inhabitants of Toytown. And, like many others, I was surprised to hear, decades later, that there had only ever been twenty four episodes.*

But however enjoyable Toytown was in my early years, and however cheering ITMA and other programmes were during the war, a love of 'good' music was not to be acquired at 161 Lee Street, for every time the beginning of an aria, concerto, symphony, oratorio or anything similar was heard, my mother pronounced it 'highbrow' and switched it off. The only exception would be for the Gracie Fields, who could do no wrong and whose voice was welcome no matter what she chose to sing. The loss of exposure to a wide range of music would not be remedied until my teenage years.

Our kind of families did not have the benefits described in so many biographies of spending idyllic summers at the familiy's holiday house at Crabtorture Cove or some such place. Instead, the only early holiday memory is of a single day by the sea, reached after 18 rather uncomfortable miles perched on the small saddle fitted to the crossbar of my father's bicycle. The memory is especially vivid because, after introducing me to the pleasure of paddling in the waves, he left me to enjoy his swim. I was then introduced to the power of the sea as a wave turned me head over heels a few times. My father cannot have been far away and I was swiftly restored to the vertical and to the beach! The pleasure in the sea, and respect for it, remain.

There were better times to come. In 1936 'Billy' Butlin opened his first 'Holiday Camp' at Skegness and we were among the first visitors. Skegness produced what must have been one of the earliest examples of advertising 'hype'. Situated on the east coast of Lincolnshire and exposed to vicious cold winds alleged to come direct from Siberia, Skegness adopted the catchphrase 'Skegness is so bracing!' I forgive them. Cold and regimented it might have been but they gave value for money beyond my dreams.

There was no need for our parents to supervise us, the Butlin's team took care of that. Part of the time we were organised by the famous Redcoats, cajoled into joining in games and competitions, teased if we were bashful, rewarded for winning, and often photographed, whether our parents could afford to buy copies or not. Best of all though, were the free individual activities. There were various fairground rides, bicycles and tricycles to ride, canoes and rowing boats on a lake, and skates of a quality I had never experienced before. Cheap skates with steel wheels clamped to ordinary shoes on a rough street are one thing, wooden wheels beneath special boots on a smooth rink were something new and wonderful. Butlin's camps are sometimes ridiculed. Not by me.

There were no kindergartens, preschools or playgroups and it is a mystery how any of us acquired a knowledge of what constituted desirable behaviour before we went to school. I do not think it was from my half-brothers for I have little recollection of them living with us either at Thoresby or Lee Streets. And at that time we did not form part of an 'extended family'. Indeed my parents usually seemed to be on 'not speaking' terms with most of their relations throughout the 1930s. Perhaps the difficulties of the relationship between my mother and her stepsons aggravated the tensions of life during the depression and, somewhere in the background, were relatives of my father's first wife who looked after Raymond and Clifford until they went, at an early age, to sea.

Wherever it came from, my peers and I had developed an awareness that life was a competitive business by the time we started school. A pecking order was soon established against criteria which seemed to come quite naturally. For instance, the Mersey Street Elementary School was about half a mile from my home. Our mothers took us to school on the first day. After that there was no doubt that from the boys' point of view desirable behaviour required mothers to let us make our own way there and back as soon as possible. That at any rate, was the view in my class and we made life a misery for those boys whose mothers continued to shepherd them for weeks. I was always pleased that mine was soon confident that I could find my own way.

School always involved trying to maintain status amongst the other boys, envying boys and girls whose parents could provide them with a halfpenny or a penny a day for sweets after school, making desperate efforts to be rewarded with the privilege of carrying in the crates of one third of a pint milk bottles which we were all given at a cheap price each morning, generally trying to please teacher, and discovering girls. We were a stable community, beginning in the 'infants' school' at 5 years old, segregated from the older children for a couple of years, then passing to the other side of the walls which divided the playground, and staying together, except for 'playtimes' during which boys and girls were again segregated, until the 'scholarship' exams at eleven.

I have no memory of any serious disharmony in the classrooms, only of competition. Rather there are happy memories such as of the reward of a halfpenny for knowing the meaning of the word diagonal at an early age and of the general kindliness of the teachers. Learning, during those early years, was a happy experience.

Being poor was less happy and it made little difference that there must have been many worse off than the Feasey's. Human nature being what it is, when my father had saved enough money to buy the materials to build a small greenhouse so that we could grow tomatoes, I was worried that he and I might be seen by someone I knew as we pushed the hired wheelbarrow along

Holderness Road, heavily loaded with cement, wood and glass. A sense of shame was a common feature of life.

Being poor meant many other things too, among them hating the smell of wet coats. Very few children had raincoats. It was considered important to provide warm overcoats to protect us from the harsh East Yorkshire winds but few families could afford both. So our blue woollen overcoats had to be worn when it rained. I can smell them still.

There were quite a few free pleasures in the Hull of the 'thirties, albeit very simple ones. Among them, my favourite, walks to the Victoria Pier to watch the paddle-wheeler ferries being loaded for passage across the Humber to New Holland. When I first saw it each car had to be rolled over slings and then hoisted in by crane, a very laborious procedure. Later a floating pontoon enabled cars to be driven onto the ferries at any state of the tide. Either way, a fascinating operation for a small boy. After watching the ferries we always walked along the wharf between the High Street warehouses and the river Hull to Drypool Bridge before returning home. A visit to Hull in 1996 showed that parts of that walk are still there and may still play a part in imparting the magic of the river, estuary and sea to small boys. Or are they all too sophisticated nowadays?

Occasionally there were rarer treats, visits to other docks to see full rigged sailing ships. Exactly why they were there I have no idea but they were probably the last survivors of the cargo-carrying sailing clipper era. And once there was a visit by a great Royal Navy warship. The image of its director tower is printed indelibly on my memory, a massive structure built around the foremast, high above the bridge, from which, I was later to learn, the guns were all aimed and fired. An image combining glamour and danger, irresistible to small boys.

Not all the memories are linked to the sea. An aunt once lived in the last house in a small cul de sac behind the Spring Bank. Right next door, at the end of the street was the entrance to the bakery of the pre-eminent grocers of Hull, Jacksons. And Jacksons still used steam lorries, Sentinels I think, great hissing, clanking, dripping, glowing, smelly, oily, fiery monsters. Visits to Auntie Ethel's house were treats indeed, even the railway engines which chugged along their preordained tracks beyond the house seemed tame by comparison.

Nor were all the memories of things mechanical. My father and mother had a few friends and one, 'Uncle Pashley' as I called him in the custom of the day, sometimes accompanied my father and I on our Sunday morning walks to the pier. Like so many other men of his generation, Mr Pashley had been wounded in the First World War, in his case losing nearly half of his face and leaving him very heavily scarred. And all too often during walks we would see ex-soldiers who had lost both their legs pushing themselves along the streets on little trolleys knocked together using old pram wheels and bits of timber. No sophisticated wheelchairs and Paraplegic Olympics for them!

There is no way of knowing exactly what triggered my interest in things mechanical and maritime, or when that interest began, though it is clear that I was exposed to the influence of both from an early age. But it is certain that the interest in engineering was well established by the time I was seven. Even in hard times comics were sometimes available and were loved by most boys but they had little appeal for me. Until, that is, something radically different appeared on the market, something for which I seemed to have been waiting all my life, the publication of *Modern Wonder* in 1937.

Modern Wonder offered an insight into the worlds of science and engineering with superb descriptions and explanations in words, diagrams and photographs. A recent visit to the British Library's newspaper repository at Colindale allowed me to browse through them again so I can record with confidence that the first edition on 23 May 1937 introduced me to Sir Malcolm Campbell's world record breaking car, the Bluebird, the 8000

Class Canadian Pacific railway engines, the casting of the 200 inch lens for the Mount Palomar telescope, plans for a polar submarine, the Canopus flying boat, the Boulder Dam, and Sir William Beebe's bathyscaphe in which he descended deeper into the oceans than anyone had ever done before. It was indeed a world full of wonders 'out there'. And what a pity that there isn't a comparable paper to inspire the children of today.

These were the early experiences which began to shape my interests in and responses to the world around me. They were commonplace, unremarkable. Soon they were to be followed by the more severe experience of war. But they had served their purpose. Although the observations earlier in this chapter have a high degree of generalisation, they reflect the fact that there never was any such thing as a homogeneous 'working class'. And they provided the foundation for my later, enduring belief that we should aim for a society in which we should all earn our keep as workers, and respect other workers, whether they operate on the shop floor or as chairman of the board, a belief which has found better expression in Australia than it ever seemed likely to in the UK.

Chapter 3.

Evacuation

Nature seems to insulate children pretty well from the full realisation of the meaning of world events, at least until the worst actually happens. Neither the expectation that there would be a war, nor that there would be air-raids, made much of a lasting impression on my consciousness. Even the issue of gas-masks and drills in their use left no sense of great fear. Rather, my memories are of the prospect of adventure stimulated by talk of evacuation to the country or even to Australia or Canada. And the latter, given my father's previous emigration to Canada, had something of the nature of going to search for the Holy Grail. That exciting prospect never materialised. At the outbreak of war in September 1939, the school was closed and with many others I was evacuated to North Yorkshire.

Almost everyone will have seen old newsreel shots of emotional farewells and chaotic evacuation scenes at railway stations at some time or other. Our evacuation may or may not have been like that. Perhaps it was because my mother made a point of never showing any emotion or affection that I took the parting and the journey in my stride. My group of children must have travelled by train to the distribution centre at Helmsley, from which a dozen or so of us were sent to the little village of Nunnington. That is where the enduring memories of things different began.

A boy called Leonard and I were billeted at the Rectory, home of the Reverend Gill and his wife, a magnificent home on a scale we had never imagined. And they had a car! How odd it must appear to young people today that Leonard and I had reached the age of nine without ever getting into a car. So began our introduction to a different world. Different in so many ways.

First, different in its social differentiations. The horror stories of mutual detestation between the townie evacuees and their country hosts are well documented in factual and fictional accounts, perhaps most amusingly of all in Evelyn Waugh's 'Put Out More Flags'. Our experience was nothing like as extreme. But, as part of the regime of living at the Rectory, it was made clear that though our hosts were kindly, we belonged in the domain of the woman who came to cook and clean. That didn't bother us. It was a far greater shock to be told that forelock touching or some similar mark of respect was to be paid if we ever beheld The Lord of the Manor, who might, or might not, be in residence at Nunnington Hall. We might have had a very limited upbringing in our little working class world, but we recognised an alien concept when we heard one. We shall never know whether we would have conformed. We never saw him.

School was different. We were accustomed to large classes. One Inspector's report on our Mersey Street School during the 1930s noted that seven classes had more than 50 pupils. But all the children in each class were the same age. Nunnington had two classes spanning all the age range of those days, 5 to 14. The change didn't cause us much trouble. Our contemporaries from the village were the ones to suffer. We were undoubtedly what would nowadays be called 'street-wise', the village children gentle creatures by comparison. And whether it was because of the competition in our large classes at Mersey Street or despite those large classes, scholastically, we were undoubtedly ahead of the villagers. We tended to dominate the classes. And win the fights!

Outside school, the locals had their revenge. They were in the own farming environment and knew a lot about it. And at an adult level too! Boys of around our age not only knew about horses, harnesses, carts and crops, they were allowed, 'expected' would probably have been a more accurate word had we realised it, to drive the monstrous beasts that hauled the

25

heavy two-wheeled tipping carts in which the mangel wurzel harvest and other crops were brought in. In that way the adult labour could concentrate on building the great, straw covered 'pies' in which the root crops would be preserved against the frosts of winter.

We hated the idea that the village boys knew so much and did our best to catch up, volunteering for any tasks involving farm machinery and the horses that provided most of the power. I don't think any of us ever took any interest in the cows. It's curious that although girls were accepted as a normal part of life at Mersey Street, I have no recollection of any at Nunnington. If there were any, perhaps they were too busy learning milking and similar 'womanly' farming skills. There isn't even a memory of them working at what was the most obvious 'unisex' job of those days, building the sheaves of corn left by the reaper-binder machines into the stooks in which they would, weather permitting, dry in the sun. Perhaps we were just too busy learning about ferreting and ratting with terriers to notice. Our closest attention we gave to the highlight of the farming year, threshing.

I wish I could bring to the description of those threshing days the skills of Kenneth Grahame. The pleasure I felt on beholding the steam traction engine as it towed the immense, box-like threshing machine into the farm yard was a combination of Grahame's depiction of ratty's raptures on the river and toad's joy in his motor car. Even though I had occasionally seen and admired the steam lorries, the size and power of the threshing machinery was, as they say nowadays, something else.

Fortunately, we were not constrained to admire from afar. There was work for young and old. Although the country was at war, farming was a reserved occupation for some men. Watching the threshing, it was easy to see why. There had to be strong young men to hoist with pitchforks, hour after hour as long as the daylight lasted, the sheaves to the top of the stack against which the threshing machine had been set, and to carry the bags of grain, which I believe weighed about two hundredweight, to the waiting carts.

We townies were given strongly worded warnings about the hundred and one ways in which we could get entangled with and injured by the threshing machine, the engine and the long, writhing driving belt which connected the two. The warnings were illustrated by horrific tales, probably much embellished for our benefit, of injuries suffered even by real farm men because they had not been careful enough. After the warnings we proudly worked alongside the country cousins, unhitching horses from the loaded wagons bringing sheaves to the thresher and transferring them to empty carts for the next trip, bringing supplies of corn sacks to the machine, and keeping the work area tidy. Bliss.

There were many other new experiences. Hero worship is the phrase appropriate to my recognition of the skill of the local blacksmith, once I had learned that it did not hurt the horses to have the hot iron shoes seared to their hooves. His were not the residual skills of some of the present day smiths but the broadest spectrum of ironworking skills encompassing shoeing horses, shrinking new tyres onto the wooden wheels of all the wagons, and mending all manner of ploughs, reapers and binders and other farm machinery. Nowadays so-called smiths produce excellent work, some of it of high sculptural quality, but all too often it is welded mild steel. The malleability of iron is almost forgotten and often people will not believe that the old smiths could produce such complex forms from bars of iron using only heat, hammer, swage and anvil.

Occasional outings in the car were among the most pleasant new experiences and the first sight of the view from the top of the Sutton Bank, about 300 feet above the surrounding country, made a lasting impression on two boys who had never experienced anything beyond the flatness of East Yorkshire. There were new words to be learned. There was no beautiful *little river flowing along one edge the village, there was the 'beck'. An entirely different dialect had to be mastered if we wished to communicate with our new friends. We had to learn that their 'gannin yam' meant the same as our 'going home. And there was an introduction to the life and ways of the Anglican Church.*

Prior to evacuation, my experience of religion had been limited to absorbing a few facts, most notably that religion was the principal cause of divisions within our family. There was an undercurrent in our home life of some earlier, rather vague, religious connection, probably through the family of my father's first wife and one of his sisters. But there was never any church-going. It was understood that church going led to hypocrisy, a very serious but apparently very commonplace sin in the family. The only manifestations of religion in the house were a beautifully bound pocket book entitled 'The Salvation Army Soldiers Guide' and an equally beautiful copy of Whiston's 'Josephus, the only book in the house which had thin tissue paper protecting its illustrations. The purpose of that paper seemed a great mystery in my early years. Then, the Rectory!

Morning service, Sunday School and Evensong all had to be attended. Leonard and I might have been regarded by some of the other evacuees, possibly even by some of the village children, as a bit hard done by, having copped that lot, but heavy duty each Sunday seemed to me not too high a price for the very comfortable weekday life at the Rectory. And there was at least one compensation, very precious given my interest in things mechanical and pneumatic. Was I conned into believing that it was a great privilege occasionally to be allowed to work the manual pump which supplied air to the church organ? If so, I was happy to be conned.

Churchgoing had its problems and these produced, for the first remembered time in my life, a sense of conflict between my ideas and those of the adult world. The first and simplest conflict came when I first saw the interior of church. Little as I knew of the Christian religion, I had somehow acquired a sense of egalitarian propriety which was offended when the social hierarchy of the pews was explained to me. Perhaps I was the more offended because I was embarrassed. I had attempted to sit at the front, thinking to get the best view of these novel proceedings. That was, of course, the Lord of the Manor's family pew. Exit Feasey, to rear of church in confusion.

After a little while, gathering greater knowledge of how the system operated, I presumed to make a suggestion. It was based on my observation that there were very few people at Morning Service and even less at Evensong. Furthermore, it was not a case of good people seeking to be doubly good by attending both services, the congregations were entirely different. Now although I regarded attendance at church as a small price to pay for the creature comforts of the Rectory, I could certainly think of more interesting things to do. So, anticipating the teachings of the management text-books of the 1980s by some decades, I suggested rationalising the two services into one. Silly me! Had I been brought up in a different environment I would have known that Evensong was the servants' opportunity to worship. I had to accept the explanation but I remember feeling there ought to be a better way of organising things, preferably one which allowed all who wished to worship to do so together.

My naivete caused me to blunder on theological as well as social matters. The Rector asked our Sunday School class what one or other of the disciples might have said when Jesus performed his first miracle. Never slow to jump in, I volunteered what I thought might be a pretty ordinary human response, 'I've never seen you do that before'. It amused the class but the Rector showed signs and made the explosive noises of one mortally offended. I learned a lesson which was to apply again years later when I was studying Old Testament theology as a lay preacher candidate of the Methodist Church. If an organisation has a 'staff answer' to its questions, free thinkers, innocent or not, are not always welcome!

The air raids which had been expected at the beginning of the war didn't happen. Perhaps our presence in the rural community caused more disruption than we realised. Perhaps our parents, whether demonstrative or not, missed us. And Christmas was coming. Whatever the thoughts behind the action, late in November my father cycled the 50 or so miles from Hull to Nunnington, talked to the Rector and pedalled patiently back again. When the school term ended some of us returned to Hull. The Mersey Street School reopened in February. The bombing started in June 1940.

Chapter 4

In Time for the Bombing.

Things had changed and continued to change when we returned to Hull. A pit about 18 inches deep had been dug in our back garden and an Anderson bomb shelter built in and over it. Sheets of corrugated iron sheets bent into 'J' shapes were set into the pit, bolted together at the top, backed by corrugated iron end pieces with a main entrance at the front and a small emergency exit, which could be removed using a spanner, at the back. The iron was then covered with a layer of concrete and the shelter completed by building a 'blast wall' about a foot thick to shield the main entrance from bomb blasts. The shelters were just big enough to allow bunks to be built at each side with a gap of a couple of feet in the middle. Comfortable enough if you didn't mind the cold and the damp.

The 'phony war', the period of freedom from the bombing which had been expected to begin as soon as war was declared, continued into 1940. The school, closed when war began, opened again on 19 February after air raid shelters for 464 people had been built, solid brick structures with concrete roofs. The school's small 'garden', it scarcely deserved the name, was dug up and vegetables planted to comply with the government's exhortation to 'Dig for Victory'. It served well enough as an excuse to chat to June, Barbara, Rita and the other girls more often, and during class time at that.

The bombing began in June and this was the beginning of years of tiredness. Families developed various attitudes to the problem. Some, working on some 'we'll all go together' principle, ignored the risk and remained in their beds. Children, we discovered, are very adaptable and some learned to sleep comfortably in their beds throughout air raid sirens' warnings, the firing of anti-aircraft guns, the rattle of falling shrapnel, and *exploding bombs, provided of course that none of these were too close!*

Most families would have regarded staying in bed as a foolhardy policy, but staying in the air raid shelter all night seemed little better because of the penetrating cold and damp. Many probably followed the pattern we used. Go to bed, get up and go into the shelter when the sirens sounded, attempt to sleep on the rough bunks, get up at the all-clear, go back to bed. Not a very good routine if there were two or three raids a night. The shelter routine had its compensations though. One of my mother's sisters and her family had moved into a house a few doors away and they shared our shelter. For the first time in my life I experienced the pleasure of comforting human warmth when I shared a bunk with my favourite cousin, Winnie. She was a couple of years older than me and I would have done anything for her, even cheerfully accepting her teasing and that of her two older sisters.

The 'Ordeal and Triumph' of Hull during the bombings are recorded in a book entitled 'A North East Coast Town', the euphemism used allegedly for security reasons in news bulletins. It indicates that although a single bomb damaged a railway bridge in Chapman Street on 20th June, the first string of eleven bombs fell in a line from Chamberlain Road to Lodge Street on the 26th. One of them fell in Lee Street, on Gardner's butcher's shop, a hundred yards from our house. No one was hurt. It did not catch fire. In that sense it was not dramatic at all but the shop and the home above it were wrecked. Everyone in the street came out to see it after the all-clear was sounded at about twenty past three in the morning. It was a long time before we settled down that night. The novelty soon wore off.

Despite the war, we had to think about our futures. The school days of working class children ended on reaching the age of fourteen unless, at the age of eleven, a scholarship to a high school had been won. War or no war, preparations for the *examinations began when we were ten. For those of us who aspired to going on to high school. the choice was between the Malet Lambert High School and the Riley High School.*

The former was a 'general' high school, I don't know how else to describe it. It was co-educational with all the 'usual' subjects, and it had the advantage of being only a mile from home. The Riley High School was the junior school of the Hull Technical College and had a strong scientific and technical bias. Three and a half miles from home, nothing nowadays when most children are delivered to school by bus or the family car, a bit of a chore then when tram and bus fares would have been a significant expense. But who cared? There was no doubt where I wanted to go.

Preparations for the scholarship examinations did not seem very onerous at the time, except for the only experience in my life which I would describe as humiliating. In addition to the local education authority's high schools, there was and still is a public school called Hymers College in Hull. Neither my parents nor I had any clear idea what a public school, major or minor, was, but my teacher, Mrs Townsend, whom I remember as a dedicated and kind person, suggested I should try for a scholarship to the college.

When anyone as prestigious as a teacher made such a suggestion to a family like mine, there could be only one response, 'You know best'. And that was undoubtedly the right response, for practical reasons, because the word scholarship had two meanings. The local education authority's scholarships were only for places in the city's high schools and although there were no fees to be paid, the expenses of keeping the child at school for two extra years had to be borne by the parents. Some families could not afford to lose the extra income which the child leaving school at fourteen would earn. That alone was enough to deprive some children of their chance of high school. Scholarships to schools such as Hymers were different. Some provided money to help keep the child at school. Winning one was highly desirable.

Even parents who could manage without the a child's earnings often had difficulty paying for the school uniform, unknown at the elementary schools but required at high schools, for travel to school, lunches, and all the other expenses involved in keeping a child at school. To pay these costs they would forgo holidays, visits to the cinema, and other pleasures they might otherwise have enjoyed. For such parents, the key word of those times was 'sacrifice'. Fortunately for me, mine were in this category, because the Hymers scholarship examination was a disaster.

We were parochial animals. Our city was too big to walk across and bus and tram fares could not easily be afforded. So crossing to the other side of the city, nearly four miles away, was a novel experience. Novel turned to daunting on entering the solemn atmosphere of the great hall in which the examination was to be held. We had nothing like that at Mersey Street! Daunted turned to horror on turning the exam paper over and realising that not only did I not know the answers, I didn't understand the half the questions. It was kind of my teacher to think that I had a chance. It would have been kinder had she prepared me better but the size of the class probably limited the time she could spend on each individual. Fortunately, it was the only experience of that kind in my life.

Life became a combination of school and bombing. The two aspects of life came together each morning when we called the roll. Absences sometimes meant that someone's house had been bombed during the night. The emergency arrangements made in these cases took time and children arrived late at school. But arrive they often did. Having ones house bombed was not necessarily a sufficient reason to stay away.

Slowly but surely though, the bombing took its toll. Advertisements sometimes show children enjoying the sight of their school burning down. The school records show that Mersey Street was damaged for the first time on 3rd March 1941. By 23rd May so many families had been bombed out of their homes and accommodated elsewhere that attendance was down to 60%. On 27th May, bomb damage made the school unusable and it was closed for a time but I do not recall any of us rejoicing. I think we were just pleased to be alive. Only one member of our class, Alec, had been killed.

Perhaps the unhappy experience of the Hymers College examination prepared me well for the local education authority's version for I won my scholarship in May or June of 1941, amid all the turmoil, with no memories of any difficulties. That was the trigger for one of the happiest experiences of my life. A bicycle had hitherto been in the realms of the unattainable but soon after the results were announced, I came home one day and there it was, not only a bicycle, but a new one. Only the faintest tinge of regret crossed my mind when I saw that it was an old fashioned one with raised handlebars and 'roller' brakes rather than the desirable, and more expensive, 'dropped' handlebars and calliper brakes. I don't think that tinge could have reached my face and come to the notice of my parents. My pleasure was great and genuine. A new era had begun.

Bicycles were the common factor of life for the next six years. Hull and the plain on which it sits are as flat as Holland. It might well have been called New Holland except that similar country on the other side of the Humber had already taken that title. Perfect for cycling, not just in Hull itself but all the way to the coast. In 1941 though, trips to the coast were some years away. Travel to coastal areas was controlled and even if we had been old enough to be allowed to go that far, wartime restrictions would have prohibited such trips.

Far more mundane, the main use of the new bicycle was seemingly endless journeys to and from my new school which was at The Boulevard, about three and a half miles from home.

There were of course days when cycling to and from school was a pleasure, even if the bicycle sometimes had to be carried over the rubble still blocking the streets after the previous night's air raids. But bombs were not the real enemy. Wind and rain were. Few children today face the necessity of starting off from home in the pouring rain, facing a bitter wind which so often seemed to change during the day to give a headwind in both directions.

It was generally recognised that some of the money saved by cycling to school should be used to buy the then familiar yellow oilskin cycling cape. Unfortunately, in the early years the money did not stretch to oilskin leggings and gloves. Not an experience to be recommended. In fact, the only time I found the experience an advantage was forty years later when I began cross country skiing in Australia. Many Australians are so unaccustomed to cold that they have difficulty getting used to stiff fingers, and whinge a great deal when they have to remove gloves for some reason. I felt a degree of smugness based on my early experiences of cold and wet.

Not surprisingly the first days at the Riley High School were a shock to the system. For instance, we all knew that we would study German. War or no war, it was regarded as the language to be learned if we wished to read the some of the best technical and scientific papers. But for some childish reason I never thought we would begin learning it on our very first day. And what on earth was Practical Plane and Solid Geometry? Soon all was revealed and became as familiar as the abbreviation PPSG.

Having qualified for high school there was soon another hurdle to be cleared. One third of our age group had a preference for what was loosely called the commercial stream. They went their own way but that left enough boys for two science stream classes and following the custom of those days we were soon divided into 'A' and 'B' streams. Those of us fortunate enough to be in the 'A' stream were left in no doubt by our masters that we were expected to live up to our privileged status. It was a 'get on or get out' system quite different to the benevolent procedures of today. And somehow or other, the 'get out' function did operate. We began with over thirty in the class. Five years later, the twenty four survivors matriculated.

There is no doubt that as the first stage of a technical education we were well served by those who selected the subjects and taught us at Riley High. Forty years after I left school, one of my engineering college contemporaries told me how much he had envied my ability to read engineering drawings as readily as a newspaper from the first days in college. The answer was of course that that was to be expected if one had started technical drawing at the age of twelve.

As usual in life, there was a price to be paid. History and geography were sacrificed to enable us to concentrate on the subjects of most use to our future technical callings. By the time we sat our School Certificate examinations, the sole survivor of the humanities, apart from English itself, was English Literature. For that I have always been grateful. Sufficient geography could be learned through travel and reading. History proved more difficult. Attempts to catch up throughout a lifetime have proved, in my case, inadequate. But life would have been much worse had we not been given an appreciation of 'Eng. Lit'. To be ignorant of two subjects might be a misfortune, not to love English would be a tragedy.

Our teachers have left my contemporaries and me with mixed views of their merits. Many were teachers left behind when the younger men had gone to war. Some left memories of excellent tuition and formed lasting friendships with students who returned later to teach. My memories of the teachers are mixed, and include recollections of age, temper, and alcoholism. Saddest of all, was the struggle of an English master, 'Chas' Wilkins, the only teacher young enough to be of 'call up' age, against tuberculosis. In addition to giving us a good grounding in the English language, he introduced us to the concept of 'expurgated editions' by throwing them away and reading to us from the original! A teacher worthy of any adolescent boy's respect.

So began and continued our secondary education. We were soon accustomed to new ideas and regimes. Homework, which had been non-existent at elementary school, absorbed much of our evenings. Caning, which varied from desultory attempts by an ineffective German master to hit our elusive hands, to really fierce 'six of the best' from the physical training master, was a commonplace occurrence. Just for the record, however much I search my memory, I cannot find any evidence that the canings, of which I think I had more than an average share and which I certainly hated at the time, had any adverse long-term effects on my development or on my attitudes. We certainly never became preoccupied with 'beatings' as so many English Public Schoolboys and thirteen year old entry Dartmouth cadets seem to have been.

There was one long term effect of the monastic technical education. Those boys who had the company of girls at school throughout the teenage years were much more at ease in their company than those of us who were segregated during school hours. And that was a grave disadvantage post pubescence, when the company of girls became so intensely desirable, and so hard to achieve for some of us who had no experience of them in the immediate family circle or at school.

With school so far from home, lunch presented a problem too. Sandwiches were to be avoided if possible because they would have to be made from rationed food. Much better to buy something which didn't require 'coupons'. There was a canteen of sorts at the school but chips were a cheaper alternative. So most lunch times for five years some of us walked to the fish and chip shop a couple of hundred yards away in Selby Street. That was the easy bit. The next was more tricky. We had no money for fish, but if the right place in the queue could be secured there would be lots of batter scraps that had fallen off other people's fish, and these would be added to the chips of the two or three lucky ones who timed it right. Not a diet to be recommended for every meal, but those lunches don't seem to have done us any harm.

Adolescence was still some way off during the early years at high school. First came the last years of toys. These gave pleasure when owned and created an understanding of the word 'yearning' when they existed only in shop windows or the home of some better-off friend. The latter included model steam engines, toy microscopes, 'oo' gauge model railways, and many others, simple enough toys by comparison with the sophisticated radio controlled cars, planes and boats of today, but equally desirable in their day.

Two types of toy enlivened my boyhood. 'Dinky' toys, scale models of motor vehicles were one source of great pleasure at affordable cost. Not surprisingly, the models were of tanks, armoured cars, Bren gun carriers, anti-aircraft guns and army lorries. The pick of the bunch, though I never owned one, was the mighty Antar Tank Transporter, never seen in real life in those early years of the war but common enough when the build up for the Normandy invasion was under way in 1944. It was easy to imagine oneself the driver of any of these mechanical monsters! That was the real pleasure. Had we been at peace instead of war, I would have been equally happy with models of ordinary commercial cars and lorries, provided of course they were big and powerful.

There was no comparison, though, between the pleasures of playing with toy vehicles and with the enduring favourite, Meccano. The catalogues showed a range of Meccano sets numbered from 0 to 10, the latter being the only one which had a partitioned wooden box. The number 2 was one of the best Christmas presents I ever had. Even today, I doubt if there can be any better preparation for a career in mechanical engineering than spending hundreds of hours designing and building models. The pleasure of realising complex designs using Meccano certainly had no equal in my time. So pocket money was invested in extra parts culminating in the pleasure of acquiring one of the most critical sets of components, the 'gears' set, a small box containing a few gear-wheels, a worm and worm-wheel, some sprockets and a length of driving chain. A new world opened up!

Some readers may have seen the film 'Hope and Glory'. It's depiction of the war as seen through the eyes of a boy of around ten or eleven years old was excellent. The pleasures of collecting shrapnel, especially if it was still hot from the explosion of shell or bomb, and the fear that the precious collection might be lost when the family home was bombed, as portrayed in the film, corresponded exactly with my memories. But there were other reasons for searching, and stealing from, bomb sites. In my case it was to find the wood from which to make a partitioned box for my Meccano set, the equal as far as I was concerned of any Number 10 box ever sold.

The principle of beginning with some small treasure and building things up slowly was soon firmly established. If a new treasure was to be acquired, an old one usually had to be sold. If new could not be afforded, second-hand must be acquired and renovated. My second bicycle was a good example. After some years of service the scholarship reward was too small but a new machine of the desired type was way out of my financial reach. So, like my friends, I bought a second-hand frame of the right size and started from that.

First came stripping and painting the frame, a brilliant red, of course. Then the addition of rather nice 'J' forks, dropped handlebars, calliper brakes and all the other items which were conspicuously absent from the first bike. Well, nearly all. Neither I nor most of my friends ever became rich enough to afford a set of derailleur gears or even a Sturmey Archer 3-speed hub. Up hill or down, we all managed with small, fixed *sprockets, a symbol of our manliness. Only girls and cissies had freewheels. And I think only one my friends owned a bicycle frame made of 'Reynolds 531 tubing', an alloy whose name had a mystical quality, beyond the reach of most of us.*

The bicycle which was to serve me until I joined the navy took shape. A favourite acquisition was an elegant, second-hand gooseneck. For those who are not familiar with bicycles, the gooseneck was a tubular bracket connecting the handlebars to the front forks. This one extended the reach of the handlebars 3 or 4 inches in front of the front forks, a practical advantage for a tall young man. But somehow there was also a belief that the greater the extension of the gooseneck, the greater the prestige of the owner. So of course I was pleased to have this desirable item. But, as any of the housewives of Lee Street could have told me, pride comes before a fall. I was introduced to that proverbial bit of wisdom and to the engineering concept of fatigue at the same moment. The gooseneck snapped while I was riding home from school and, with much of my weight being carried on the handlebars, I plunged head-first towards the road surface, one of many falls, none, I'm glad to say, at all serious.

The fall which could have been very serious occurred not on the roads but in the gymnasium. For many of us, 'Gym' was a welcome relief from serious studies and a chance to let off steam. Even better were the few minutes during which those who changed quickly enough could do what they liked in the gym before the gym master, a strict disciplinarian, arrived. My greatest pleasure was swinging on one of the rope ladders about twelve feet long suspended from hooks on the ceiling. I have few claims to records, at school or elsewhere, but I don't think anyone else ever managed to swing so high that the 'free' end of the ladder caught on the next row of ceiling hooks, conveniently placed exactly one rope ladder's length from the first row.

Unkind friends said I was lucky to land on my head and I have to admit that it suffered only a small cut in spite of being the first contact with the floor. A broken left arm was the more serious injury and I was taken to the infirmary to have it set. Times change. There was never any question of compensation for injury caused by negligent design and certainly no question of my parents taking any legal action over the matter. They wouldn't have known where to begin. Nor, as far as I can recall, were the offending hooks ever removed or modified during my time at the school. However, I was able to use the incident when lecturing on Occupational Health and Safety decades later as an example of very bad design.

There were two other activities which claimed my attention and gave great pleasure during the early high school years, fretwork and Scouting. Fretwork had the advantage that it could be done on a frugal budget provided fretsaw machines operated by a treadle, superior drills with inertia weights and fretsaws with cam devices for tensioning the blade were avoided. Fretwork is sometimes the subject of jibes and it is true that the items I produced were of no artistic merit, though in those days everyone needed a box which rather mysteriously produced a cigarette when pressed in the right spot. But three reflections on the hobby have relevance today. First, hobbies could only be done thanks to tolerant families. When the living room is only thirteen feet by twelve, has to accommodate the settee, the easy chairs and the table and chairs, the competition for space can be intense. Fortunately, for me, not for them, Raymond and Clifford were in the navy. And my parents allowed the cutting board to be clamped to the table..

The second reflection is of the pleasure, after emigrating much later in life, of being lucky enough to have all the space my wife and I need for our activities. Without our early experience of cramped conditions, we might not realise how lucky we are. Finally, I wonder whether that early interest in working with wood, which was to become a major interest later in life, had genetic origins. I have recorded earlier that my father's woodworking was more likely to deter than to inspire good craftsmanship. But was there an inheritance from my cabinet maker grandfather and some of his cabinet maker forebears? Is there some genetic link between them, my nephew Roger who has made woodwork a major part of his life, and myself?

Scouting was a major interest for two years. I joined the Saint Aidan's Troop, which took its name from an Anglican church just under a mile from home. We played rough games, we played 'wide games', we learned signalling, knots and lashings, we hiked, we camped, we marched, we were proud if selected to be the flag bearer at Church Parade. We did all the things which have made scouts, in the eyes of some people, figures of fun. And we learned self reliance, co-operation and elementary leadership, qualities which have earned the scouting movement respect in so much of the world.

Although the greatest catch phrase of the day was 'Business as Usual', it must have been very difficult to keep scouting going during a world war. The most obvious problem was to find young men as leaders while ensuring that soldiers who volunteered to assist scout troops did not include homosexual paedophiles. Many of us were accosted at some time during those years by a rampant exhibitionist in the local park but it is to the credit of the scouting organisation that it's filtering system never allowed any suspect characters access to our group.

Then, as now, some youths viewed the scouts only as a target for abuse and a fight. The consequence was a very scared Geoff Feasey at times. There was such a shortage of helpers that I was asked to assist another troop at Marfleet. Fools rush in and I enjoyed helping. But not the solitary two and a half mile walk through the blacked-out streets, most of it through alien territory by our parochial standards, an area moreover which was thought by relatively gentile Lee Street to be 'very rough'. Was it not near the docks and the Hull Prison?

Looking back, it is easy to ask the question, 'Why then did we always wear our uniforms, which were generally sufficient to provoke an attack'? The only answer is that it would have been unthinkable in those days not to do so. Plus, perhaps, the fact that our uniforms included staffs, in my case, an ash pole nearly six feet long and an inch thick. Fortunately the concept of 'an offensive weapon' had not yet become part of the law. Still, I'm glad I never had to use it.

Scouting provided an excellent introduction to responsibility and I have always been pleased that my parents judged me responsible enough, just before I was fourteen, to cycle with a friend two hundred miles down the Great North Road to camp in London for a few days. Given the wartime setting, and even allowing for the lower levels of vehicle traffic in wartime, it was a great act of faith by our 'olds'. They might have been less confident if they had known that after completing the ride in two days we would become separated as soon as we reached London. Being young men, 'it couldn't possibly happen to us' so we had no contingency plan. At times like that there is no substitute for a streak of self confidence. I camped on Dulwich Common for a few thoroughly enjoyable days, then rode back to Hull to find that Fenton had done more or less the same. My parents made no fuss, which make it unthinkable to be irresponsible ever again.

As soon as I reached the minimum required age of fourteen, I completed my First Class scout's qualification and then, having added the extras required to qualify as a King's Scout, I resigned. It was time for something new.

The air raids continued throughout the early high school years. Everyone became accustomed to them but boys of my age became frustrated as the months and years passed. Other boys only two or three years older became bicycle messengers for the Air Raid Wardens, a job which entailed being out on the streets, braving dangers, rather than being cooped up in the shelter.

Parents just didn't understand how much we wanted to be heroes. But the memory made it easy to understand in later years how easy it is for fanatics anywhere to persuade boys of ten, or even less, to take up arms and fight for a cause.

Boys were not the only ones willing to do their bit for 'the cause'. One of the most savage memories is of the passion of the mother of one of my friends. A gentle person in every way except one. She prepared for the possibility of a German pilot being shot down and having to land by parachute in her vicinity by studding her wooden potato masher with three inch nails. Do not doubt that in the climate of those times she would have used it. As the song from 'South Pacific' says, 'You've got to be carefully taught', but if taught, anyone can hate.

Like so many other aspects of war, the air raids were ninety per cent boredom, we suffered nothing more than tiredness. There were always stories of horrific experiences, like seeing a policeman's helmet lying in the road and, on coming closer, finding that there was still the policemen's head in it. But such dramas always happened to a remote friend of a friend of a friend, never to someone that we actually knew. Most of us had to make do with nothing more than gawping at the much bigger craters made by the land mines which replaced bombs on some raids, and sneaking into the part of the RAF airfield at Sutton where the remains of British and German planes which had been shot down were kept, to satisfy ghoulish curiosity and steal a few souvenirs.

The closest I came to real action was during the first daylight air raid on 1st July 1940. A lone German aircraft approached the city from the west and the authorities had no time to sound the sirens. The raider made machine gun attacks on some of the city's barrage balloons and as there was no anti-aircraft gunfire the pilot probably enjoyed the sight of the tracer ammunition igniting the hydrogen filling. I was riding home through Swinburne Street as the raider dealt with our local balloon tethered in the nearby Garden Village. The sound of the machine guns certainly livened me up. Not knowing how far away the firing was or in which direction the plane was flying, but well aware how fast planes moved, I first performed the classic manoeuvre of dropping to the ground, then reflecting that that didn't really help at all, I leapt back onto my bike and pedalled for home as fast as I could. Even though the firing never came close, the incident taught me the difference between wishing to be in danger and actually being there. There was a strange sequel to the incident after I joined the Navy years later.

Drama may have been rare but the tiredness was real, especially after a near miss damaged the roof and bedrooms of our house and we had to sleep elsewhere until repairs were completed. There was an organisation for that. Each evening busloads of people in similar predicaments would be taken to a church or school hall at Bilton, about six miles away. There we made ourselves as comfortable as we could and slept on the floor. As I recall it, 'as comfortable as we could' didn't amount to much. It was good to get back to the house and shelter routine when repairs were completed.

The war dragged on, schooling was always a mixture of the exhilarating promise of learning and the drudgery of learning it. Girls were on the horizon and although hair cream was unobtainable we had to do something to make ourselves beautiful for them. I shudder to recall that the affordable and available substitutes for the Brylcreme, which allegedly all went to the RAF's fighter pilots, were Vaseline and liquid paraffin. Yuk!

My half-brother Raymond had joined the Royal Navy as a Seaman Boy in the mid-thirties and served in submarines throughout the war, having a lucky escape when illness kept him in Bighi Hospital in Malta thus missing the last fatal patrol of HMS Turbulent commanded by Lieutenant Commander 'Tubby' Linton VC. Clifford had left the Merchant Navy when the war began and joined the Royal Navy. He was the Coxswain of a

Motor Torpedo Boat which was sunk in the Straights of Messina in 1943 and was a prisoner in Germany for the rest of the war.

In May 1945 the war in Europe ended and there was never a greater regret than that of my generation on VE night. It was not a regret that the war had finished without our participation. By then we knew very well that war was not an heroic business. It was a regret that although we were old enough to go into the centre of Hull to join in the wild rejoicing, we were too young to take a more active part in it. A fraction older and we might have shared in the generous giving, learned a lot that night and been able to answer Michael Caine's question 'What's It All About?' Having missed the chance we had to wait a long time for the next!

VJ Day was quiet by comparison. The atomic bombs had been dropped and my friends and I were glad because we had no doubt that many thousands of lives would be saved. We had heard the casualty figures as the allies patiently liberated island after island in the Pacific. There was no reason to suppose that the Japanese would not fight on their own doorstep. So the alternatives were to occupy Japan at the cost of many more lives or, an option which isn't discussed much even today, mine their waters, blockade them and wait for them to starve to death or surrender. Either way, the bomb saved lives. ours and perhaps even some of theirs! Relief that it was all over was the emotion of the day.

Were we children changed as a result of our experience of the air raids and the 'war on the home front'? The answer must be yes. First, above all, there has been a lifelong thankfulness that I survived. The advocates of 'adventure training' believe that undertaking some hazardous experience, even under carefully controlled conditions to minimise the risk, is enough to change people. World War 2 provided many of us children with that experience, all the more character forming and thankfulness promoting, because the conditions and risks were not at all *controlled.* Second, there was for many years a reaction to the whistling sound which had been made by falling bombs, but that was not as they say nowadays, a big deal. Third, many of us acquired a lifelong dislike for any form of wastage of food, not a bad thing at all!

I did not link one other fact to the war until I read Michael Caine's autobiography, 'What's It All About?'. There I learned that we share a lasting distaste for the smell of rubber. He attributes this to his experience of gas masks which combined fear of the undiscriminating nature of the poison gas, which we all believed might be dropped on us, with an attempt, fortunately not shared by all of us, to breathe when wearing a mask from which the inlet plug had not been removed. He may well be right for I have no recollection of revulsion for the smell before the war.

All in all, given that we did not know the word trauma existed and that stress counselling would not be invented for many decades, we didn't come out of it too badly.

Chapter 5

The Rites of Passage Years

Into the dull and depressing realities of the last years of the war and the early post-war years there intruded two aspects of the same new interest: sex. The powerful physical changes of puberty and the sweet discovery of girls. If those words betray to the reader that the transition to adolescence was not a smooth one, they serve well, for our ignorance was immense by the standards of today. Most of us were well aware how little we knew but the conventions prevented us admitting it. Perhaps 'twas ever thus.

The very first intimations of changes to come are quite clear in memory. I was still young enough to be reading 'Biggles' books when I became old enough to have a warm glow when I read the one, the only one I think, in which Biggles had a girl friend. Then came surreptitious collections of photographs of pin-ups from various sources and later still an interest in the only accessible magazine of the day with naked women in it, the nudist journal 'Health and Efficiency'. 'Men Only' was still a long way down the track. Needless to say, these sources failed to give any warning of the magnitude of the changes awaiting us. Nor was there any other source available. Parents had nothing to say on the subject and at our single sex school we lacked the worldly wisdom that girls always seemed to possess.

The first violent eruption of sexual activity occurred almost spontaneously one night as I undressed to go to bed and my first response was a strong feeling of guilt. Why, I have no clear idea, but I have no difficulty in recognising that that's how it was. Guilt, and lots of it. Fortunately, it didn't take long to realise that this phenomenon gave me great pleasure and, there being no clear reason for it, guilt was put away. There remained the sad truth that young men are at their most active so early in life, when, in those days at least, there were strong prohibitions on practicing our new competence in the most natural way.

I'm glad to say there was no prohibition on the enjoyment of the company of girls albeit at a much more innocent level, nor was there any shortage of girls wishing to enjoy our company. 'Our' is very much the right word because the custom of the time in our circle was that intermingling often began on a group basis. There may have been some boy-girl relationships lasting more than a few weeks or months among the boys and girls of the co-education schools but for the rest of us, a group was the usual basis of the time. 'Safety in numbers' it was sometimes called by mothers of daughters.

Our group evolved from a number of individual friendships into 'The Gang'. Despite the title there was nothing sinister about us. We were probably more than averagely law abiding and respectable, but we liked the name and it served us for more than three years. 'Joe' often took a leading role and Sid, Arthur, Harry, Rowland and I were the 'permanent' members. Others came and went. Arthur was at the Nautical College preparing to become a Merchant Navy Officer and I was at the Technical College. The others had left school at fourteen and had jobs, Sid apprenticed to his shoe repairer father, the others in manual work of various kinds.

It is years since I became convinced that in our society the fundamental process involved in adolescence and the teenage years is simply 'hanging about waiting for maturity to happen'. How else can the observed evidence be so easily explained? Some mothers of daughters have suggested that the correct verb should be 'moping' or 'drooping' but the principle is the same. We were no exception.

In the earliest years we hung about in the spacious East Park. We played cricket and made the wide variety of swings and roundabouts in the children's section perform beyond any young child's wildest dreams and probably beyond their worst *nightmares. Those monstrosities of tubular steel and cast iron had their genesis in the nineteenth century school of design which believed that everything should last at least a hundred years. It was just as well. Though intended for younger children, they could take our abuse and allow us to establish the pecking order of bravado based on willingness to take each apparatus to its limits. Nowadays, it's fashionable to suppose that all young people believe they are immortal and can come to no harm. The war had taught us otherwise. But that didn't stop us taking risks!*

There were two other pastimes during the week. The Maybury Road Youth Club, and promenading up and down sections of the Holderness Road. Neither required much money which was just as well for even those who had jobs had very little. The phrase 'disposable income' hadn't been invented which didn't matter because no-one had much of it anyway. No-one directed advertising at us. No-one exhorted us to spend our money on records or drinks, for we had little and we needed the little we had for Sundays.

Sundays were different and they formed the foundation for much of our lives. It's true that sometimes Saturdays were as good as Sundays but they were the 'optional extra' of our lives. Saturday was part of the five and a half day standard working week for the workers of the gang. Saturday mornings were perhaps the only part of my life they envied. But Sundays were the main event and whenever the weather allowed they followed a set pattern for some years.

The bicycle was the key to our weekend pleasures and the coast was our usual Sunday destination. Our motivation had two interconnected components. The first was to exercise the passion of young men for physical prowess. The land between Hull and the coast, known as Holderness, was more or less flat and it took no great effort to cycle the sixteen miles to Hornsea or Withernsea. The term 'macho' was not used until about thirty years after my youth ended but that's more or less the concept that drove us to extend our trips to Bridlington, about thirty miles from home, and even to Scarborough, over forty miles. These longer trips taught us what hills really are.

The other motivation was our desire to attract young females and showing off to attract is undoubtedly part of the concept of 'machismo'. The problem was that few of the girls wished to exhaust themselves cycling thirty or forty miles each way. And although there were girls aplenty in Bridlington and Scarborough, they were not what we sought. We were looking for girls from Hull, preferably from our own area, so that we could enjoy their company during the week with a minimum of effort. So our longer rides tended to be boys only but they provided us with the blase boasts 'You should have come to Bridlington with us last week' which we hoped would impress the girls the following weekend when they joined us on, or were 'chatted up' during, the Hornsea and Withernsea rides.

The favourite memories must be of rides to Hornsea. Before reaching the sea, there was the delight of Hornsea Mere, a beautiful lake well over a mile long with rowing boats for hire. We could only afford half an hour there but no matter, the lake was followed by the Amusement Arcade. We recognised from the start that the machines were there to extract our money with a minimum chance of giving a good return but that didn't matter. Our optimists knew that one day the grab on that little crane would hook the only valuable prize on their favourite machine. It never did.

More importantly, the arcade gave us access to music of our own choosing. Even if a family had a gramophone, very few records would have been available. The Juke Box in the arcade allowed us to choose from a wide selection. Better still, someone else might put their penny in the machine and choose it. Was the popular music of the day better or worse than that of today? There's no way of knowing. To our shame we enjoyed 'Mareseatoatsanddoeseatoatsandlittlelambseativy' but need not *be ashamed of our delight in Harry James playing 'Trumpet Blues and Cantabile', still enjoyable today.*

Most importantly, the amusement arcade was the accepted place for making contact with girls. Even if we had 'brought our own' there would probably be other girls there that they knew and if we boys could attract them, our circle would be enlarged and enriched. What more could any young man wish, given that neither Porsches nor the permissive society had yet been invented? The answer to that followed the ride home to Hull.

Every Sunday evening 'The Gang' went to the cinema. If money permitted, anyone might go to the cinema on another day too, but Sunday was a ritual observance. Our favourite cinema was the 'Astoria' on the Holderness Road opposite Craven Park, the home of the Kingston Rovers Rugby League team. We tried to get there in time to get seats in the back row, not always successfully for the competition was fierce. Disappointingly, occupation of the back row did not imply anything torrid.

By the standards of today we were astonishingly innocent and gentle. An example? Our gang, with its major interest 'girls', formed when we were fifteen. That fact alone might suggest that we were all behind the young of today in our sexual development. In my own case, a combination of natural diffidence accentuated by sequestration in a single sex school and plain old shortage of money made the process of getting to know girls even more difficult. So I benefited greatly from the custom of belonging to the group of boys and girls. Never more so than one evening at the Astoria cinema when Shirley, notionally Joe's girl at that time, slipped her hand into mine, ceased being Joe's girl, and began my first encounter of a close but wholly innocent kind.

Affections and partnerships changed frequently and these changes never caused any animosity. There was only one couple, Sid and Betty, who remained paired off for many years, despite which increasing maturity brought diverging interests and they never married. Looking back on the period, it was generally one of happy experimentation, typified by a catchphrase, 'Hold hands till love comes'. Given a bit of propinquity we could fall in love with almost anyone. The frustrations of knowing that we had to restrict our experiments just had to be accepted. Mothers in our area brought their daughters up with a very clear understanding that the only infallible method of birth control was crossed legs.

We were all aware of the convention to be brought into play if we got carried away: marriage without any option. Daunting enough for any boy, doubly daunting for me, for I already knew I wanted to explore the world far beyond Lee Street. Whatever the theoretical merits or deficiencies of that old convention, it worked in my group. None of us fathered a child during those teenage years. Which is why, as a crusty old man in a different world, I grumble about paying taxes to support, often in greater comfort than we ever enjoyed, the thousands of very young, unmarried Australian mothers whose irresponsible young men freely donate their sperm but not their wages.

Our group had other conventions, not so serious, for which I was grateful. We were quite communistic in our financial affairs, practicing 'from each according to his or her means' so that we could all enjoy our modest amusements. And there is no doubt that as a student I was a great beneficiary of the custom. If anyone of the old team ever reads these words they can be sure that I have never forgotten their generosity. Financial support was not always a gift or loan. Sometimes it was a matter of trading. Years later, Betty, who became my wife's bridesmaid, reminded us at our Silver Wedding celebrations that she used to buy my sweet ration coupons for a shilling and sixpence a week to swell my funds. And even though Yorkshire folk, young or old, are noted for their directness, there was a subtle convention that when a boy and girl agreed to go to the cinema and he said 'See you inside' it meant he couldn't afford to pay for her ticket.

Cinema was not only entertainment. Though almost all the films we saw were Hollywood products of little artistic merit, they introduced us to a wider world of music and singing. Set against the home background I mentioned earlier, in which anything except the popular music of the day was classified as 'highbrow' and switched off, our films had much to offer. Many of my generation will always be grateful to the conductor Jose Iturbi who began our musical education by introducing us to classical music via Tchaikovsky's first piano concerto and to Beniamino Gigli for bringing us a love of opera.

Gigli had the greater impact of the two and singing became, however badly some of us did it, part of our lives. We sang as we walked along the roads, we sang at the youth club. We loved it. The only problem was that we all wanted to sing like Gigli and it was a long time before most of us were reconciled with our baritone voices. No matter. I remain wedded to the view that everyone should sing. Those who are lucky enough to have good voices and to be trained to do it properly just have to suffer the rest of us as best they can!

By any standards our conduct was conventional and usually very proper. There were exceptions of course. There was never any alcohol in our house during my childhood but there was no parental resistance to the idea of having cider to drink at my sixteenth birthday party. The war was over, we were a little better off, it could be afforded. Great. And it was. At least until my girl friend, one of the earliest, exchanged the atmosphere of the crowded little room in Lee Street for fresh air. Megan went out like the proverbial light in the taxi taking us the half mile to her home. As far as I can remember I arranged her sleeping form in a tasteful pose across her doorstep, saying to myself, 'In the morning, Megan's mother and father will wake up, open the door and find their dear daughter. And they'll be so pleased'. Exactly why I should have thought the last bit, even having much cider taken, I've never been able to work out. They weren't. I never darkened their doorstep again!

Having got past that first hurdle, drink was not a problem. Cider was repugnant after the birthday party incident. Drinking wine was unheard of in our circle, and spirits suffered more than beer from the basic problem of drink, that it had to be paid for. Nevertheless, the idea of drinking was very attractive, and when an older friend occassionally invited us to drink at the Merchant Navy Club, it made us feel very sophisticated.

The grind of high school years neared its end and 'Tiger' Harrison, the Headmaster, interviewed us to find out what we wanted to be. By that time my mind was clear on the subject. 'I want to join the Royal Navy, Sir'. I didn't tell him that my underlying wish was to combine engineering and seagoing. The Royal Navy bit was only a desire to explore the unknown, a reaction to living in a Merchant Navy city.

Then came my first experience of the kind of limited thinking which helped slow the rate of change of British life. 'We'll enter you for the Artificer Apprenticeship examinations', said he. 'But I want to be an officer, Sir', said I. To his credit, he took my remark in his stride, reflecting only that he didn't think anyone had ever joined the navy as a cadet from 'The Tech', but I wish he had not automatically assumed that I couldn't possibly be aiming for Wardroom rank. I encountered a similar attitude eighteen years later when the Rector of my son's school at Helensburgh in Scotland said he didn't bother to invite lawyers to tell his pupils about careers in the law, ' . . . .because we don't get many children who want to go in for the law'. Surprise, surprise. And tough on the children who do not have a stubborn streak!

My interview with the Headmaster made me realise that above all I was studying for my own good, just in time for some last weeks of study which resulted in School Certificate passes in all subjects, 'Credits' sufficient for Matriculation in all necessary subjects except English, and one 'Distinction', in Applied Mathematics. The deficiency in English was rectified at the September examinations in Leeds. Another hurdle had been cleared, just!.

When the procedure for entering the RN had been digested, it was agreed that I would apply to begin the London University external degree course at the Tech. By doing the first 'Inter BSc Engineering' year I could prepare myself for the Civil Service Examination for navy cadetships. It was to be the first broadening of my education.

Sometimes, during our years at the Riley High School, we had left our quarantine at The Boulevard to spend some time at the main part of 'The Tech' in Park Street. We knew it was a different world. There were so many older students doing so many different things. Superior young women were doing their 'Pre-nursing' training. Friendlier women known as Dilutees occupied the machine shop learning to turn and mill so they could work in the local factories in place of men away at the war. All very exciting and as a bonus, it was a mile less to cycle each way. The experience boosted our morale. Perhaps, despite the oft repeated predictions of one of our more cynical masters, our destiny was not to be hung.

When our engineering class assembled my expectation of differences was confirmed. There were nine of us. The oldest, George, was twenty eight, a tradesman who had spent five years in the army. Two others from the Blackburn Aircraft Company at Brough were beginning a 'sandwich' course which combined the last part of their apprenticeships with working for a degree. I met my first public schoolboy, from Sedbergh in North Yorkshire. He exuded the confidence which I later learned was a common product of public schooling but there seemed little to back it up and I never heard whether he turned into a half decent engineer. I was the only 'kid' in the engineering class. All my *contemporaries who stayed on to get degrees had chosen chemistry.*

Pure and applied maths, physics, all the usual subjects were still there albeit at a higher level, continuing the impression that this was still 'school'. The subject that really made me feel like a budding engineer was engineering drawing. We had studied it since the age of eleven, but not like this. We no longer did drawing at our desks. Instead there was a real drawing office, a big drafting machine for each of us. We were half way to being real designers. The hot summer afternoon on the boards, when George produced a pint bottle of beer for each of us from the poacher's pocket of an entirely superfluous raincoat, completed, as far as I was concerned, the rites of passage from schoolboy to serious student.

The year passed quickly. Kindly members of the staff tried to persuade me to stay, get my degree, and then join the navy if I still wished to do so. They were wiser than they knew. The navy assumed that graduates would be at least twenty one years old, and fixed their pay and seniority accordingly. An external London student starting at sixteen and completing a first degree at around twenty could have scored a rare victory over the system.

The advice of mentors went unheeded. Adventure called, and after resisting tempting advertisements for the Palestine Police, a short-lived body formed mainly to prevent Jews getting to Israel until that country existed officially, I did the Civil Service Commission's navy entrance examinations, achieved a reasonable mark, and was called for interview. I knew that if successful in joining the RN I would be entering a different world. But I had no idea how different it would be.

The differences in education and background were not too apparent when our group of interviewees left London for Brockenhurst, home of the Admiralty Interview Board, and our home for three days. Why not? The last act of the medical examiners in London was to dilate the pupils of our eyes until any letter of the alphabet smaller than three feet high, viewed from further away than six feet, seemed just a blur. We wondered if managing to get off at the right station was a first small test in the selection process. But not for long. There was too much else to think about.

Was the Lieutenant Commander who said that he was merely our guide, nothing to do with the selection process, to be trusted? I thought not but enjoyed playing billiards with him on a far better table than those in the hall above the Savoy cinema on the Holderness road. Would it be wise to leap to the front and assist a rival who was making a mess of one of the practical 'get that one ton load across that chasm using only the pair of chopsticks and ball of string provided' tests? Or should I allow a rival to make a mess of it?

Most curious of all. Why did the Admiral presiding over the Board think it so strange that I did not wish to join the navy unless I could be an engineer officer? I did not know then that all would-be naval officers were expected to want to stand on the bridge on dark and stormy nights saying 'Left hand down a bit' or something similar. Nor that many candidates who failed selection for seaman officers, or whose eyesight was not good enough, were invited to become engineers. When I did find out, I was affronted. How could anyone do engineering if they didn't love it? Subsequently I reluctantly admitted that some 'failed seamen' became competent engineers. Nevertheless, it gave me and other engineers some pleasure when, years later, increasingly complex technology required all General List engineer officers to have degrees, and some officers who were not up to it became seamen.

Meanwhile, back at the interview, there was a small Meccano model into which a few simple faults had been introduced and we were timed as we diagnosed and remedied the faults. Pathetically easy. Not so the questions on geography.

Where would you take on fuel if you had to steam from England to Timbuktu?

Lieutenant John Pratt, alias John Winton, wrote the definitive description of the Board in action in his book *'We Joined The Navy'*. Definitive, but rather hard on ex-Scouts. I hope I was not quite as idiotic as his candidate Machonochie! The only thing worth adding is my experience of the Admiral's final question, *'What will you do if you fail this interview?'* I hadn't the slightest idea so the only available answer was, *'Try again, Sir'*. I never had access to the records but I'm prepared to believe that he said *'If he tries again, give him an extra mark for perseverance and let him in. If he doesn't, good riddance!'* I did try again, but nothing is ever that simple.

The world is small now. Not so in 1947. So while I was over two hundred miles from home it made sense to visit brother Raymond, now a Chief Petty Officer with a home at Whitstable, a wife Ruth whom I had rarely met, and three children. The idea of having a family in a wider sense than just a mother and father had become very appealing. Raymond and his family fitted the bill, not least because Clifford had settled in his wife Marian's home town, Oldham. Raymond and I became friends, and having never had younger siblings, I loved my nephew Roger, his younger sisters Rowena and Elizabeth, and later, Linda, born in 1950. I enjoyed my few days there, days which laid the foundation for much that happened later.

Readers who did not share those years may wonder why, when shortage of money was such a pervasive problem, I didn't take a part time job while I was still at high school. The answer is in two parts. First, the tiredness which was part of our share of the war, and second, the lack of opportunities. Jobs in those days were for full time workers, usually fathers of families. In Lee Street even the newspaper deliveries were done by the son of the owners of the local corner shop, a man of forty or more with a handicap known then as St Vitus' dance which caused his head to roll every few seconds. There were no part time jobs for school boys in the Lee Street area.

After the interview, there was at last a chance to earn some money. Most young men were still away in the Services and an acute shortage of strong labourers made it easy to get a job as a 'navvy' building the roads for a housing estate in Laburnum Avenue, close to home. It's a good job it was a small estate and narrow roads because the only machinery used was a concrete mixer, and that had to be fed by hand shovel. The gang comprised the 'gaffer' and four men all around sixty years old, one young man who had been invalided out of the Army, and me.

The standard hours before overtime were 55 per week and the pay two shillings and a farthing per hour. Riches indeed for an impoverished student and I was quite fit enough to share with the ex-soldier the hardest work, feeding the concrete mixer. I learned not to rush at the work in the manner of the young bulls, instead working economically in a slow steady rhythm. The sun shone and all was well. Until Friday. Then I found that the first pay packet of my life contained only three-quarters of what I expected.

The gaffer gave me my fare to go to the office and sort it out. The office had it right. The gaffer had assumed that I was over eighteen. Very good for a young man's vanity until I learned that the rate of pay for a seventeen year old was one shilling and sixpence an hour. Though disappointed, I would have been happy to continue sharing the hardest work but the gaffer would have none of it. His sense of natural justice relegated me to tea-boy, fetcher of cigarettes from the local shop and every other menial task on the site. Three-quarters of a pay packet is better than none and I stayed with the gang until it was time to try again to join the navy. I gave the required notice of leaving. Two hours, either way, was the custom of the industry then!

The result of the Civil Service Commission examination wasn't so good this time. I had been enjoying the money I earned instead of revising as much as I should have done. So when called for interview to demonstrate what were known then as 'Officer Like Qualities' I had a backlog to make up. I did my best and returned to Hull to await the outcome.

Trams had gone, replaced by trolley buses but they still needed conductors and my father soldiered on. The excited, almost revolutionary mood of some ex-servicemen with its 'Joe for King' graffiti, had largely passed. Joe, of course, was Joseph Stalin, still a friend and ally in many eyes. Churchill had been discarded at the 1945 general election, being replaced as Prime Minister by the austere Clement Attlee. Re-examination of the newspapers of the day shows idealistic hopes for a better society quickly fading. Homes and jobs for heroes seemed as hard to come by as at the end of the First World War. The sun was sinking rapidly on the remnants of Empire. Rationing was as strict as in wartime with no sign of an end to it. The 'We are all in it together' spirit, never as strong as the propaganda machine wished everyone to believe during the war, was soon lost. Depression all round. What was there to be cheerful about? In my case, being old enough to get a licence to ride a motor cycle!

Young men and women today almost invariably learn to drive a car as soon as they are old enough to qualify for the necessary British Provisional Licence or Australian Permit. Someone can usually provide a car. They have no idea of the frustration we suffered in a carless society, especially those of us who understood how cars worked. We knew we could drive if only we could lay hands on a vehicle. My chance came when I heard that 'Jackson's the Printer' needed a driver for a delivery tricycle and I got the job.

The machine was a curious contraption. The back end of a two-stroke motor cycle pushed a two wheeled box carrying about a cubic yard of payload. It was steered by a handlebar attached to the box, had three gears and was quite fast enough for work in the Hull traffic. It had no pillion seat and no reverse gear. That allowed it to be driven, unaccompanied, by the holder of a 'Provisional' motor cycle licence. Five shillings, paid by the boss, for my licence, a couple of 'L' plates and I was in business.

My belief that I could drive was justified. I had imagined driving for so many years that I knew exactly how a clutch would feel as it was 'let in'. Bliss! Something, however humble, to drive at last. The machine was called a 'DOT' which stood for 'devoid of trouble', a bit of a misnomer for not only was the engine hard to start, a common feature of two stroke engines at that time, but it also gave me my first experience of driving without a clutch when the cable broke far from base.

But that was all part of the learning experience. Two other parts were equally memorable in different ways. Jackson's had an almost wholly female workforce and although sexual harassment legislation was unheard of, sexual harrassment of men in workplaces with a majority of women was commonplace! It's true the women at Jackson's did not have as fearsome a reputation as their sisters at the pickle factory or the Metal Box Company. In those places, it was said, young men were held down on a bench and exposed for inspection. Total quality assurance, circa 1947.

Life at the printers was genteel by comparison, but still sufficiently explicit to embarrass most seventeen year olds. certainly enough to embarrass me. But if the sexual teasing looked like getting out of hand and causing me a real problem, the cook-cum-canteen manageress came to my aid. She was a gentle person who never had to raise her voice to get her workmates to stop. A born leader, perhaps, for her wishes were obeyed and her interventions were not resented? Or was it that anyone flouting her authority would find themselves with the smallest portion of lunch for the next week? I never discovered the answer but I learned that leadership comes in many forms and not always from conventional sources.

The other learning experience came at Christmas. It was the custom for delivery boys to present a card offering the 'Compliments of the Season' when making the last delivery to each firm before the holiday. The hoped for response was a tip, usually half a crown, sometimes five shillings. I had two problems with this system. The first was that although I needed the money desperately, for how else could I hope to take out any of the girls so plentifully available at Jackson's, I was nervous about 'begging'. Left to myself, I might have foregone the extra cash but an especially nice card befitting a printer's delivery boy had been produced and everyone told me very forcefully to suppress my diffidence, my words, not theirs, and make the most of the opportunity. There wouldn't be any difficulties, they said.

They lied of course, and my second problem was that the people who were unwilling to offer a tip usually expressed their refusal in the crudest and most personal terms. More embarrassment, but good for the development of a thicker skin than I then possessed. Unfortunately, a thick skin is not the same as self confidence. It was the latter I really needed but if you haven't got it, a thick skin is a good second best!

Jackson's also opened up another opportunity. One of the few men there invited me to play rugby. I had some previous experience of playing rugby league in the '13 to 17 year old' league for a team called Hull Kingston Rangers. Now, without anyone bothering to give me an explanation of the different rules, I found myself playing union. A few kickings soon taught me that the last thing you should ever do when playing the union code is to hang onto the ball when tackled. Fortunately I was unaware that it 'simply isn't done' to play rugby union after playing league and continued to enjoy playing 'coarse rugby' for the next eight years. I think I enjoyed, more than most people, watching *the league versus union matches televised in England in 1996. A healthy sign if ever I saw one.*

Perhaps the Admiralty Interview Board did give me a few extra marks for persistence. I was accepted, and in due course thick envelopes arrived with instructions about uniforms, requests for parental assurances that I would not run home to mum after the first week, and a hundred and one other matters. Suggestions that I stay on at Jackson's fell, like suggestions that I complete my degree, on deaf ears.

Christmas 1947 was good.

Chapter 6

I Joined the Navy

If you are allowed to join an organisation as prestigious as the Royal Navy it is best not to be late. When my father and I studied the mass of paperwork which accompanied my acceptance into the service, somehow we both understood that joining instructions would be sent later. Working class families did not have telephones so when I was two days overdue, the navy sent us a telegram. It made it clear that the instructions had been somewhere in the package. Once again, I had to catch up. Perhaps that is the reason why so much that happened during that one term at the Royal Naval College Dartmouth is a bit of a blur.

There was much to learn, not only about things maritime but about my fellow cadets and about the world. The RN cadets were mostly from public schools but there was one other working class boy from Saint Helens in Lancashire, one or two from Grammar Schools, and a couple of navy-wise ex-artificer apprentices who had earned selection for commissioned rank. In addition to these RN cadets there were Commonwealth cadets from India and Pakistan wearing medals commemorating the independence gained during the cadets' initial training in 1947, and from pre-apartheid South Africa, and foreign cadets from Egypt, then still a monarchy, and a solitary representative of the Irish navy.

Learning sometimes involved shedding the misconceptions and parochial nonsense with which we had been indoctrinated. I had been taught that our British ways were the best in the world. So it was a shock to learn, for instance, that the Indians considered our practice of bathing a dirty habit. We did not have any Australian colleagues at that stage, they would join us later in the Cadet Training Cruiser. Had they been there to bring their national love of showering to the argument, they would doubtless have supported the Indians' line.

While we learned from one another the navy got down to the job of teaching us the basics of naval life. We learned how the navy is organised, how to march, salute, make our beds and sling hammocks the navy way, and all the thousand and one bits and pieces of navy detail. We were taught to tie the knots some of us had learned years before in the Scouts but the process was nothing like the cruel parody in 'We Joined the Navy'. We began to learn the Navy's strange language beginning with simple words like port and starboard for left and right, through numbers which might mean anything from a cure-all pill to a punishment drill, to esoteric expressions like 'salt horse' for a seaman officer who had not specialised in gunnery, navigation, communications or some other subdivision of the branch still called at that time 'the Executive branch'.

Not surprisingly we were given a fairly thorough medical examination soon after we arrived and the assessments of the merits of our physique, upper and lower limbs, heart, eyes, ears, and musculature were entered as a 'PULHEEMS' score, with details of weight and height, in our Pay Books. The final 'S' for mental stability was kept from us. Characteristically, no one bothered to explain the rating system to us. Nevertheless I was pleased to have a row of '1s' and the entry weight of 164 lb served as a lifelong benchmark. Less pleasing was the barbaric dentistry.

Our parents had to present us to the navy with any necessary dental treatment completed and a Hull dentist had done the two or three fillings I needed. He was a gentle old man who still used a foot treadle operated drill to remove the minimum of decayed matter and produce neat little fillings. I was not best pleased when, only a few weeks later, the Dartmouth dentist roared his displeasure and drilled them all out into great craters which he *then filled. I should have protested but I had already been taught not to criticise the Navy's way of doing things. I kept quiet.*

The navy had strong views about criticism and loyalty. It was self evidently improper in a disciplined service to criticise any aspect of naval life to our subordinates and we had no trouble with that idea. Next came not criticising the service to our superiors. That sounded like simple self preservation to anyone who wasn't completely naive. Then the teaching tried to put a prohibition on criticism between contemporaries. That seemed to me to be asking too much of mere mortals and, if obeyed, likely to stifle discussion of possible improvements. And even at that stage I couldn't believe that the navy was perfect.

Loyalty as taught at Dartmouth was a simpler concept. We could expect the loyal support of our seniors, even when we made mistakes. We were to give loyal support to our subordinates even when they made mistakes. The good superior was always the one who shouldered the responsibility for subordinates' errors when reproach by higher authority was in the air. That principle stood the test of application in service and civilian life over the next forty years.

Looked at from a strategic point of view, our training was based on two important items of navy philosophy. Though we did not appreciate it at the time, the navy was trying to heal the breach, which had opened a century earlier when steam propulsion was reluctantly introduced, between the seamen officers and the engineers. The Admiralty's strategy, which had been introduced by Admiral Fisher in the 'Selbourne Memorandum' of December 1902, was based on the idea of inculcating mutual knowledge and respect by giving all cadets the same training for the first eighteen months or so. Therefore we cadets who proudly had a (E) for Engineering after our rank had to learn as much seamanship, navigation, meteorology, etc as our executive colleagues, the executive cadets were exposed to the rigours of life in the boiler and engine rooms, and we both had to get a sound appreciation of the arts and crafts of those destined to be supply officers. It was, to say the least, a very expensive strategy. It would be five and a half years before we engineers really earned our keep.

The other bit of naval philosophy was that the best introduction to the ways of the sea is to go upon it in small boats. I never bothered to consider the wisdom of this, I was too busy enjoying the experience. In any case, given the principle of common training during our early years, we could all expect to serve as Midshipmen driving liberty boats full of sailors returning from the delights of shore, or perhaps manning a sea-boat to rescue a crashed pilot in gale force seas. We soon appreciated that small-boatmanship is very different to big-shipmanship. For my part, I was entranced to spend part of almost every day afloat on the River Dart, learning to handle boats under sail or power. Even the introduction to 'pulling', the navy's word for rowing, in boats weighing up to 3 tons using oars up to 17 feet long was almost a pleasure once the blisters on bottom and hands had healed. This was definitely what I joined for.

Better still when a Battle Class destroyer, HMS Sluys, and subsequently the sloop HMS Burghhead Bay, arrived to give us our first experience of being at sea for a few days. I soon realised that the most important item issued to us in those ships was a bucket. I was not one of those hardy souls who eat hearty meals during gales, and I experienced for the first time the twin torments of seasickness, the illness itself and the wish to curl up and die that goes with it. But with our buckets always at hand I and the others steered the ship, manned the sea-boat, became acquainted with the gun turrets, and were introduced to how the whole ship operated. I did not know it at the time but, like many others, I would be sick for the first few days of each period at sea in a small ship throughout my career.

There was only a little foretaste of the great gulf between life in Lee Street and life in the wardroom during those early days at Dartmouth. However, there were some explicit indications of the way officers should behave and we learned a lot from the attitudes of the officers charged with our instruction. The basis of those attitudes was that it was a privilege to serve in the navy. And so, in many ways, it was. As cadets we did not 'sign on', we did not agree to serve for any specific number of years, we did not swear any oath of allegiance. We were joining the King's navy and our loyalty was presumed to be beyond question. For decades, even when employed on highly classified and sensitive matters, we were not required to sign the Official Secrets Act.

Our status might have had its origins in the navy's special relationship to the Sovereign but some of the attitudes we observed appeared to be based simply on British, officer-class snobbery. It was suggested, for example, that we should never query our pay. The King would give us some money each month and it would be bad form to count it, let alone to question whether the amount was correct. That attitude may have been reasonable around the turn of the century when all nominations for cadetships had to satisfy the First Lord that the parents of prospective cadets were of suitable background and sufficiently well off to support them during their years as subordinate officers. But our pay was two shillings and sixpence a day, reduced after a few weeks by one day's pay each week as a contribution to the newly introduced British National Health Service. And I had to save some of my pay to spend during my leave. I had serious reservations about the instructors' attitude to money!

One other characteristic became clear very early in our naval experience. The officers who taught us considered the Hostilities Only officers, who had borne much of the burden of fighting the recent war at sea, a horrible bunch and were united in their pleasure that the 'HOs' had almost all gone by then.

There was a feeling that now we could get back to being 'a real navy' again. At that stage it was far from clear what 'a real navy' was meant to be in their eyes. They were keen enough to teach us of the glorious traditions that we were to inherit. But there was no indication that they recognised the appalling deficiencies of the navy's preparedness for World War 2, of which I had learned from my brothers, from seamen in Hull, and from Mallalieu's book 'Very Ordinary Seaman'. Nor was there any indication that the navy was critically examining the lessons to be learnt from the war to ensure a better performance in future.

We learned about the ways of the navy as propounded by our officers. The navy way was the only possible way of doing things, the navy deserved the best, regardless of expense. Some of the teaching stood the test of time. Despite the navy's long experience of choleric admirals, we were taught that it was absolutely unthinkable for an officer to lose his temper when dealing with a subordinate, control was required at all times. But we were also taught that there was no objection to acting out a tremendous show of rage if that would help to make a point. Both proved admirable lessons.

Commander Geoffrey L Lowis' book 'Fabulous Admirals' refers repeatedly to the expression 'On Service' or 'Off Service'. I never heard it during my time at Dartmouth, nor for that matter during the next thirty one years. The idea was instilled though, especially in the context of giving or receiving 'bottles' or 'blasts', the Navy's words for a telling-off. It was good teaching that each incident of criticism or reprimand should be complete in itself, not to be forgotten, but to be contained and therefore no obstacle to living harmoniously in the ship, and in the case of officers often to having a drink together a couple of minutes after the fiercest of blasts.

In London, while we were beginning to learn the ways of the navy at Dartmouth, their Lordships struggled to ensure that there would still be one in future despite the austerity necessary in a near bankrupt Britain and the uncertainty about the future value of conventional forces in the age of the atomic bomb. I do not know whether they shared the ideas of our instructors. Probably, as at most times of navy history, they were a mixture of conservatives wishing to restore the past and reformers looking to the future. Both groups, if two there were, would have agreed on another very important principle underlying our training, namely that we had not joined a navy which gloried in war, but one which aimed to preserve peace.

Though virtually isolated from the 'Darts', the cadets who had joined Dartmouth at the age of thirteen, we too were treated like schoolboys. There was no leave to go into Dartmouth for the first half of the term and lights out was about half past nine. It seemed a great step backwards after being treated as an adult during my last year at the Tech, but it didn't matter very much. Given that our day was intensively organised from early morning to an hour or so before 'Pipe Down' and that almost every move had to be done 'at the double', we were usually too tired. We didn't know how much more tired we would feel when we joined the cadet training cruiser HMS Devonshire.

The Devonshire was much in our thoughts. We knew we were destined to spend two cruises totalling eight months in her, getting a good grounding in all the practical skills necessary to operate a warship, while continuing our classroom training. We would take the place of some of the seamen, stokers and stores ratings and learn by working alongside the remaining nucleus. Our cruises would be to the Baltic and the Mediterranean Seas. News had reached us that the cruise currently underway in the Caribbean had been interrupted by an operational requirement to transport army reinforcements to Belize to counter Guatemalan pressure on British Honduras. There was a possibility that the cadets who had left Dartmouth only a few weeks earlier would see action on their first cruise. We hoped to be as lucky.

Before moving on to Devonshire, however, there were examinations to be passed. They were not onerous but there was a strange event during a communications exam which left a vivid memory. Sitting at a desk in a conventional classroom in peaceful Dartmouth College, I suddenly heard machine-gun fire. Reflexes took over and I was under the desk in a flash. Reflexes then returned me to reality and I felt very silly as I climbed back onto my chair and, having realised what had happened, got on with the exam. The machine-gun-like noise had been created by a car on a gravel path and my brain had returned me to the day in 1940 when the German daylight raider had shot at a nearby anti-aircraft balloon in Hull. I'm glad I had that experience of how fast the brain can work in a real or imagined emergency.

Easter leave saw me returning to Hull and feeling depressed because most of my friends were becoming better paid as they moved up from juniors' wages to adults' at the age of eighteen. One was positively affluent having shelved his ambition to become a deck officer in the Merchant Navy. He had about twenty eight pounds to spend at the end of each three weeks at sea as a 'deckie learner' in a trawler. I had no doubts about the shortsightedness of his choice compared to the long term benefits of a career in the Royal or Merchant Navies, but I did wish the RN rewarded its cadet entrants a bit more generously.

I made sure I joined Devonshire on time. Captain John Wells' excellent book 'The Royal Navy: An Illustrated Social History 1870 - 1982' records that 'Geographically, most officers originated from those English counties south of a line from the Humber and Mersey and nearest to naval ports'. Those 'most officers' were wise. The journey by rail from Hull to Plymouth in the conditions of the late nineteen forties was very slow and the high excitement of really joining a ship for the first time was compromised by weariness. There at the end of the journey was the impressive hull towering over the naval bus which had brought us from the station, her three rows of scuttles and superstructure brightly lit. Great excitement.

The predominant memory after boarding the ship is of the noise. We took in our stride our distribution to various messes, issue of hammocks, allocation of slinging billets and so on. But the noise of the forced ventilation fans which kept us supplied with fresh air was something for which I was entirely unprepared and I remember wondering how anyone could ever sleep amidst such a din. I soon found out. The pace set at Dartmouth had been quite a gentlemanly preparation for the more strenuous life at sea and falling asleep was never a problem. Getting enough sleep was.

Sleeping in a hammock did not prove difficult. The hammock is so often displayed in films as a droopy sling in which the occupant is bent double. In that form it looks, and I'm sure would be, most uncomfortable. Hammocks as used in the RN were slung, tightly stretched between hammock bars roughly 17 feet apart, along the fore and aft line of the ship. Wooden 'spreaders' forced the edges to remain about the width of a pillow apart. The result was comfortable bed which had the advantage of remaining vertical when the ship rolled, and out of which it was impossible to fall in a rough sea. What more could one ask? Only perhaps that maritime museums such as the otherwise excellent one in Amsterdam would display hammocks the way sailors used them!

We continued our naval studies during the day and early evening either in the classrooms, with which Devonshire was well equipped, or had practical training in the myriad functions of a major war vessel. However, there were two differences between this and the Dartmouth routine. The first was that our studies were preceded by scrubbing the teak decks, barefooted, before breakfast every morning winter and summer, polishing the brightwork and generally smartening the ship up. The trouble was that except for the effects of sea air on polished brass the ship didn't really get dirty enough to warrant the effort involved. It was explained that ships had to have so many men to man all the action stations that work had to be found for them at all other times, which was of course almost all the time in peacetime. That needed thinking about.

The second difference was our introduction to watchkeeping during the night, on the bridge, in the boiler or engine rooms or elsewhere, mercifully reduced to two hours instead of the usual four. Starting even a couple of hours of extra work at ten PM, midnight, two or four in the morning took a bit of getting used to and left a convicttion that permanent tiredness is the normal condition of the later teenage years.

Such 'spare' time as we were allowed usually had to be devoted to polishing boots and blancoing webbing for the many drills we practiced and guards we mounted. And nothing I did was ever quite right. Perhaps my Divisional Officer, being the Gunnery Officer, felt he had to be the strictest. Whatever the reason, there always seemed to be something he could complain about. Unfortunately it would be many months before, as a relatively rich Midshipman I would be able to buy my first book, a volume of Kipling's poetry collected under the title 'The Seven Seas'. The words of 'The 'Eathen' would have reassured me that I was not the first to have this problem. And like Kipling's soldier who one day found himself with a 'full and proper kit', one day the Gunnery Officer inspected me and passed on without criticism. I felt as though he had forgotten something and almost wanted to call him back, but perhaps he hadn't, for he never complained again.

We 'Special Entry' cadets were joined in the Devonshire by our peers from the 13 year old entry stream, the 'Darts'. Some exuded tremendous confidence, they seemed to have been brought up in the 'born to rule' tradition. A few were extremely nervous and seemed unlikely to last long. Either way, even though they were on average only a few months younger, the Darts seemed rather immature. In reality, we were all inexperienced and the Service in its wisdom provided the rigorous routine which carried us all along during our first year. Later, beginning with our time at sea as Midshipmen, self-discipline would have to take over. That was when some of the more nervous cadets broke down and left the navy. But for the time being we were all in it together, sharing the excitement of going to sea.

Nor was our first taste of seagoing a routine affair. The cruise began with a visit to Bantry Bay on the south coast of Ireland. That excursion provided time for our instructors and the cadets who were on their second cruise to teach us many of the rudiments of working our ship. There for the first time I set foot on foreign soil and for the first time encountered the half wheedling and half bullying tones of a local alcoholic, not exactly begging outside the pub but expecting to be rewarded for balancing a heavy cart axle on what was left of his nose. If he thought I was a rich man's son who could reward him handsomely he was much mistaken. At Bantry, apart from visiting the local pubs, we painted the ship and readied her for the highlight of the cruise.

That highlight was providing a British naval presence at the eightieth birthday celebrations of King Gustav of Sweden in Stockholm. Little as I knew of international politics in those days, even I recognised some of the complexities of the Scandinavian situation. Sweden had been neutral in the war, and Denmark had surrendered without significant resistance to the invading German forces, whereas Norway had resisted strenuously. Altogether, a recipe for mutual detestation. And although two and a half years had passed since the war ended, I quickly learned that that was a very short time indeed in the timescale of international feelings. But reconciliation has to begin somewhere, somewhen, and as usual it began with a symbol, King Gustav's eightieth birthday celebrations.

Stockholm and the archipelago through which we approached it must be one of the most beautiful combinations of natural setting and man-made environment in the world. We steamed between dozens of tiny islands, some of which appeared near enough to touch, certainly near enough to give the navigator of any large vessel a few nervous moments. When all were gathered at the moorings it was a memorable sight, ships of many navies and the two of the most beautiful of all, the Danish Royal Yacht and the Norwegian navy's Sail Training Ship Sorlandet. I had been impressed as a child by the occasional full rigged ship in Hull docks but there was never one like the white hulled, gold trimmed Sorlandet. I have seen her several times since and she remains a magical vessel.

Beauty apart, the visit meant lots of ceremonial, gun salutes, guards, and one evolution which is impossible in today's warships. Known as 'manning ship', it invoked the memory of sailing ship days and involved climbing the Devonshire's modern tripod masts and manning the yards as if we were back in the days of sail. I loved it and having no fear of heights sought the highest position I could. I might not have been so keen had I realised that it was symbolic of the navy's wish to cling to the old customs and if possible turn back the clock, or at least slow it down.

Naturally, there was plenty of entertainment organised for us in Stockholm which introduced three lifelong delights into my life. The first was the different food, especially the many kinds of mayonnaise-laden salads. They could not have been more different to the soggy lettuce leaf and tomato sliver with which I had been brought up. The second was 'proper' coffee. The weak and watery English coffee was bad enough at that time but at home we usually drank 'Camp Coffee', well known, but mostly chicory rather than coffee. But by far the most notable discovery was that long haired blondes abounded at the Swedish naval academy where we were entertained at a dance. Great fun, apart that is from the discovery that unless you time your discrete stroll in the shrubbery carefully, to take advantage of the half hour or so of dark, you might as well not bother. That's summer life in high latitudes!

We soon learned that parties are not always for pleasure. We were expected to play a part in entertaining the many VIPs at the official receptions held onboard Devonshire.It was a daunting experience, typified by the incident in which an imposing figure in the uniform of an Admiral of the Royal Norwegian Navy walked up to two of us who were wondering what we should do next, held out his hand and introduced himself with the one word 'Knut'. I think we had it right when we worked out that that meant he was Prince Knut, the Norwegian king's brother. Needless to say, he knew exactly how to deal with two nervous young cadets. For that we were grateful and the incident gave us confidence that we could cope with just about anything after that.

There was a rare occurrence when Devonshire was underway in the Baltic in the aftermath of that wonderful visit. A ship was sighted approaching us and soon it was revealed to be King Frederick of Denmark's Royal Yacht with the king aboard. Usually, we would have been aware through diplomatic channels of the possibility that we might meet the yacht and would have been prepared to pay the appropriate respects. In this case, with no warning, we had about twenty minutes to prepare to fire a twenty one gun salute and parade a sovereign's guard and band. We made it. Whale Island would have been proud of us. There was no similar event in my next thirty years in the service.

The cruise continued with visits to other Baltic ports, most notably Oslo, the home of even more blondes, the frightening Olympic ski jump tower, museums housing a Viking ship and the Kon Tiki raft, cafes offering smoked salmon and strawberries at ridiculously cheap prices, and a host of hospitable and kindly people. I was taught a lesson there by one of the blondes, not of the sexual variety, but social. She came to collect me from the ship and insisted that in conformity with local students' custom I rode her bicycle while she sat on the carrier behind and stretched her long legs out to the side. Naturally, being English and being a cadet compelled to wear uniform to go ashore during that visit, I was embarrassed. What would officialdom think? I decided not to worry about that and to 'relax and enjoy it'.

The reason for giving official receptions when visiting foreign ports was fairly obvious even to someone with my parochial upbringing. But during my time in Devonshire I was also introduced to the sight of the ship's officers and their guests knocking back the booze at Wardroom cocktail parties and for some reason I was shocked by the sight. I still cannot explain why. I knew that drinking played a part in ordinary working class life and no one brought up anywhere near Merchant Navy and fishing fleet circles could remain ignorant of the part which drinking played in the life of a major port. So I must assume that it was not the drinking but the setting for it which shocked me, though I really cannot think why it should have. One fact emerged from a recent conversation though. Clive, my old friend from a similar background in Hull experienced a similar reaction when he served as an officer in the RAF.

Presumably we progressed in knowledge of things naval as the first cruise ended and after another leave the second began. Now we were the senior, experienced cadets. Not that it made much difference, we still scrubbed the decks at six each morning and did all the same chores as on the first cruise. The setting was different though. This was a Mediterranean cruise, and one of the first calls was at Villefranche where I discovered two things. First, that the 'Med' could appear pretty rough if one chose to go sailing outside the harbour in one of the Devonshire's 14 foot 'RNSA' - Royal Naval Sailing Association - dinghies on an unsuitable day.

The harbour at Villefranche was small and windless when my friend Keith and I set out so the answer was obviously to take the boat out of the harbour. But there was no wind at the harbour mouth and, because it 'simply wasn't done' to use the oars, I hopped over the side and swam, pushing the boat out in a literal sense. No sooner had I hopped back in, removed my wet trunks, and wrapped a towel around my waist, than I realised that the dinghy was screaming along a sea running at about 4 feet. No problem for anyone who didn't mind crossing the Mediterranean from north to south, but a challenge for an inexperienced sailor wishing to return to Villefranche. Though embarrassed when I lost my towel and the local tourist steamer altered course to see what was happening,, we managed to keep the boat upright and turn it back to the harbour.

Money was as usual the pivot of my decisions. Should I go ashore to see this or that attraction or should I save what little I had for my leave. Sometimes I made the wrong decision. I shall always regret deciding not to go ashore at Sorento, of which beloved Gigli had sung so often, and giving up opportunities to see the ruins of Pompeii and the aging splendour of the Monte Carlo casino. Fortunately, I did invest in a miniature bottle of Courvoisier cognac which provided an introduction to the lifelong pleasures of good brandies.

Many cadets probably shared the introduction to cognac. I doubt if any others shared a contribution to my naval education like that made by the submarine Chief Petty Officers when Devonshire arrived in Malta. Raymond was the 'Spare Crew Coxswain' in the submarine depot ship, HMS Forth, and invited me to visit his mess. There was definitely a touch of two cultures in the situation. Was it proper for a cadet to visit a Chiefs' mess? I had little difficulty with that question. Having been brought up virtually as an only child I was keen to strengthen family links and as far as I was concerned that took priority over theoretical questions of propiety.

There was also a practical question to be faced but I was reasonably confident that my experience in the Hull Merchant Navy club would prove a sufficient answer. The centrepiece on the sideboard in the Chiefs' mess was a bottle of rum. I never learned what the procedure was for keeping it full but I was soon introduced to the rule for serving it to guests, especially those, like Cadet Feasey, with some novelty value. Fortunately, their hospitality was generous but not excessive and my confidence in my ability to survive it was justified.

That visit to the Chiefs' mess not only reinforced Nelson's lesson that there are some things in naval life that it's best not to know but also taught me that naval life embraces every kind of person and every aspect of life. Not only was I liberally entertained in the mess and taken out to dinner later that evening, but I was invited to join Raymond and a couple of other Chiefs at the Floriana Methodist Church on the Sunday evening. I accepted and was rewarded by the discovery that these Methodist Christians, of whom I knew practically nothing, included some very good and kind people who belonged to a church whose somewhat austere architecture and furnishing emphasised the spiritual nature of worship rather than the grandeur of ritual. I resolved to learn more about them.

In November that second cruise contributed a never to be forgotten announcement. One night I put on my overalls to go on watch in the boiler room at midnight and went on deck for a breath of fresh air before going below. A rather excited Liverpudlian Petty Officer rushed up and asked "'ave you heard the news? Liz 'as dropped a sprog". Few announcements of the birth of the heir to the throne can have been so simple and dramatic. I have often wondered whether Ma'am and Charles would be amused by this vernacular version. I hope so.

More simple exams completed, with promotion to Midshipman in prospect, we went home for Christmas.

Chapter 7

'Snottie'

The principle and practice of training Midshipmen, always better known as Snotties even though most of us knew quite well when to blow our noses, were both good. The principle has been described many times in factual and fictional books about the navy but it is rarely found in management text books. Many young people are willing to seek positions which bring early responsibility. Some organisations recognise that these people must be allowed their share of mistakes as they learn their jobs. Few organisations have entrenched that principle as deeply in their corporate culture as the Royal Navy.

By the time we were promoted Midshipment in January 1949, Dartmouth and the Devonshire had taught us enough for us to begin to be useful in many ways, substituting for Leading Seamen as Coxswains of boats or Stokers in the boiler rooms for example. But we lacked experience and were grateful that the system encouraged everyone from the youngest Leading Seamen and Stokers to the oldest Chief Petty Officers to help us avoid mistakes if possible, and tolerated those which occurred despite our best efforts. It was another naval lesson which stood the test of application in many different circumstances years later.

For me, the practice of being a Midshipman began with another long train journey to join the battleship HMS King George V, invariably spoken of as 'KGFive', at Portland. I had learned to read travel instructions very carefully so when they issued me with a railway warrant from Hull to Portland, a place I had never visited before, I did exactly as instructed, even though it involved arriving at Weymouth late at night and sleeping on a station bench to await a train to Portland the next morning. When I finally arrived onboard, bedraggled and weary, I was less than pleased to be told that 'they' should have told me to get a boat from the Bincleaves jetty in Weymouth the previous evening. Lesson learnt, 'they' don't always get it right, even in the RN.

KGV was part of the Training Squadron. With her sister ship HMS Anson and the aircraft carrier HMS Victorious she shared the task of training the Young Seaman entrants. These joined the navy at seventeen, unlike Seaman Boys who entered at fifteen and did their initial training ashore at HMS Ganges. Like the Training Cruiser Devonshire, KGV operated with a reduced complement of trained personnel to make room for the trainees. Unlike Devonshire, she spent most of her time in harbour.

The optimism generated in Britain by the end of World War 2 had been replaced by the austerity of an almost bankrupt nation. There was liitle money for fuel to take big ships to sea and the squadron spent months swinging round mooring buoys in Portland Harbour. Officers who had spent years in command during the war, especially those who had been in submarines, 'paced the teak' as rather embittered Officers of the Day.

Whether the ship was going to sea or not, joining KGV was a big thrill. Everything was on such a massive scale. Acres of scrubbed teak decks, superstructure rising like an eleven story building from the upper deck to the main gunnery director. And, unseen by most of her ship's company, the side protection, fifteen inches of armour over much of the ship's length and inside the armour, three compartments each about a yard wide containing water, air and fuel respectively. These protected the four engine rooms and boiler rooms, numerous auxiliary machinery rooms, the cordite magazines and shell rooms, and the 'Transmitting Station'. The latter was the equivalent of today's computer room. Bearing and elevation settings for the guns were calculated mechanically by combining the position of the aimers' binoculars in the gunnery directors with ballistic, meteorological and ship motion data.

We were not there to gawp at this wonderful piece of naval architecture but to consolidate the knowledge we had gained during our first year by serving in every department of the ship and taking part in all aspects of its life. In addition to these general duties, those of us who were Mids (E) had to get an Auxiliary Watchkeeping Certificate and a Boiler Room Certificate. The first covered duties normally done by Stokers or Leading Stokers such as operating steam turbine and diesel driven generators, hydraulic pumps for the main armament, evaporators and all other auxiliary machinery. The second authorised us to take charge of the watch in a boiler room, normally the duty of a Petty Officer or Chief Petty Officer. We were slowly moving up the scale.

The thoroughness of the training was exemplary. Our engineering studies required us to identify and draw diagrams of every system in the ship: oil fuel, diesel fuel, boiler feed water, fresh water, main steam, auxiliary steam, hydraulics, high pressure air and many others. It was a pleasure to produce neat Indian ink drawings. And the training objective was achieved. I knew that whenever I joined a ship I must learn all the systems thoroughly .

Moving around the departments taught us to appreciate the efforts of all who contribute to running a capital ship with about twelve hundred men aboard and most of the training was a pleasure. One exception was writing a daily account of naval, political or other events which seemed important to us in a Midshipman's Journal. I hated it, probably because my narrow education encouraged me to succumb to the failing of some engineering specialists, imagining that the world outside engineering is someone else's business. It was years before I realised how valuable keeping a journal could be. By then there were many other demands on my time.

Driving the ship's power boats was the most pleasing duty of all. Alongside berths for the biggest ships only existed in the main naval ports. At Portland they were moored to buoys in the harbour and depended on boats for movements of men, mail and materiel between ship and shore. There were plenty of opportunities to become proficient in handling power boats ranging from the utilitarian launches and pinnaces with their uncommon Kitchen Rudder controls to my favourite, the graceful 45 foot picquet boats with their little bridge and twin Gardner diesels. Boatwork also taught us quite a bit about about human nature, particularly when picking up libertymen after their evening of drinking ashore. Training it might have been, but the responsibilities were real. A few months before I joined KGV a pinnace returning from Weymouth to a ship in Portland Harbour on a rough night had capsized with considerable loss of life.

One problem with this training regime was that the ships didn't go to sea oftren enough. In eight months we had one excursion to Torbay, another to Portsmouth and a channel crossing to Jersey. Consequently, we could often finish our departmental work during the forenoon and then, with the blessing of the Lieutenant Commander responsible for our training, always known as the 'Snotties Nurse', spend the afternoon sailing. His condition was that we took a crew of Young Seamen and taught them sailing. Not surprisingly, many of them loved it. They may have joined the navy to see the world but learning the joys of sailing was a good second.

This routine had consequences for me. The first was on a Wednesday in February, a race day with boats from all the ships in the squadron competing.After we had done all our preparations the race was cancelled because the weather in the harbour was too rough. I didn't think it was that bad so I took my dissapointed crew for an exhilarating sail outside the harbour. In Weymouth Bay the wind and waves were from different directions and we came up 'in irons' when we tried to go about in the usual way. Instead we had to 'wear' round, to turn with our stern to the wind. That involved gathering up the mainsail, 'brailing up' as it was known, and anyone who has ever sailed a whaler knows that if you give the order 'Let go the brails' too early, the boat capsizes. I did and it did.

We were unable to right the boat and spent a cold forty five minutes hanging onto the hull. It was especially tough on the one non-swimmer who, although wearing a lifejacket correctly, did not have the swimmer's knack of not breathing in when the waves swept over him. As we were towed back I thought nervously about the consequences but the Snotties' Nurse made no adverse comments or recriminations. Capsizing a whaler was just one of those misjudgements a learner was allowed to make. Perhaps it helped that thirteen other naval boats had capsized in the harbour, a Borstal boy escaping in a stolen boat only managed ten yards from the Portland Naval Base jetty, and a couple leaving England for a cruise in their yacht were wrecked on Portland Bill and the husband drowned. Quite a day.

The second consequence of my love of sailing was revealed when I was promoted to Sub-Lieutenant and received a copy of the reports which had been written on my Cadetship and Midshipman's time. The Snotties' Nurse, a seaman officer, had written, among other things, 'Feasey is very keen on sailing at which, with more experience, he should become very good indeed'. The head of the engineering department struck a drier note, 'Feasey is perhaps too keen on sailing and should ensure that he pays full attention to his engineering studies'.

There was little social strain in life as a Mid. When we joined the KGV it had the traditional three officers' messes, Wardroom, Gunroom and Warrant Officers' Mess. Mishipmen lived in the Gunroom under the presidency of a Sub-Lieutenant. We had all heard stories of the despotic ways of some Subs who caned Midshipmen for trivial offences, a continuation of an English public school way of life practiced at Dartmouth and recorded vividly in various books. Personally, I would have regarded an attempt by the 'Sub of the Gunroom' to cane me as one slight too many. Fortunately, our Sub had already learned to preside without fuss. The mess was a happy one.

Not all the Mids had a happy time though. The highly structured routine of Dartmouth and the Devonshire had to be replaced by self descipline. The immaturity of some of the ex-Darts began to show. For years they had been told what to do and a few could not make the transition, becoming withdrawn socially and neglectful of ordinary personal hygiene. They usually disappeared quietly from the navy though not always before they had been scrubbed by some of their fellows. The Australian Midshipmen seemed particularly keen on that kind of summary justice. It was not an endearing characteristic.

During the first year in the navy there were no signs of homosexuality between cadets and, apart from leave periods, no spare time in which to seek girl friends. Most of us were just too busy minding our own business and trying to keep up with the pace set by our mentors. As Mids, there was more time for individual characteristics to be revealed and two who were obviously close friends were 'removed from training'.

For those of us who had been accustomed to female company before joining the navy, the relaxed routine of the Training Squadron was a great pleasure. There were many attractive girls in the Weymouth area, some had access to their fathers' cars, and Mids were generally assumed to be suitable escorts and partygoers. That did not prevent some parents making the groundrules very plain, like the 'old' Commander, he must have been over forty, who warned me in Churchillian tones to remember that, 'My daughter may have reached the age of consent but she is not yet allowed to do so'. Our time ashore was very restricted. We usually had to return onboard by eleven PM or midnight but sometimes Portland's notorious rough weather came to our aid. When 'All boats are cancelled' was the message at Bincleaves, there was not much to do except go back to the party. Those were the days.

The absence of social strain was partly due to improved finances. Never again have I had a 300% increase in pay. Instead of fifteen shillings as a Cadet, Midshipman Feasey had two pounds ten shillings a week to spend. Comparative riches, celebrated by spending fifteen shillings on the book of Kipling's poetry, 'The Seven Seas'. Credit must also be given to the Captain of the KGV and his family. Some officers have written of the dread with which they went to breakfast, lunch or dinner with their Captains. I have only memories of a man whose equable temperament and relaxed manner soon gained my respect and made attendance at his table enjoyable, and whose wife and young children made invitations to their family picnics a real treat.

Entertaining in the Gunroom wasn't always a pleasure. The most important event of my eight months in KGV was a visit to Jersey. As we understood it at the time, the people of the Channel Islands were not best pleased that their islands were the only British territory occupied by the Germans during WW2. They appeared to believe that if Britain had tried harder they might have been spared the experience. Some years had therefore been allowed to elapse before a senior representative of the British government paid a formal visit to the islands. The time was now ripe and the representative was Admiral of the Fleet Sir Algernon Willis accompanied by Lady Willis. It did not escape us that Lady Willis was said to be Prime Minister Clement Attlee's sister.

They embarked for an uneventful passage to Jersey where a vin d'honneur was held during which, according to the headline in a local newspaper the next day, 'Midshipman Makes History'. I was the Mid. Hungry in mid-morning and titbits being a bit scarce below the salt, some of us scouted for extras near the VIP table. When it was time for the Bailiff, Sir Alexander Coutanche, to lead a procession to the next stage of the ceremonies, the parliament's mace-bearer could not be found. 'Lets have a

Midshipman to carry the mace' said Sir Alexander. Flash go the pressmens' cameras and a suitably serious looking Feasey is recorded for the papers. So far so good.

Later a VIP invited me to lunch at a superior restaurant. The hors-d'oeuvres were impressive. My host insisted that I try the artichokes. I had never eaten an artichoke, didn't know there were two kinds, and certainly didn't know what to do with the prickly thing before me. My kind host perceived my difficulty and quickly started to tackle his so I could see what to do. But no one who has had the advantage of learning the social graces during childhood should underestimate the embarrassment such incidents can cause.

Admiral and Lady Willis visited the Gunroom for a pre-lunch drink during the return passage. The Sub detailed me to organise their drinks. Lady Willis ordered a glass of sherry, the austere Sir Algenon half a glass. Our steward brought them to me on the customary salver. By this time two conversation groups had formed and naturally I presented the tray to Lady Willis first. She took the half glass so I offered the full glass to Sir Algenon. He looked coldly at the glass, even more coldly at me and said, 'I asked for half a glass'. Such a silly remark on such a trivial matter would never have made much impression on a thick Yorkshire skin but I didn't need to react at all. From the other group came Lady Willis's voice, 'I've got the half glass, you drink that one'. Thank goodness for common sense.

A page of naval history was turned during my time in KGV. In the interests of economy, the Warrant Officers' Mess and the Gunroom were closed and we all moved into the Wardroom. If any of the Wardroom officers secretly disliked having us in the mess they hid it well. We were made welcome and treated as responsible members. There was the occassional embarrassment of course, like the mess dinner at which a fellow Mid sat next to the dashing young Lieutenant who had just charmed his girl friend away. Tim drank a little too much, broke the rule of not mentioning women in the mess, and then asked me why I was kicking him under the table.

Membership of the Wardroom enabled us to be present on a unique occasion. The Soviet navy was returning a cruiser which the Americans had leased to them during the war. They spent one night in Portsmouth and the officers were invited to dinner. Presumably they were hand picked for their loyalty but that did not prevent them from following our Captain of Marines and the rest of us around the mess in a conga line after dinner, singing heartily the words he had taught them, 'We are the King's Navee'. We never learned what the Political Commissar reported when they returned to base.

There is no denying although the post war navy could be criticised for apparently wanting to revive the pre-war social life for the officers and sport for the troops, it was a pleasure to take part in well organised naval sporting events. The highlight of these for us was the Training Squadron Pulling Regatta. The boats were cutters weighing 3 tons and having four oars at each side, and whalers of 27 hundredweight with three oars on one side and two on the other. There were races for many classes of entrant. We formed a Gunroom whaler crew, trained hard, and treated our sore bottoms with methylated spirits to harden them. It paid off. Early in the day we won the Midshipmens' race.

The organisation of the regatta was undoubtably a real treat for officers and men. Betting was allowed and HMS Anson ran a tote linked to all ships by radio. That gave us our chance. We used our modest winnings from the Mids' race to back ourselves in one of the most prestigious races of the day, the 'All-comers Whaler' race. Few expected a bunch of Mids to win. Certainly the toughest Stokers and the most experienced Seamen didn't and they placed their bets accordingly. It was our day. We won and collected silver oars as our prizes and quite a lot of money as our winnings. KGV became 'Cock of the Fleet', the trophy for the winning ship being a silver cockerel to adorn the Wardroom and a seven foot high wooden one to place on a gun turret for the next few days to flaunt the ship's success.

We were pretty fit young men. I certainly thought so and was annoyed when the Medical Officer doing my annual medical altered my PULHEEMS assessment from a line of ones to a line of twos. When I asked why, he answered that only Commandos got ones. It was not difficult to get a surreptitious look at the criteria for assessment. One criterion was on the lines of 'Should be able to march 20 miles in a day and to repeat the performance the next day'. Many of us were fit enough to satisfy such criteria but protest would not have enhanced reputations. I contented myself with relegating naval doctors to the low regard I had for naval dentists.

Further justification for that low regard followed. I was lucky enough not to inherit in any serious measure my father's psoriasis but my skin reacted badly to shaving. The ship's doctors tried all sorts of remedies which failed, then sent me to the Portland Naval Hospital where another doctor failed before a Petty Officer sat me under an ultra-violet lamp for a few minutes and, in a few sessions, solved the problem.

Our Church of England Chaplain didn't fare much better than the doctors. He was responsible for teaching us elementary psychology, which he did quite well, and some of us sang in his rudimentary choir. For all I know he may have been a boon and a blessing to those with whom he served during the war but we saw him as a 'Jack me hearty' clergyman who used the word 'bloody' frequently to show he was one of the boys. His idea of humour was to amend the words of the Te Deum to 'The sea is His and He can keep it'. The Anglican Church had not improved since evacuation days. It was not for me.

Many years after leaving the KGV I realised how large a part chance plays in many careers. It was already at work during my time as a Mid. The KGV's three turrets with ten 14 inch guns were impressive enough from the outside, but the *barbettes supporting the turrets were far more so. They extended down into the ship the equivalent of about eight stories of a building. In remote machinery spaces, steam turbines the size of a sloop's main engines drove hydraulic pumps which pressurised a 12 inch hydraulic ring main to power the guns' elevating and training motors and the hoists for the massive shells and their accompanying four silk bags of cordite propellant. Many functions were interlocked by complex mechanisms and isolated by flash proof doors to ensure the correct relationships between various parts of the system during normal operation and to limit damage in the event of a hit by an enemy.*

Although the battleship concept had been overtaken by the increasing capability of naval aviation, big guns were very impressive. We were duly impressed and two of us explored the department so carefully that we discovered, within one of the barbettes, an empty recess of which the Ordnanace Officer was unaware. We earned particularly good reports for the gunnery segment of our training. Much followed that simple incident.

As Mids (E) we knew that after a common grounding in marine engineering, we would have to specialise in marine, aeronautical or ordnance engineering. We also knew we would only get our preferences if they coincided with the navy's requirements. In my term they didn't. There were too many preferences for marine engineering, too few for ordnance. The good report from the Ordnance Officer of the KGV probably swung the balance. I was later conscripted into the ordnance specialisation. It was one of the best things that happened in my career. But I didn't know that at the time.

A Touch of Two Cultures

The present owners of the Lee Street house, June and Roy, with their neighbours Betty and John and, on the next page

The Rectory, Nunnington
To which Geoff was evacuated in September 1939.

We lived in Two-Bedroom Semi's
and, on the next page

And three bedroom semi's
The Villa Camasen, Malta

Welcome to Australia Peter

Our Aussie Home in Yampi Place

Thirty one homes in 27 years in the UK. This one since 1979. Bliss.

Frivolous in Yampi Place

Serious in Study 1998

Chapter 8

College

The Navy's plan for our education as professional engineers was finely tuned to the navy's needs. We would spend two years at the Royal Naval Engineering College in Plymouth doing a 'Basic Course' of subjects common to marine, aeronautical and ordnance engineering, promotion to Acting Sub-Lieutenant occurring after the first term. Then back to sea for about eight months to qualify for our final Engine-room Watchkeeping Certificates. Returning to college, after a few weeks in which to consolidate our marine engineering knowledge, we would study our specialist fields for just over a year. Examinations at the end of the Basic Course would prove our suitability to continue. Conspicuous success would be rewarded with accelerated promotion to Lieutenant.

The courses, which had been introduced a year before we joined, were so well tuned to the navy's needs they were not acceptable for the award of external university degrees. We would have preferred to obtain a degree but that was only to come years after we left. However, the Institution of Mechanical Engineers had examined the facilities and the qualifications of the staff of the old Keyham college perched on the wall of Devonport Royal Dockyard and on the new site at Manadon on the outskirts of Plymouth. They concluded that after the inclusion of 'Economics of Engineering' they would recognise us as professional engineers and accept us as members in due course. Economics of Engineering was duly added.

We had competed hard to be allowed to join the navy, had survived twenty months of rigorous training, and were about to begin serious tertiary study. There were some rewards. We lived in single cabins within the huts at Manadon during our first term and were tended by servants, most of them ex-navy. I have *pleasant memories of their kindness and interest. Once again the navy made its teaching plain and once again it was absolutely right. The servants, we were reminded, did not earn a great deal. Some officers had quite a lot of money. Our mentors did not say whether theft had ever occurred but the lesson was clear, if any servant succumbed to the temptation to steal because an officer left money lying around, it would be the officer's fault.*

In some respects we were again treated like schoolboys. For the first term or two we were only allowed to 'go ashore' until nine o'clock at night on weekdays. And the lesson here is that if young men are treated foolishly they will respond accordingly. As a nineteen year old I wasn't going to tell a girlfriend that I had to be 'home' by nine. I frequently followed well worn routes through the fences surrounding the college, considerably later than the rules allowed.

We were still a mixed bunch of Brits, Australians, Egyptians, Indians, and Pakistanis. We were Mohammedans, Anglicans, Hindus and Catholics. It would have been surprising if we had not had a wide range of interests. Drinking was probably the most popular common factor. There was a strong 'rugger' tradition at the college with the usual connotations of beer and bawdiness. The college club held in the highest regard by some was dedicated to drinking beer by the quart rather than the pint. I preferred to go my own way. The main reasons were a belief that 'the mating game' was the most interesting recreation, and an increasing interest in the Methodist Church. Fortunately, they were compatible.

While walking in Hull during my leave I had paused to read the posters outside a Methodist Church on the Holderness High Road. A man of about thirty whose most obvious feature was his premature baldness invited me to the next Sunday service. I thought this was very much the spirit that should be abroad in a Christian church and accepted. Douglas and his wife Enid were two of the nicest people you could meet. Devout but practical,

Douglas did not wish to be involved in the killing during WW2 and joined the Royal Army Medical Corps. His baldness occurred soon after he became one of the first rescuers to tend the living skeletons in a concentration camp. He and his family would have been a fine advertisement for any church.

Doug and Enid's influence motivated me to attend the Methodist Central Hall in Plymouth when I joined Manadon. It had only three features in common with the small church in Hull, simplicity of architecture and worship, and friendly people. Otherwise the Central Hall was a different world. The architecture was simple but elegant. The hall's organ, recently rebuilt after the bombing of WW2, was arguably the finest in the West Country. The grand piano had been Paderewski's. The congregation on Sunday evenings numbered about twelve hundred, a far cry from the faithful few in Hull. A bonus was the use of the hall for concerts on weekdays and I was introduced to organ and piano recitals, oratorios, concert version of operas, and performances by singers of distinction such as Joan Hammond.

The friendliness of the people of the church was exemplified by Stanley Foot. Before retirement Stanley had run the family law practice while his brother, the Right Honorable Isaac, and nephews, Hugh Macintosh Foot, later Lord Caradon, and Michael Foot, later the leader of the British Labour Party, and other members of the family were in politics. Stanley lived at Ladywell, a large Victorian house hidden behind a high wall in Ladywell Place, near the city centre. On Sundays he kept open house for any young people who didn't have a home of their own in Plymouth, mainly navy men but also au pair girls and a Nigerian pre-medical student. Anyone was welcome.

I felt awkward at first because I was the only officer but I felt I could be friends with fellow members of the congregation without prejudice, as they say, to good order and naval discipline. I was right and made some good friends, one of whom, a Petty Officer, later asked me to be Best Man at his wedding in Liverpool. Ladywell contacts also improved my understanding of aspects of life on the 'lower deck', knowledge which would have been hard to acquire any other way. One example was learning how easy it was for sailors wishing to extend their leave to virtually 'buy' medical certificates from certain unscrupulous doctors.

Methodist services at the Central Hall were characterised by the simplicity of the worship and by the wholehearted participation of the congregation and about sixty choristers in hymns which, even though some of the words wouldn't stand much critical analysis, often had magnificent tunes. The Methodists' approach to theology was equally simple. It accepted that belief in some Christian doctrines did not come easily and merely advised reacting to doubt with a simple prayer, 'Lord, I believe. Help Thou my unbelief'. Given this understanding approach and seeing that so many members of the congregation were obviously admirable people, it was not difficult for me to decide to join the church.

It has taken me a long time to introduce the subject of our studies. That's because there is not very much to say about them. My reaction to study at the college was similar to that at the Tech: immense pleasure that I was learning the mathematics, physics, chemistry etc, which are the foundations of engineering, co-existed with frustration that learning was such a laborious business. A few bright contemporaries found their studies easy but most of us had to work hard and long. The rewards of success seemed a long way off and there were many temptations to be succumbed to. Not surprisingly we sometimes got into trouble.

At one stage, when the nine o'clock curfew was a thing of the past, our tutors talked to us in our cabins so we could continue working until they arrived. Unless of course he arrived so late that all he found was a note pinned to the cabin door,

'"Much study is a weariness of the flesh" (Eccl 12.12). Gone ashore to recover.' Using biblical quotations in naval messages was common practice but my tutor was not best pleased with that one. I admitted it was a mean-spirited gesture. He probably had a wife waiting to enjoy his company when he finally reached home around half past nine. Nevertheless the incident illustrates the general weariness which some of us with very ordinary brains experienced during our studies. And it was the forerunner of a belief that there are times when we are wise to listen, if circumstances permit, to our brains telling us to defer difficult tasks until we really feel ready to deal with them.

Their Lordships believed that our engineering education should be leavened with some exposure to 'the humanities' and it fell to a solitary Instructor Lieutenant Commander to represent them. He had a hard task, not because we were unwilling to study life, the universe and everything, but because like engineering students everywhere we were already heavily committed. At first acquaintance he appeared to be a gentle Cambridge graduate with much 'Footlights' experience, whose genteel style contrasted sharply with that of heartier fellow bachelors, and whose productions never failed to win the Royal Navy Drama Festival. We bestowed the nickname 'Gloria' on him but learned there was much more to him than theatre.

One of my friends did not comply with Gloria's order to write a letter giving his reasons for failing to return an overdue library book, a punishment designed to improve familiarity with drafting of formal letters and perhaps also to instil the thought that in naval life there is no such thing as a trivial offence. Furthermore, when taken to task for his omission, Brian failed to take the reprimand seriously. This released the most crushing 'bottle' he had ever received, delivered with a fine rage never before displayed by this gentle officer. The mystery was solved when we discovered a book which revealed Gloria's wartime role as a seaman officer and eminently successful destroyer captain.

Mixing with more people from other backgrounds increased my awareness of the narrowness of my education and I began trying to remedy some of the deficiencies. I met people who still believed that 'God made them, high or lowly, And ordered their estate' and that 'the poor didn't mind being poor'. I minded, and I disliked those aspects of British social structures. I needed to learn more, and thought a good starting point would be the Industrial Revolution and its aftermath.

For one essay I wrote about the growth of the Trades Union Movement and the establishment of its parliamentary wing, the British Labour Party. The general climate of Wardroom opinion appeared to be true blue Conservative and I was uncertain how my subject would be received. I am pleased to record that although 'Gloria' rightly criticised it severely as an essay, the only suggestion he made on the content was that I should consider 'The Socialism of JB Priestley' as a subject for a future occasion. I had read quite a lot of JBP's works and it is a measure of my ignorance that I had not recognised the thinking behind his words. I remain grateful to 'Gloria' for encouraging my self-improvement even though the political direction I chose has usually been, and perhaps still is, a minority one in Wardroom circles.

There were other non-engineering aspects to life during the Basic Course. We all tried our hands at the controls of one of the college's Tiger Moths, the idea being to identify those who then began to lust after a career in aeronautical engineering. In my case, one flight was enough to satisfy everyone that even if a shortage of volunteers forced me to be conscripted for aeronautics, I would never be successful or happy as a pilot. Fortunately the aeronautical books were balanced without me.

Team sports were another great component of college life and, for the first time since playing rugby league in Hull, I began to enjoy them. High school sport had been desultory. Dartmouth memories are chiefly of unwelcome cross country runs and *although they may have served some purpose because I eventually came to enjoy cross countrying, it was the engineering college experience which provided a lasting, and I believe correct, attitude to sport. A lot of attention was given to the activities of the First Fifteen in winter and the First Eleven in summer, but that did not detract from the encouragement given to everyone to enjoy sport. It was an excellent example for the role we later played in our ships, encouraging everyone to 'have a go' even if they were not very good.*

Some of us were very well qualified for the 'not very goods'. Even the Second Fifteen played fairly high class rugby. The 'Thirds' were different. Coarse rugby as ever was. Sloping grounds, indifferent markings, missing corner flags, absent referees, all differentiated our game from the couth variety. Sometimes we even played for the opposition to ensure an even match. And although the sharp practices in scrum and line-out were not applied forcefully enough to break bones, it was good rough and tumble stuff. I look back on it with pleasure. If sport were limited to those with elegant skills, the Services would be the poorer for it.

The same principle applied to all the other sports. Although sailing, rugby and cricket were the mainstay of college life most of us had a go at soccer, hockey, rifle shooting and riding. The only sports conspicuous by their absence were baseball, which US troops stationed in Hull had taught me to enjoy, basketball which had not yet entered British life, and polo, so often lauded by naval writers describing prewar naval life.

For many, one highlight of these years at college was buying a car or motor cycle. Most of us believed, and still believe, that every mechanical engineer should be a good mechanic and the repair or modification of old cars provided a lot of practical experience. The range of vehicles was immense from stately sedans and MG sports cars to Austin Sevens, one of which became an unusual entrant in the Land's End Rally, run in those days on the public roads of Cornwall. The days when I could buy even a share in a car were still a long way off, but in the summer of 1950 I managed to get some driving experience at last.

The Rector of Stepney, 'Father' Peter Booth as he liked to be known, invited volunteers to spend a couple of weeks of summer leave helping him to look after the 'East Ender' families who moved, young and old, in sickness and in health, to the hop-fields of Kent and Sussex every summer. Each family lived a room about twelve foot square in long corrugated iron huts. Half of each room was bare and the other half formed a rudimentary bed for the whole family. The toilet and sanitary facilities were primitive and acoustic privacy non-existent, but the care with which families garnished these hutches was remarkable. Some even wallpapered the corrugations! They worked hard stripping the hops from the bines during the day and looked forward to a 'knees up' or a booze-up every night. We were there to help them in any way we could. Our privilege was to have a hutch each!

When I arrived Peter asked me a question and followed it with an instruction without waiting for an answer. 'You can drive I suppose? Take that three tonner and go to the farm two miles down the road to pick up so and so.' Twenty years old and I had never had a chance to drive a four wheel vehicle. Unthinkable by present day standards. And the truth was, I could drive. Admittedly, I didn't have a licence but he hadn't asked me that. I got in and drove. I had imagined doing so for so many years it wasn't really difficult, even though I only had twenty yards practice before having to pass through a five-barred gate only slightly wider than the lorry. And it was a day or two before I got the 'crash' gear box into top in the narrow Sussex lanes. No matter, no-one noticed and I was appointed driver for the duration of my stay.

It was one of the best holidays I ever had. I was busy taking people and stores here, there and everywhere. A typical task was driving granny to the railway station on her way back to the hospital from which she had discharged herself. She had probably never missed the hop picking since Mafeking was relieved and resented the infirmity which prevented her remaining now. Another useful function was emptying the pubs at closing time. Some Londoners regarded a police presence as an invitation to a punch-up, but Peter Booth's team were friends, especially when, unlike the police, I could offer the drinkers a lift back to camp in the lorry. That holiday gave me enough driving experience to pass the test after a couple of lessons in a driving school car soon after I returned to college.

Although I did not have a car of my own, the licence was important, because in November 1950 I met my last girl friend. I had enjoyed the company of several girls during earlier terms, some being exclusive affairs, others friendly arrangements that a girl and I would team up whenever we lacked a special partner. But one night this long haired blond appeared at the church arousing the immediate interest of at least three young men. I was one of them. Marlis Lina Sophie Honig was well aware of the interest and decided that whoever was the first to appear when she decided to leave could take her home. My naval training stood me in good stead. I was first and the elderly motor cycle I had acquired ensured a quick get away. The others never had a chance.

Marlis was German, one of the fairly adventurous girls who came to England on a scheme which allowed them to work in a hospital or private house for two years. She had already worked in a hospital for tubercular patients, so she elected to become a forerunner of the au pair girls, the only significant different being that she was not allowed to change her job. Her nationality presented no problems for me. Only unthinking believers in vengeful Old Testament doctrines would seriously charge anyone who was fifteen when a war ended with any responsibility for it. But people don't always behave logically.

Some people resented the presence of any Germans in England and expressed their feelings forcefully. My new friend coped with such people without difficulty.

Marlis and I were different in many ways. She was a country girl from the village of Bad Munder near Hannover. I was a city boy. She had left school at fourteen. I was still studying. But we had strong drives in common. We had both begun to explore the world beyond our parochial birthplaces and wanted to see more. Another common factor was that neither of us had any money, nor any expectation of inheritance. We recognised that if we teamed up, we would be on our own.

The significance of the driving licence was that I could occasionally borrow a car. For the loan of his little red MG I shall always be grateful to Peter, and for his spacious Hotchkiss, to an Aussie friend Blair, generally known as 'Bleary'. Marlis and I picnicked in favourite spots, and she provided the food and the coffee. Her employers were the owners of a local grocery chain so she was able to indulge her generous ideas on how much to bring. On a typical occasion, we ate our fill of her delicious food, then fed six Boy Scouts and a couple of hungry dogs. The scene was being set for decades to come.

Within a couple of months of our first meeting I had proposed. The conversation on our way home one night had turned to the time, six months ahead, when Marlis' work permit would expire and she would have to return to Germany. The idea of losing her concentrated the mind wonderfully and the question was asked. I didn't get an answer but at Easter 1951 we took the next step, a visit to my home for my 21st birthday. My parents were happy to invite her to stay though my father injudiciously hoped that when I 'settled down', it would be with an English girl. That got the proverbial dusty answer from me. Nothing more was said and within a year or two he had become very fond of her. I kept that bit of our history to myself for many years.

Marlis' visit to Hull for my 21st birthday was the first time the two strands of my life came together. Before then, my Hull girl friends had not shared my naval life and no-one who knew me through the navy had visited me in Hull. Was I ashamed of my Hull background? That is not how I look back at what happened. A more accurate description is that I recognised the vast differences between the two worlds in which I had a part and had discovered how little the officers who taught me the ways of the navy knew about working class life. To these facts I added my own perception of how uncompromising that naval world seemed to be.

A good example of the gulf between the facts of life in Hull and those of the Wardroom occurred decades later. Marlis and I had begun to explore the worlds of theatre and opera and on the eve of my 21st birthday we went to the theatre in Hull with our friends Betty and Bernard. Following the usual naval custom, I wore 'plain clothes', the navy's phrase for 'civvies', that evening. About thirty years later, at a dinner party on the other side of he world, Betty mentioned that I sometimes worn uniform when taking her to the theatre in Hull when her boyfriend was doing his National Service in Germany. The reaction of one of my ex-navy contemporaries was instant and intense, 'Why were you wearing uniform', he snapped.

I didn't bother to tell him that any young man brought up in Hull who acquired the right to wear a uniform was expected to wear it on every possible occasion. Nor that the suit which had been bought for my Admiralty Interview Board was worn out and I couldn't afford a replacement. Such questions could still irritate me even if the friend was an ex-Dart who occasionally hinted at a belief that Special Entries were not quite 'proper' naval officers.

When preparing to write this book, I wrote to the Hull Daily Mail seeking to re-establish contact with friends from my youth. One respondent was Marlene, my last girlfriend in Hull. She implied that I was always telling her to behave on occasions when I wore uniform. But, for better or worse, her most enduring memory of me was of me sitting on the tail-board of a lorry when I helped her family to move house, singing a popular song of the time, 'The Spaniard That Blighted My Life'. Their Lordships may be relieved to know that I was not wearing uniform at that time.

Back at the college, the terms left pleasant memories. A special place among these will always belong to Genoni's restaurant in the centre of Plymouth. The original premises had been destroyed during the bombing and our Genoni's was a couple of Nissen huts decorated with Italian posters and Chianti bottles. There were two different approaches to eating there. When friend Tim and I had been out sailing, for instance, the Head Waiter, immaculate as ever in stiff shirt and black coat, would remind us that 'The roast duck is very good tonight, Gentlemen'. We had only to indicate that it was not that kind of an evening and he would serve us, with unfailing care, egg and chips, two shillings, and coffee, threepence, replenishing the plate of free bread, and accepting a threepenny tip with grace. But, when courting and no expense was to be spared, it was a pleasure to see his smile when we said 'Roast duck tonight, please'. Sadly, the site of those happy memories now lies beneath a traffic roundabout.

There was another development during my last couple of terms which was to influence my thinking for some years. In the countryside around Plymouth and around Saltash in Cornwall, there were many tiny Methodist Churches which lacked anyone to lead their services and they looked to the Central Hall to find people willing to help them out, even if they were not qualified Lay Preachers. Anyone with any pretension to be a leader in the navy could hardly refuse a request to become one of these helpers and Marlis and I often combined attendance at the evening service of some obscure village chapel with our *courtship. As I commented earlier, the Methodist Church recognised, as most churches probably did, that membership and 'the mating game' are entirely compatible.*

I must have had some sort of answer to my proposal of marriage during the next few months though I have no recollection of anything specific. Perhaps a clear cut answer becomes superfluous as understanding becomes more definite. The records show that I completed the first two years of study satisfactorily, albeit with only the lowest class of pass, a 'third'; that the only subject in which I scored the highest marks in the term was 'Practical Engineering 1'; that I was to be conscripted into the ranks of the ordnance engineers; and that Marlis and I announced our engagement at my term's 'passing out' dinner at the Dorchester Hotel on 27th July 1951. Not surprisingly, I was the first in the term to do so. Be that as it may, I had passed, and the doors to the next stages of life were open.

Chapter 9.

Back to Sea.

The Admiralty sent me to HMS Indomitable to get my final marine engineering certificate, a Fleet Carrier with two decks of aircraft hangers and three steam propulsion units, an impressive vessel by any standards with a far more complex organisation than a battleship. I had many reasons to be happy with the appointment. But there was no reason to be ecstatic.

Indomitable was the Flagship of the Home Fleet and was absent from its home port, Portsmouth, for three cruises totalling about nine months each year so Marlis was soon to be introduced to the separation inevitable in naval life. To minimise the separation, we completed the formalities permiting her to remain in Britain and to move to Portsmouth. There she took lodgings on the Havant Road and a job at a clothing factory. We would then be together for about twelve weeks of the year instead of six.

There were six Sub-Lieutenants (E). We shared a cabin and were allowed the privilege of living in the Wardroom. That should have been a pleasure, as it had been in the King George V, but with the Commander in Chief's staff and two squadrons of aircraft aboard there were ten Captains and seventeen Commanders in a Wardroom of over two hundred officers, of whom we were the most junior. If we risked our careers by being pushy we could get to the bar on alternate Mondays after Michaelmas, or so it seemed. Meanwhile, 'Indom' still had a Gunroom Mess where a solitary seaman Sub-Lieutenant enjoyed a life of relative luxury, even though it had to be shared with Midshipmen.

For the first time in my career, I had the financial burden of a normal Wardroom messbill. This part of commissioned life has daunted many ratings considering taking Commissions but most

Wardrooms were not extravagant, and bills were rarely excessively large. Rather, it was the annoying loss of control over expenditure. It was difficult enough balancing income with the essential outgoings without having the wild-card of a 'mess share' in the equation. Lise and I managed as best we could.

The two most obvious features of carrier operations were the extremely hazardous nature of naval aviation and the continuing need for economy in operating costs. Indom's squadrons flew Seafires, later to be replaced by Sea Furies, and Firebrands, piston engined aircraft all. The British inventions which made carrier operations significantly safer had not yet been developed: the steam catapult which propelled aircraft more reliably off the flight deck, the mirror landing sight which improved their chances of getting safely onto it again, and the angled flight deck which enabled jet engined aircraft to abort a bad approach and 'go round again'. In 1951, if the aircraft did not engage the arrester wire hook properly, it slammed into the crash barrier beyond. Aircrew celebrated survival with a phrase still used in our family many years later, 'Oooooh, it's Friday!'. We generally kept clear of the Wardroom that night. The aviators had earned their right to a celebration.

Economy in operating costs is difficult to achieve during flying operations, especially when nature fails to contribute enough wind speed over the flight deck. Unlike the Light Fleet Carriers, Indom was capable, when really cranked up, of using her own speed to operate in almost calm conditions but it was inevitably a costly operation. Lateral thinking was called for, long before Edward de Bono coined the phrase. There was no night flying then. The solution was therefore to save fuel at night. Instead of returning to harbour or steaming around all night, four of the six boilers, two of the three sets of turbines and as much auxiliary machinery as possible were shut down. Two red lights were hoisted indicating that Indom was 'Not Under

Command and Stopped'. We wallowed until first light. Never done before or since, as far as I know.

We qualified for our Engine-room Watchkeeping Certificates by working with all sections of the engineering department and watchkeeping as a second Engineer Officer of the Watch. Watchkeeping is understandably unpopular. Few enjoy going to work at midnight or four o'clock in the morning, even if each watch is only for four hours. The engineering department was manned on a three watch basis. Even so, eight hours of watchkeeping a day plus normal duties when not on watch filled our days and our nights. I soon realised how lucky I had been. Ordnance Engineers rarely kept watches. Marine engineers serving in big ships might be watchkeeping for years.

The Admiralty has systems of reports on officers and ratings as a basis for selection for promotion. The navy tries hard to be just and the most important rule, from the recipient's point of view, is that any adverse report which is within the person's power to correct must be made known to the person and recorded accordingly. The system is as good as most, despite the idiosyncracies of some reporting officers, like the Admiral who classified a character trait which he had in common with a subordinate as, '....in my case, tenacity of purpose, in X's, sheer bloody stubbornness'.

We received brief extract from each report, known as a 'Flimsy'. When I left Manadon, my Captain wrote, amongst other things, that I was ' .... rather lacking in self confidence. He must learn to stand on his own judgement ....'. Fair comment, I thought. The confidence with which I had approached the idea of becoming an officer had ebbed quite a lot. I was keen to improve my self confidence, but it was easier said than done.

Early one evening I was alone in the Engineers' Office. The telephone rang. It was the Fleet Engineer Officer. 'What is Indomitable's fresh water storage capacity?' I had studied the systems carefully, knew the answer, and told him immediately. The storage capacity was very small, the ship depended heavily on its distilling capacity for its fresh water. The Captain (E) told me I must be wrong. I had confidence in my knowledge and insisted the figure was right. My words were obviously ill chosen for after I had taken the authoritative references to his cabin and proved my point, I was left in no doubt that had I been wrong I would have been in big trouble. It's not always easy for young Yorkshiremen to learn to be tactful as well as self confident. Fortunately, given time, it can be done.

Few things are so good for building confidence as knowing ones job thoroughly and it was a pleasure to learn in Indom. Each of the three steam propulsion unit's comprised an engine room housing the 'ahead' and 'astern' steam turbines and the gearing driving one of the propeller shafts, and a boiler room with two boilers and the appropriate auxiliary machinery. Each unit was in the charge of a senior Engine Room Artificer, and each unit had more shaft horse power than the 250,000 ton 'supertankers' designed many years later. The ERAs with 'Charge Certificates' carried very significant responsibilities and it is little wonder that the best of them were so highly respected. Our first task was to achieve competence equal to theirs.

But power must be controlled, especially during flying operations in an aircraft carrier and especially when things go wrong. The Engineer Officer of the Watch was based in a Machinery Control Room adjacent to the three units. Over 120 gauges enabled him to monitor conditions in every machinery space. When things were going well his need to intervene in the running of the units was minimal. The only routine exception was to control the build up of shaft revolutions when going to flying stations because unco-ordinated increases by the outer propellors might slew the ship off course and hazard operations.

As second Engineer Officer of the Watch we did rounds of all the machinery spaces, checking that all was well and keeping the junior watchkeepers in remote locations on their toes. Sometimes these rounds posed questions which never appeared in the textbooks. What, for example, should the response of a young officer be when offered a roast lamb sandwich cut from a fine looking joint cooked on one of the turbines during a night-watch? The 'Pussers' rations were less than generous in those days and the provenance of that leg of lamb might not have borne much scrutiny. But the heat of engine rooms and the tedium of watchkeeping is a great leveller. It's risky trying to climb on a high horse when slippery with sweat. The job which had to be done was being done well so my answer was, 'Thanks, I'd love one'.

Indom was a pretty reliable ship at that time and neither watchkeeping nor working in the various sections of the department presented many difficulties. Keeping up the supply of fresh water for domestic purposes and feed water for the boilers was the biggest problem. Gaining the experience required for that final certificate was pretty painless. Even so, my first watch after it was awarded was memorable, not because anything went wrong, but because I was in sole charge, come what may. Those hundred and twenty gauges in the Control Room were scanned continuously, and a bit anxiously, for the first few watches!

Life was relatively simple in the engineering field but the Non-conformist Christians in the ship soon introduced plenty of complexity. There were so many officers in the Wardroom that there was no room for the Fleet's 'Church of Scotland and Free Churches' Chaplain. So although I was a relative newcomer to the Methodist Church I was asked to conduct some simple services and the Chaplain agreed I should do so. Fools rush in and all that. The mixture of Presbyterians, Congregationalists, Baptists, Methodists, and minority groups like the Plymouth Brethren soon taught me why churches divide and subdivide.

The classic example was the Brethrens' wish that I and some others join them in a Communion Service. Most of us belonged to churches which restricted the sacramental services to ordained Ministers. The Brethren did not practice ordination and held their simple Communion Services without clergy. That offended some of the members of the larger groups. In these ecumenical days it may seem little to get passionate about. Not then. I remember a loyal member of the Anglican Church telling me he would regard entering a Roman Catholic Church as a grievous sin. It became clear to me that the good nature of the people who had attracted me to Methodism was not shared by all members and denominations. It was wise to avoid getting involved in sectarian squabbles. And, in case involvement could not be avoided, be able to take a position on the basis of having studied theology.

Those studies had to wait their turn. My return to Manadon for specialist course studies was scheduled for mid-May 1952. That would be the beginning of a fifteen month period ashore, our only chance to begin married life without the threat of separation. That threat was real. Separation could be for up to the two and a half years on a 'Foreign Service Commission'. The navy disliked early marriage by officers and limited financial support to a fraction of a normal Marriage Allowance until the officer's 25th birthday. The Service's attitude to marriage was not endearing but it did not deter us.

The Royal Navy did not require its officers to ask permission to marry, only to inform the Commanding Officer. The information was usually accompanied by an invitation to 'The Commanding and Wardroom Officers'. Not a problem for families planning to hire the customary marquee and capable of providing sufficient champagne. The response was equally customary, a suitably engraved silver tray presented by 'The Captain and Officers'.

This customary practice wasn't a problem for us. The difference between that practice and our circumstances didn't allow any decision except to keep the two parts of our lives *separate. It was impossible to bring all the trappings of a naval wedding to Lee Street. To complicate things further, I experienced the first of a number of episodes of inflammation inside my eyes during my time in Indom. It involved having my eyes covered with bandages for three weeks at a time, sometimes in the ship's Sick Bay, sometimes in the Military Hospital at Gibraltar or the Bighi Naval Hospital in Malta.*

Being in hospital was no problem, they provided hospital issue pyjamas. But when stuck in the ship's Sick Bay for weeks at a time I had a problem. I only possessed one pair of pyjamas and had no money to buy another. Fortunately I was the only patient in the two berth part of the Sick Bay which was used as a Medical Officer's Consulting Room and Officers' Ward. When my pyjamas needed washing I hopped out of my bunk in the middle of the night, washed them in the handbasin, dried them as best I could using the ship's ventilation system and put them on again. All blindfolded of course.

Bandaged up behind the curtains of my bunk, with nothing to do except listen to the doctor interviewing patients, I learned that there were other officers with far more embarrassing conditions contracted across the Spanish border in La Linea. It made my problems seem relatively minor, especially when I learned that my inflammation would subside in about three weeks no matter what the medicos did. A comforting thought.

The stage was set for as quiet a wedding as a naval officer ever had. The ship brought me home from Bighi Hospital in Malta, I said goodbye to the team in Indom and returned to my old life in Hull for leave. The trouble was that in beginning to take up my new life, I had lost contact with my contemporaries in the old one so there was no close friend from either world to act as best man. Raymond got the job. Later experience showed that he had many faults, but he had a strong sense of family loyalty which I greatly appreciated.

Lise had similar problems. She was giving up her old life too, to live in a country with which Germany had been at war seven years earlier. Her mother had rarely travelled far from her home in Bad Munder and did not propose to start doing so, even for our wedding. Her brothers and sister were equally stay-at-home so it gave us especial pleasure that our old friend Stanley Foot travelled from Plymouth to Hull to give Marlis away and that the one remaining friend from the days of 'The Gang', Betty, agreed to be her bridesmaid.

A few relatives and friends Doug and Enid from the church completed the small congregation at the Methodist Church on Holderness High Road. A kindly retired officer lent me his sword so that I could at least be properly dressed for my part. And though flowers in the church were few and there was no choir, the hymns were sung in the best Methodist tradition and a few photographs were taken to record the event. There cannot have been many weddings at that time at which the groom wore the uniform of a Sub-Lieutenant and the best man that of a Chief Petty Officer.

There was some champagne at the wedding breakfast at my parents' home, but there was no dancing till dawn. Stanley Foot had to return to Plymouth that night so Lise and I saw him off at Hull's Paragon station and then walked back to Lee Street, rejoicing that although we couldn't afford to go away on a honeymoon, we were married, we could take on the world. And I remember we were rather smug that people walking past on the street would find it hard to believe that we had been married only six hours earlier.

The next day my parents departed for a silver wedding holiday leaving the house to us for a week or so. When they had gone we did the things all honeymooners do. During the week we also did one thing that most honeymooners don't. We laid a lawn for my parents in their back garden. The memory is all the clearer because the weather was so good that Marlis, now more often known by the pet name Lise, wanted to wear a sun dress. She didn't possess one so she wore the nearest thing, a black taffeta cocktail dress with a strapless white Broderie Anglaise top. Sadly, we did not have a camera to record the sight.

At the age of twenty two, we had been adults under the law of the time for a year. We had voted in our first General Election in October 1951, one in which over half the population still wished to give the Labour Party another term in government but which, owing to the distribution of population and the 'First past the post' electoral system, gave them four per cent less seats than the Conservatives. We were in excellent health, I had embarked on a career, and although Britain was still an austere place to live, we had no reason to be unduly pessimistic about the future. There were many worse off than we were. After all, we had eight pounds between us after paying for the wedding. It would have to be enough.

Chapter 10

Getting Started

Getting started didn't seem too difficult at the time. We had to return to Plymouth, where I would begin another year and a half of studies and training, most of it at the Royal Naval Engineering College, find a flat, and live happily ever after. We were newly weds with a monthly income of twenty eight pounds, simple tastes and a determination to manage somehow. We had a good friend in Stanley Foot whose house 'Ladywell' became our home until we found a flat.

The first few weeks of studies were devoted to consolidating marine engineering knowledge. It was not onerous and the four of us who were to become weapon specialists, ordnance engineers in navy jargon, knew there was some far more interesting engineering ahead.

Specialisation brought us into entirely different technical territory. There was some fairly conventional work on subjects like stresses in 'thick tubes', guns by another name, but the heart of ordnance engineering was electro-mechanical engineering applied to computation and servo-control mechanisms. These were the technologies which revolutionised weapon systems designed after WW2. Goodbye thermodynamics, hello electrics and electronics. We studied 'mechatronics' and 'systems engineering', long before those terms became common usage.

Most Royal Navy gunnery systems in use during WW2 were relatively simple electro-mechanical calculating devices delivering their answers to the pointers of elevation and training dials at the guns. There, men turned handwheels, which controlled the high powered electrical or hydraulic machinery required to move the guns, attempting to align pointers representing the actual position of the guns with those indicating the required positions. It was very inaccurate.

The problem for the post war years was to calculate where shells should be placed to allow their radar fuses to be triggered by fast moving, jet-propelled aircraft, and to point guns in a turret weighing 45 tons, mounted in a pitching, rolling, yawing, heaving and somewhat flexible ship, within very few minutes of arc of the calculated position. The answer to the problem was known as the Flyplane 3 System which was being fitted in the new Daring Class ships. The theory required to understand how this and similar complex systems were designed and maintained at optimum performance was the main strand of the final phase of our engineering education. It was good to be studying, at last, theory with applications on which our careers, or in extreme cases, many lives, might depend.

On the home front, Lise and I found somewhere to live and experimented with our limited income. We found we could survive on an absolute minimum of a pound a week for housekeeping. We could afford two, so we had some flexibility. We bought a bicycle which I rode to college. We adopted a simple system of envelopes into which we put money for other expenses such as clothes, insurance and my mess bill. There was usually enough left over for an evening at the cinema every week. So far, so good, but it still seemed odd that my Chief Petty Officer brother could afford a higher standard of living. Jam tomorrow, perhaps.

It may seem incredible how many foods were still rationed so long after WW2 and how small the rations were. Britain was still suffering from debts incurred to pay for the war and lacked funds even to buy sufficient food. Meat, eggs and sugar were certainly still rationed, perhaps other foods as well. The size of the rations can be gauged from Churchill's response when he asked to see a typical food ration. He remarked, 'Not a bad meal'. He was looking at rations for a week. Rationing finally ended in July 1954.

Far from the government's worries about food supplies, Lise and I had our first quarrel over the egg ration. We were allowed one a week each. I had eaten mine and Lise tried to give me the second one for breakfast the next day. When I refused to eat more than my share of such delicacies, Lise tried to insist and we quarrelled. However, after my return from work and our evening meal she was not only restored to good humour but seemed positively smug. It was not difficult to guess why. She had used the egg in a dish we had shared. Like it or not, I had eaten half her egg!

While I attempted some serious study Lise faced the introductory rituals for young naval wives. Custom at the engineering college required new wives to telephone the Captain's wife. Lise was somewhat nervous and not very enthusiastic but recognised that such protocols were part of her new life and must be observed. She was even more nervous and even less enthusiastic when a 'plummy' voice responded to her call with, 'I suppose you want to come to tea'. It seemed to Lise a strange way of welcoming a newcomer but her simple 'Yes, please' brought an invitation. That was the beginning of Lise's efforts to reconcile her own wishes with the Navy's.

Mrs Captain made it quite clear that she regarded it as her role to make new wives fit the 'correct' naval wife mould. Lise's question to me after her first tea party was, 'Do I have to learn to speak like that?' That was easy to answer, 'No'. Other matters were not so easily settled. Like most newly married people we wanted to spend as much time together as possible. Lise, knowing that my lectures finished quite early, tried to leave one of the tennis parties in time to be home when I arrived. She remembers the rebuke to this day, 'Do you see any of the other wives leaving?' Lise countered with a wish to be home to make tea for me. Mrs Captain responded with 'Do you carry the bread with you?' followed by, 'My husband gets his own tea, so should yours'. That wasn't exactly true!

In retrospect it was surprising that any of the wives, whether of students or staff, put up with a regime like that, but that was the way of things then. If Mrs Captain complained about officers' wives being seen shopping without stockings, high summer or not, only the most rebellious would go stockingless in future.

The stuffiness was accompanied by kindness. One day I went to college and was suddenly attacked by a recurrence of the eye infection. By nine o'clock I was in Stonehouse Naval Hospital. At about nine thirty, Mrs Captain arrived in my cabin. She had been to our flat to tell Lise what had happened, and discovering that she was out, had come to the hospital to find out if I had been able to tell Lise that I was off to hospital. There cannot be many organisations which show a higher regard for the welfare of their families.

The practical aspects of kindly concern were demonstrated again when Lise became pregnant. When morning sickness had reduced her to a pitiful heap, she was horrified to see Mrs Captain arriving. She would have liked our landlady to say she was out but was too slow. She was not dressed, the place was chaotic. But she need not have worried. Mrs Captain merely sized up the situation and with the aplomb of one who has been there and done that more than once herself, put the kettle on, washed the dishes, made a pot of tea and settled down for a friendly chat about the great news.

We took Lise's pregnancy in our stride. That was one of the advantages of marrying young. If healthy and united, you can face anything. We would not have been disappointed if pregnancy had been delayed for a year or two but really effective birth control was still in the future. We didn't even have a comprehensive knowledge of what there was, at least not in the statistical terms so common today. At that time it was odds on that any healthy young couple would produce a child a year or so after marriage. We were no exception.

Apart from Lise's morning sickness, life was very good. I had never studied so contentedly. I knew where and with whom I was going to bed, so I could get on with my work each evening without any restless urge to leave my books and frequent clubs like the one nicknamed 'The Groin Exchange'. If we couldn't afford to go out very much it didn't matter. We enjoyed radio plays, music and each other. For a few months that is. Then it was time to pack and move.

The navy had decided that in addition to studying relevant theory and practice, ordnance engineers should do introductory courses on the life and work of the customers for their future services, the gunnery officers and torpedo and anti-submarine officers. These specialists were very different creatures from the marine engineers with whom we had spent most of our time and it was good to meet our new colleagues on their own ground, the shore establishments HMS Excellent on Whale Island in Portsmouth Harbour and HMS Vernon near the harbour entrance.

The general rivalry between the gunnery and TAS branches has been well documented in naval histories. Gunnery officers did everything with great gusto and believed in making their presence felt on all occasions. The quieter race of TAS officers recognised that although guns could batter, and sometimes disable, enemy ships, torpedoes were best for sinking them. And, as Churchill recorded, it was the anti-submarine war which had so nearly determined the outcome of World War 2. On the other hand, it was the gunnery officers who faced the challenge of combating the rapidly increasing power of aircraft and their weapons.

Our problem as ordnance engineers was not the traditional rivalry between our two groups of masters but their attitudes to our existence. Enormous technological changes were occurring in the posr-war gunnery world and, generally speaking, the gunnery officers recognised the value of having specialist professional engineers to maintain the new systems. The changes in the TAS branch were not so far reaching at that time. Furthermore the TAS officers considered themselves a technical branch in their own right. They had maintained the electrics of ships from first introduction at the turn of the century until the Electrical Branch was formed in 1947. In spite of the customary courteous reception at the personal level, professionally, we felt less welcome at Vernon than at Whale Island.

'Whaley' came first. The gunnery school was legendary for its ability to turn out a Royal Guard or a Sovereign's funeral party at short notice, and for the strictness of the disciplinary methods which enabled it to do so. Parade training, parade training and more parade training was at the heart of the system. Was Whaley going to treat engineers differently? The answer was 'No'. The only concession was that on our first morning, the great overlord of training and standards, the Commander 'G', not only gave us a rationale for parade training but gave us one we could not refute. 'Parade training is not the only way of instilling discipline and developing self confidence' he said, 'It is probably not the best way. But it is certainly the cheapest and you will take part in it.' To recall the catchy sentence from one of Bernard Miles' old monologues, 'We couldn't answer that!'.

I had reason to be grateful for the training. When I finally finished my time at engineering college, the Captain's report included the words ' .... a strong character who inspires confidence'. It was a pleasant change after the remarks at the end of my first stint there and I have no doubt that the time spent in front of the small squad of my fellow engineers contributed to my increased self confidence.

Our training was similar to the introductory courses which all seaman officers did as Sub-Lieutenants. The routine was simple, first a morning parade of the whole establishment, known as Divisions, classes all morning and parade training almost every afternoon. It was a piece of cake compared to engineering theory but we didn't complain.

While at Whale Island took part in the strenuous naval 'sport' of field gun running. The intense competitions at the Royal Tournaments, in which field guns of the sort used by the navy in the Boer War are taken apart, swung over chasms, carried over walls, put back together, raced around obstacles and generally thrown about, are well known to the British public. Those crews trained for months to provide a great spectacle. Whale Island had its own field gun competition for crews from the Portsmouth area and although training opportunities were limited the event was taken very seriously.

Three of us joined the Sub-Lieutenants' course team. Our Australian member was a county standard athlete and could not be risked in such hazardous sport. There's always a lot of competition between the officers and the ratings on such occasions and it was satisfying to be part of the team which won the officers' cup and also the Brickwood's Trophy for the overall champions, especially having managed to do so without crushing a few toes or fingers. It's a pity they didn't have a tote on that occasion.

Another insight into the navy's attitude to marriage occurred at Whale Island. A gunnery officer about twenty eight years old was appointed our 'Course Officer', responsible for all aspects of our life and progress while we were there. That was customary practice. At least it was until he told Brian, who appeared to be on the verge of getting engaged, that he was too immature for marriage. That was going too far. Naturally, Brian protested, asking, 'What about Feasey, He's married already'. I'm told the response was, 'He's more mature'. I suspect it meant, 'I can't do anything about Feasey, but I can about you'.

Although it illustrates the extent to which the navy gave itself a right to intrude into officers' lives, this incident would not be worth retailing if it were not for what happened after that.

The Course Officer said he would ensure that Brian would be sent to a ship serving on a foreign commission, thus separating him from his fiance for a long time. We had no way of knowing whether or not the appointment was a result of the Course Officer's recommendation, but Brian was sent to a ship of the Mediterranean Fleet and was away for a year. I hope the navy has learned better.

The next course, at HMS Vernon, didn't produce anything so dramatic. New technology was being applied in the research and development establishments to two long-standing surface ship problems. A much improved sonar set for surface ships would enable a target submarine's depth to be established, and a bigger and better anti-submarine mortar would be capable of firing bombs in any direction instead of only a few degrees either side of the ship's centre line. These equipments had not yet reached the fleet but advance information was available. Like the new gunnery systems they depended heavily on servo-mechanisms for their accuracy. Unlike the gunnery officers, the TAS officers appeared to feel that they could do all that was necessary to tune and maintain the new weapons.

There was even less to study on the torpedo side of the house. The first British designed homing torpedo had not yet arrived in service. It was to be primarily an anti-submarine weapon capable of being launched from surface ships and submarines. Until it arrived we could only study the navy's anti-surface ship torpedoes and a German design of homing torpedo. The Mark 8 anti-surface ship torpedo for launching from submarines and the Mark 9 from surface ships had both been designed long before WW2. Both were to be in service for an extraordinary number of years, but they were not exciting to study.

New weapons were not in service but there was enough going on at the Torpedo Experimental Establishment at Greenock, on the Clyde, to teach me how easy it is to misjudge *of engineering possibilities. We were told that the TEE was already working on a second homing torpedo which would dispense wire as it travelled through the water, along which corrections to its course and depth commands could be transmitted as it approached the target. I was sceptical about the chances of success. The problems of maintaining the integrity of the insulating coatings on wire thousands of yards long, while still keeping the wire thin enough to be stored in a manageable volume, seemed too great. It was to be the first of a number of 'they'll never do it' misjudgments that, to my shame, I made.*

One experience at Vernon which I wouldn't have missed for anything was diving. First we dived in the old fashioned 'hard hat' helmet with its little window screwed in the front, the cumbersome suit, the lead boots, the air pipe and the life line, tugs on which were the only means of communication. It was exactly as it has been portrayed on cinema screens so many times. The self contained diving equipment which followed had nothing in common with the sleek wet suits and SCUBA sets developed later. We dived in the Sladen suit, a 'dry' suit which had an umbilical about eighteen inches in diameter through which the diver 'entered' rather than 'put on' the suit. The feet and legs went in first, then the top was pulled over the head, a tight rubber collar making a seal at the neck. Finally the umbilical was folded and secured with a strong clamp. It was said that more people felt claustrophobic in Sladen suits than in submarines. We could believe it.

Lise and I were in Portsmouth when our son Michael was born at Saint Mary's Hospital, a bastion of authoritarian medicine and nursing. No possibility there of a father's presence at the birth but nor was it permissible for a young officer under training to miss a day of instruction just because his wife was having a baby. We were grateful to our friend and landlord for driving Lise to the hospital at about half past eight in the morning while I went to work. I couldn't resist a mischievous remark when I said goodbye to Lise. I have never been forgiven for saying, 'Have a good time'.

The birth went well, Lise and Michael were both in good health and life was uncomplicated. The only unfortunate aspect was the timing. Lise was unable to attend the Coronation Review of the Fleet. Whale Island had a target-towing tug available to take officers and their guests to the review lines in the Solent. It was a great day and although Lise couldn't be there I invited my parents. They were made very welcome and thoroughly enjoyed it. The occasion showed that simple people like my parents do not necessarily feel out of place when they enter a different social environment because they are content 'to be themselves'. Hybrids feel the differences more keenly.

I returned to Plymouth when the courses ended. Lise remained in Portsmouth until I found a flat. That was more difficult now that we had a baby, but it didn't take too long. When Lise arrived at North Road Station, I tried to enter the carriage to help her. I need not have bothered for I was thrust aside by an entourage of Royal Marines she had collected. 'Stand aside, please. Can't you see we're helping the lady with a baby'. Looking blond and helpless can become an art!

Another iritis flare sent me back into hospital. This time the ophthalmologist attempted to hasten recovery by the use of one of the early antibiotics. The drug was believed to be effective only if the patient had a high temperature so I was given four times the annual TAB vaccine dose, straight into a vein. Anyone who has had TAB injections will have no difficulty in believing that a quadruple dose was nearly lethal. My temperature peaked at a hundred and three and I hallucinated. My head was hollow. A man had his hand through the empty socket of my left eye and was hammering the inside of my skull. The drug didn't accelerate recovery. As usual, it was three weeks before I could see tolerably and a further week before the effect of the dilating drops wore off.

The medical aspects of the infection were not particularly worrying. I had been told that provided the eyes were dilated with atropine when the flare occurred, there should be no permanent ill effects. Far more worrying was the possibility of the navy dispensing with my services because I had been unfit for work for a month each year for three years. I raised the matter during the customary call on the Surgeon Rear Admiral before my discharge from hospital. His answer was vague, a forerunner of the remark of a paternalistic Queensland Premier many years later, 'Don't you worry about that'. I would have preferred something like, 'These infections tend to die out, or at least become dormant for years, and the navy has invested a lot of money in your training so you will not be discharged unless there are several more recurrences. Get on with your training and we'll see what happens'. The vagueness left me uncertain whether I had a future in the service or not but there was little point in making a fuss about it. I had learned not to expect straight answers.

Shaving had always irritated my skin and I grew my first beard while in Indomitable. In hospital, unable to see, I grew my second and a friend submitted my request keep it after returning to college. The Captain's Secretary replied, 'The Captain has asked me to inform you that he does not consider the growing of beards a suitable form of self expression for young officers under training'. I have always regretted that King George V's example was not continued by his successors for I might then have been spared the Captain's pomposity. The beard was grown again as soon as a convenient opportunity occurred but I was always conscious that bearded General List officers above the rank of Commander were scarcer than hens' teeth.

Having a beard occasionally brought strange reactions. Lise's logic puzzled me when she said, 'I don't mind you having a beard before we are married and I don't mind you having a beard after we are married but I don't want one on our wedding *photographs all our lives'*. The photos show a beardless boy! Number one son therefore grew up believing that when daddy was young he had no beard and mummy had long hair. One morning I shaved and hopped back into bed. When Michael woke and came into our bed he exclaimed, 'Daddy, you're young again'. Lise started growing her hair.

There was a sad end to my rare shaves. When I retired from salaried work I wanted to see if anything had gone mouldy underneath. Shaving off a beard should be greeted with, 'You look ten years younger without a beard'. All I got was, 'You look ten years older, you'd better grow it again'. Lise explained that when she last saw my shaven face it was thirty two years old, now her illusions were destroyed by a sixty three year old. She added that not only would she not have recognised me in the street, but she would not have fancied the passing stranger. One shave was enough. Never again.

Despite a concern that eye problems might prevent me continuing in the Service there was nothing to do except get on with 'business as usual'. Studies and enjoying being a family were the staple diet but there were occasional treats. One was a week at the Military College of Science at Shrivenham, later the Royal MCS, because Manadon lacked the equipment for some essential laboratory work on servo-mechanisms. That week gave us an insight into the comfort in which the army lived and we enjoyed their custom of working in plain clothes, changing into uniform only for the weekly mess dinner.

There were about six officers from almost every regiment at the college. No one could accuse the army of being a uniformed service on dinner nights. Every regiment and corps had its own dress uniform, ranging from the simplest designs to those with chain mail and spurs that jingle jangle jingle. Collectively they were a fine sight at the four long tables with a top table for the senior gentlemen. Not that all the senior ranks sat there. A cheery Brigadier joined us at the low-life end of one of the tables *and enquired, 'How's that idiot brother of mine?' We soon learned he was referring to our Director of Studies, a powerful force in our lives.*

The treat of the week was an afternoon driving tanks on the training range at Bovington. A Comet and the later Centurion were available and with only four of us in the course we had plenty of time to try our hand. The 800 BHP Centurion remains the most powerful vehicle I've ever driven and it was a memorable experience, not least because the course had deep mud in many places. The sergeant in charge told us that the worst was a sort of cliff which we had to topple slowly off, in first gear, into a deep chasm. He implored us to floor the accelerator when half way down, otherwise we'd never get up the other side and he would be put to a lot of trouble towing us out. The message that sergeants don't like being put to trouble was clear enough but he didn't tell us that before we got to the bottom, mud would cover the driver's window and we would be driving blind. An act of faith was called for. Working on the principle that sergeants know what they are talking about, I floored the accelerator and climbed the other side. The mud slid away. You can rely on sergeants.

The most memorable of the domestic treats were our visits to the opera. Stanley Foot invited a party of about a dozen when the Carl Rosa company came to Plymouth. They may not have been the most prestigious opera company but they brought their bit of magic to many people who had never experienced it and they'll always be fondly remembered for that. Not surprisingly, our first two operas were La Boheme and Madam Butterfly. What better choices for beginners?

It was a time for experimenting. I enjoyed a normal part in the sporting life of the college and the frequent mess dinners. Drinking alcohol was the common factor and I wondered how Lise would react if I had too much to drink one night. My experiment, burbling cheerful nonsense while lying outside the

French windows of our bedroom after returning from a dinner, proved that I could not rely on a sympathetic reception. Lise swears she knew I was faking, so it was not unkind to prod me with her foot. I have never been sure.

The few months of accelerated promotion earned from the examinations at the end of our Basic Course had taken effect. A second stripe accompanied the first on each sleeve. That gave great pleasure. A young cadet entry Sub-Lieutenant wears an invisible 'L' plate, not so a 'Two striper'. And our finances improved a lot. We could buy our first car. It was a 1933 Morris Ten, about as roomy a car as anyone could get for forty pounds. It was useful in many ways. Lise visited a friend one evening each week while I looked after Michael. With a car we were no longer dependent on Ann's father to bring Lise home. And if Michael's insomnia threatened to disrupt my study, I could put him on the back seat in his carry-cot and drive him around the block a couple of times. It always worked.

Cars were not a wasting asset in the early 'fifties, there were too few new ones to meet the demand. Ours was no exception. It served us well until I was about to return to sea. Then the question was, 'Could we afford driving lessons for Lise'. Our answer had to be 'No'. So, on a warm day, we cleaned the car carefully and gave it a new coat of maroon paint. It was brushed on but we had chosen our day well. The paint flowed beautifully, the car looked good. We sold it for fifty five pounds.

I survived the examinations and qualified as an ordnance engineer, the country survived the austerity of the post war period and the deliberations of eminent British politicians who wondered whether Britain should become the 49th state of the USA and concluded that such an extreme step was not required. We hoped the worst was over, for the country and for us.

Chapter 11

The Real Thing

Five years and seven months after joining the navy, my education and training were complete and I was sent to HMS Decoy to do some real work. The appointment suited us very well. We had escaped the dreaded possibility of two and a half years of separation. Decoy was a ship of the Home Fleet, based in Devonport, away for 'cruises' of three months each three times a year. Lise and I did not have to move house, and we would be together for three months each year. From our family point of view it was the best we could expect.

It was also the best appointment from the technical point of view. Decoy was a new ship of the Daring Class. These ships were said to have firepower equal to small pre-war cruisers but by any commonsense standard they were destroyers. They were fast, and armed to attack surface targets with guns and torpedoes, submarines with a 'Squid' anti-submarine mortar, and to defend themselves with their anti-aircraft gunnery capability. The most interesting was the Flyplane 3 gunnery system, two orders of magnitude more complex than any previous system.

Decoy had recently completed its trials and was ready to join the Fleet. The ordnance engineer who had had the worry of building her was ready for some leave and another job. He was one of the 'old school' who had specialised in ordnance after several years of marine engineering. Under the new scheme, despite our long training, we were still young and very inexperienced when we were 'thrown in at the deep end'. For the first time we became heads of small departments and carried the full responsibility for the technical efficiency of the ship's weapons. Many marine engineers served their first appointments *in big ships, where the guidance of senior officers was available if needed. No such luxury for the O/Es.*

It was far from ideal that the navy's most inexperienced officers should be responsible for the efficiency of its most complex gunnery system. The navy's Chief Ordnance Engineer later told us how concerned he had been. But there was no alternative. Having just left engineering college we were better prepared to cope with the new technology than more senior O/Es and we had to get on with it.

There was also a cause for concern at the practical level in the ship. The maintenance of the Flyplane 3 electro-mechanical tracking and computing system was best achieved by having a specially trained electrical artificer working, with the six ordnance artificers, under the direction of the ordnance engineer. This did not please some electrical officers of Daring Class ships. They may not have possessed systems engineering experience themselves, but they didn't like to see their recently established 'empire' threatened. There was an uneasy truce in Decoy. As usual in life, I had delegated authority to succeed, but not to fail.

Life in Decoy seemed likely to be pleasant enough. The main influences on my life, the First Lieutenant, and my boss, the Gunnery Officer, were cheerful personalities. They wanted good results but believed that a relaxed style was more likely to achieve them than domineering autocracy. They were good role models and my staff and I were keen to succeed. There were eleven other officers, twelve if we had a Reserve Medical Officer doing his annual seatime, or an officer under training. My interaction with the other officers was social rather than professional. However, social contact can be close when you share a cabin with someone for a year.

The Daring Class ships were not formed into a destroyer squadron and they all had Captains in command. That was not the ideal 'small ship' situation. Our first Captain was a bachelor and he was no fun. By tradition, the Captain leads a solitary life. As a courtesy, he is invited into the Wardroom quite frequently. Ours not only wanted to be invited very frequently, he monopolised the conversation with tales in which he was rarely certain whether he has been in Hong Kong or Singapore at the time, whether he had been serving in the Rodney or the Renown, or whether the incident had occurred in '33 or '34. It was trying.

When Lise attended her first Wardroom cocktail party, the Captain remarked how pleased he would be to get away from Devonport because his officers seemed to spend all their time ashore. He had no appreciation of the feelings of officers who, no matter how loyal they were to the navy, were going to spend the next three months away from their families and was taken aback when Lise, less intimidated than some young wives might have been, responded with, 'It's obvious you're not married'. Perhaps he was one of the old school who had been brought up to think it indecent to marry before the age of forty. Later we learned that he had been persued for years by a nursing sister who was determined to have him, and that she finally had her way. I hope he mellowed.

We may not have had a congenial Captain but we certainly had an experienced one. He had served gallantly during WW2 and had excellent ship handling skills. We joined the Fleet and sailed for Exercise Mariner. That was really the point at which I began to study the way the navy did its business. My busiest times were always going to be in harbour, testing and tuning the gunnery system. At sea I had the time to look and learn. And question.

The political climate of the time was, as usual in those years, quite tense. The threat of action on some scale or other was never far away. Yet here we were, sailing off to a major tactical exercise without first ensuring that our weapon systems were effective. I tucked that thought away in my mind.

The first part of the exercise was the deployment of British and US naval forces to prevent HMS Swiftsure, pretending to be a Russian cruiser, breaking out into the Atlantic through the gap between Iceland and Greenland. The biggest enemy, as so often, was the sea. For days we struggled in a gale, Decoy's hull proving a great credit to her designers. A maritime patrol aircraft photographed her with the foremost third of the ship out of the water, the sonar dome clearly visible. Despite the conditions she rode well. Some of the US destroyers were less fortunate, suffering hatches torn away and other damage.

It became clear that the force might not be able to 'cut the enemy off at the gap'. The 'enemy' might have slipped through, so some ships turned their tails to the gale and moved to a new position at high speed. It was one of the two most exciting rides in thirty one years. Under those conditions the sea threatened to turn the ship broadside on to the waves and to roll it onto its side. There was little risk in the situation because the response was simple. The ship's two best helmsmen took the wheel, putting the rudder over from lock to lock trying to keep the ship on course. When they could not hold her any longer, the Captain eased the ship's speed until they regained control.

The rudder was turned by powerful hydraulic rams, but the navy had retained a traditional control system which made steering hard work, performed, equally traditionally, standing. The result was that when steaming at high speed before a heavy following sea we had to have two Chief Petty Officers taking ten minute tricks on the wheel, stripped to the waist and dripping with sweat. What a contrast to the simple electrical system of the WW2 German destroyer which became known as HMS Nonsuch or to the hydraulic tapper gear used in RN submarines by seated sailors to control hydroplanes and rudders.

Worse was to follow. During a later phase of the exercise Swiftsure joined the Fleet and became part of a force escorted by a screen of smaller ships. It was more by good luck than good practice that no one was killed when Swiftsure and HMS Diamond collided during that part of the exercise. 'Twas a dark and stormy night and, as usual, all the ships were blacked out. Several hours passed before those of us in the escorting ships were sure that Swiftsure would not sink that night.

The basic reason for the collision is well known. A signal ordering a particular manoeuvre was misinterpreted, a matter of 'left hand down' or 'right hand down'. Decoy was the next ship to Diamond on the screen and I was an interested hanger-on in Decoy's operations room. I was able to look over shoulders at a close range radar display showing the Diamond and the Swiftsure converging. They were almost certainly in each other's 'radar ground clutter' and therefore unaware how close they were to each other. We watched as the echoes merged, Captain, Navigator, ops room team and hangers-on.

Radar had been in use for several years and we were watching the Decca Navigator, an admirable second generation radar, reliable, easy to use, with simple controls and a very clear display. The presence of our Captain in front of the display rather than on the bridge indicated his confidence in its use in hazardous situations. But no one in the Admiralty, the Specialist Schools or the Fleet had thought to recognise radar's value by introducing a radio message equivalent to the old flag signal 'You are standing into danger' .

My subsequent conversations with our Navigator, an experienced officer for whom I had a great respect, failed to produce a convincing reason why not. Peter's argument could be summarised as 'An attempt to warn might cause more confusion and make the situation worse'. We should all hope that air traffic controllers never follow that line. I have not seen any published account of the accident which discusses the possibility that the costly collision might have been avoided by a timely warning over the radio.

Even serious events are accompanied by lighter moments. The best known was the response of the Captain of Diamond to a signal from the Admiral in Swiftsure asking, 'What do you intend to do next?'. As he backed his foreshortened ship out of the hole he had made in Swiftsure's side, he responded, 'Buy a farm?'

The Daring Class may have had excellent sea-keeping qualities but few things are perfect and a longitudinal stiffener at the break of Decoy's forecastle had cracked in the heavy weather. We were ordered to accompany Swiftsure and Diamond to a remote fjord in Iceland to assist them with first aid repairs and await suitable conditions for our return passage to the UK. That order had a significant effect on my career, but first came a couple of footnotes to the history of the collision.

As soon as we anchored in the fjord, the Deputy Supply Officer of Swiftsure was sent across to Decoy to tell us how we could help. It was 1800 by Swiftsure time and, not unnaturally in the circumstances, he expected to be offered a drink before he told his tale. Faces have seldom fallen as far as his did when offered tea. It was 1600 in Decoy. Swiftsure had not altered her time when she changed from 'enemy' to 'friend'.

One of our youngest engine room ratings returned from Swiftsure's sick-bay. He had been assisting an experienced artificer to strip a large steam valve a week earlier. The senior man had a mental aberration and failed to use a safe procedure. Steam blew the cover off and the youngster was scalded, seriously enough to have him transferred for treatment by Swiftsure's doctor. He was then practically tipped out of his hammock by Diamond's intrusive bow and had his first experience of a major fire. We wondered whether he would return a nervous wreck. Nowadays, he might have needed extensive counselling, and might have sued the senior rating, the ship's Marine Engineer Officer and the Admiralty for negligence. We learned that he wrote home on the lines of,

'Dear Mum, It's great being at sea. I've had so many adventures . . . . '

Having done what we could for Swiftsure, we waited for reasonable weather for our return to UK and tried to make good use of the time. Some new jet aircraft called Sabres at a US base in Iceland were willing to practice attacking us while we defended ourselves. Our main radar had to detect the aircraft and point the specialised gunnery radar in the right direction before our computing and gun aiming systems could get to work. It was no contest. We could rarely get beyond the first step.

Reservations that I had about the effectiveness of guns against modern aircraft were justified. Conventional gunnery thinking was that although aircraft might be too fast for us in tracking exercises, if they were really attacking us they would have to slow down to reduce the stresses when they launched rockets. It did not seem like an argument that could be sustained for long. It wasn't.

A lack of confidence in gunnery opened two lines of thought. The future of anti-aircraft warfare lay with the development of missiles, and surface ships would become increasingly vulnerable to submarine attack even if they won the anti-aircraft battle. Missile development was the preserve of engineers with the highest examination results. I had no illusions about my place in the engineering pecking order, my results were the lowest in my group. Given my ingrained Yorkshire desire to win, underwater warfare was the area for me.

Speculation on career directions was put aside when we returned to the UK. We were due for an Admiral's Inspection, always an occasion to make career conscious officers nervous. It involved detailed technical and administrative examinations by the Admiral's staff but the finale, the sea inspection, was the most important. We would be exposed to air, submarine and surface attack, would have to rescue a 'man overboard', take a stricken ship in tow, and perform many other evolutions.

My action station for daytime operations was at the back of the bridge, close to the Gunnery Officer. Just as the first air attack turned towards us the Admiral 'killed' the Gunnery Officer. I am very much in favour of having officers who can and do think, but when there's no time to do so, training takes over. Pick up the microphone dropped by the dead GO and rattle off the commands, 'Alarm aircraft starboard. Director follow sight. M1, M3 engage'. Continue to be a gunnery officer to the end of that exercise, making sure that the guns did not shoot down the aircraft towing the target. It went well. I was again grateful for the training we did at Whale Island.

'Guns' was pleased with the team until his senior rating, the CPO Gunnery Instructor, ruined it all. The ammunition for our 4.5 inch guns was old WW2 stock and 5% of the propellant charges misfired. If repeated attempts to fire the gun failed, the gun had to be pointed in a safe direction for an hour. If it had not 'cooked off' by then, the charge was to be removed and dropped over the side. No examination of the firing circuit, no removal of the primer or cordite for examination in a laboratory, just straight over the side.

It was customary for the Gunnery Officer to remove misfires. In Decoy, I opened the hydraulically operated breech slowly, Guns removed and disposed of the cartridge. Sometimes we fired hundreds of rounds a week. Guns and I had plenty of practice at removing misfired cartridges. Perhaps the GI thought he was being helpful when he appeared at the back of the bridge where Guns. now restored to life, was talking to the Admiral son after the firings. Saluting smartly, he reported that he had taken the misfired cartridge from the gun, opened it, and taken the sample of the cordite which was now sprouting like a sheaf of corn from the pocket of his shirt. He had broken every rule in the book. Poor old Guns. The GI left the ship soon after.

We learned that our ship had been selected to do a trial of the Flyplane 3 System. The objective was to see whether a typical ship of the Fleet obtained results as good as those of the prototype system fitted in the Trials Cruiser, HMS Cumberland. It was a great challenge but also very frustrating.

The frustration of Admiral Sir Percy Scott, the father of modern gunnery in the RN, has been recorded in many books. When he was the Commander of HMS Duke of Edinburgh, around the turn of the century, he was in trouble because gunnery, like steam machinery, tended to dirty the decks. He wrote, 'So we gave up instruction in gunnery, spent money on enamel paint, burnished up every bit of brightwork on board, and soon got the reputation of being a very smart ship'. Similar attitudes were still found in the 1950s. Preparations for the great trial required that we check the tuning of all the servo mechanisms. Those which controlled the computing were no problem, they were tucked away down below, but the guns had to be trained and elevated for hours to get their controls right. That required the forecastle and quarterdeck awnings to be removed. That would make one ship of the Fleet look different to all the rest. And that was rarely permissible. Too often, appearances were still more important than efficiency in gunnery.

Testing and tuning was different to most other shipboard engineering tasks. The artificers of the navy, skilled tradesmen and diagnosticians, were highly respected. The role of the engineer officer was often to manage a team that could do most individual jobs as well as he could. But the Flyplane System required new skills which, at that time, only the OEs possessed.

Obviously, a keen young OE should teach the new methods to his staff, but experience showed it was not always possible. While tuning 'A' turret one afternoon, the wriggley lines down the centre of the metres of paper flowing from the recording instruments proved that the 'acceleration feedback unit' was defective. I explained it all to the thirty seven year old artificer responsible for that turret and ended the day by asking him to remove the unit. Next morning, Guns entered our office apoplectic with laughter. During his walk around the department, he had seen the OA removing an access plate from the side of 'A' turret and asked what he was doing. 'Humouring the Ordnance Engineer, Sir', was the reply. As far as he was concerned it was all much better in the days when they just 'followed pointers'. I learned to be more selective in my teaching.

There were no set periods for maintenance and testing weapons but somehow or other the preparations were completed and the Operational Evaluation Trial conducted. Success was measured by the percentage of shells which passed close enough to a target towed behind an aircraft to trigger their radar fuses. There was much wailing when it produced results consistently 'x' per cent lower than those achieved in the Cumberland. After being made to feel that I had bitterly disappointed the designers of the system, I ferreted about a bit and discovered that their crack team had had six weeks of uninterrupted effort preparing for their trials. We had only the few days when it was convenient to have the Fleet's awnings in disarray. A move to underwater weapons seemed better all the time.

Life wasn't all gunnery. They were days of widespread discontent among the ratings of the Fleet, a discontent expressed by the 'gauge glass smashing' incidents especially in the aircraft carriers and cruisers. It was easy for a malcontent to go down to an unoccupied machinery space and smash the glass of pressure gauges.

Decoy, being by definition a 'small ship', was a closer community. We had less trouble but we had to be sensitive to the feelings of our ship's company and also to the possibility that there might be a trouble maker aboard. We did not wish to repeat an experience of the Invergordon Mutiny in 1931 when a

138

Ship's Company was told by their Commanding Officer, explaining the drastic pay cut, 'The country is in trouble. We must all tighten our belts. I have written to my wife to sack one of the maids'.

Sports helped to remind us of Drake's 'all one company' principle and provided good opportunities for officers and ratings to get to know each other better. To the disgust of our Welshmen, Decoy was a 'soccer ship'. It was hard to raise a rugby team but it could be done. The best rugby player in the ship, a tough Able Seaman, was always in trouble and was confined him to the ship almost indefinitely unless the First Lieutenant gave him a dispensation to go ashore, under the eye of an officer, to play sport. So 'M' had to persuade enough people they wanted to play rugby. He never seemed to have much trouble doing this. It was a very practical system. The First Lieutenant had my neck on the block if 'M' misbehaved. I could allow 'M' a pint in the canteen before returning to the ship after a match, confident he wouldn't misbehave because if he did there would be no more sport for him. We enjoyed our rugby, infuriating opposing teams by our gimmick that everyone was called Dai. Most of them were.

Another chance to see sailors in their off duty hours occurred when the Home and Mediterranean Fleets joined forces. After the exercises, the aircraft carrier, HMS Eagle and six destroyers and frigates visited the Algerian port of Oran. Everyone had been at sea for two weeks, it was pay-day, about 2,000 men were free to go ashore. I was one of the two Officers of the Patrol.

In the Royal Navy, away from the major naval ports, every junior rating except Sick Berth staff could be detailed for shore patrol duty. The principle behind the policy was sound. Experience in other navies showed that if professional naval police were used, a lot of heads got broken. But if tonight's sober patrolman is potentially tomorrow's drunk, treatment is *even handed. The objective of patrols was simply to ensure that sailors behaviour did not prejudice the Royal Navy's reputation.*

Engineer officers rarely became involved in matters like shore patrols and I had not had any training in the duties of an Officer of the Patrol. Nevertheless, I looked forward to the role and was prepared to use common sense in lieu of experience. Leave had been given from early afternoon and we landed with the first libertymen. The senior officer of the patrol and I had six patrols, an office and some cells in the police headquarters, a Landrover and its Leading Airman driver, a French police interpreter, and a map showing the brothels of Oran. We found the police station, worked out patrol routes and sent out the first patrols. There was no time to wonder what to do next. The first incident occurred within an hour and from then on we were reacting to events until six the next morning..

The first incident was illuminating. A cafe owner reported that a British sailor had been robbed and the police asked me to go with them. The sailor was an old 'Stripey', still an Able Seaman after nearly twenty years service. He had been drinking at the cafe with two young sailors, his cap on the table, cigarettes and lighter on top of the cap. A young local selling newspapers rested them on top of the pile. When he had gone the lighter was missing. Stripey was already quietly maudlin, 'I should have known better, Sir. I'll never see that lighter again'. He was wrong. The police said,' Ah, that'll be so and so' and went to look for him. A few minutes later the lighter was back.

The lesson from that incident was clear. The French police were efficient but their methods might not bear close scrutiny. And so it proved. When some sailors were brought to the station in the French police paddy wagon, the headquarters police wanted to beat them up with their batons as they got out. We persuaded them it was not the way we did business.

It was more fun responding to calls from the brothel owners. Some of them thought they ought to have their own patrols to keep their customers in order. We certainly didn't have enough patrols for that. In fact all patrols were soon committed so my driver and I, with the interpreter, took the next call ourselves. This place was in a dark alley. The driver took us past the entrance. Experienced or not, I knew better than to venture down alleys in the dark. The Land Rover was turned, the headlights shone on the queue of prospective customers, and the problem was half solved. We were invited in, toured the establishment and negotiated. Madam wanted only the rough customers removed from the queue. Instead I invited her to chose between letting them all remain and having me tell them that she was not going to let anyone in for two hours. She chose dispersal and all except one young sailor went quietly. He had to be grabbed, put in the Land Rover and prevented from jumping out. It was the only time I manhandled a sailor in 31years.

I never had a chance to compare notes with the other officer. He was supposed to be the senior officer of the patrol but we were so busy we never saw each other during our night of interesting duty. In his absence I had to decide whether the misbehaviour for which the sailors had been put in the cells warranted charges against them in their ships. Like most sailors who have had a drop too much to drink the night before, they were a sorry looking and quietly respectful bunch in dawn's early light. There were no charges.

Other new skills had to be learnt during the time in Decoy. One of the most useful was the keeping and auditing of accounts. We all had to take our turn at running 'non-public funds', the wardroom wine fund for instance. The method of learning, 'pick it up as you go along', was good enough if you wanted to learn but some officers never took accounts seriously. Later experience showed how important it could be to belong to the serious brigade.

Personally, I still had to be serious about anything involving money. Although I had acquired a second stripe in

December 1952, I was the second lowest paid member of my small department when I joined Decoy in August 1953. A few months later the most junior artificer was rated up to Chief Petty Officer and I became the lowest paid. My prospects were better than those of my staff, but I carried the responsibility, not them.

When the most junior artificer was promoted, he celebrated by buying a motor cycle. He had only a few weeks experience when he announced he would ride to Portsmouth and back the next weekend, about 200 miles each way. Several of us tried to talk him out of it but he was adamant. At seven o'clock on the Monday morning a hospital reported that he had been killed. We were reproaching ourselves for failing to dissuade him when he walked up the gangway. He had only been slightly injured in his accident. Another motor cyclist had died and the hospital had mixed the names. By the time we had finished with young Ivor he probably wished he had died. Deaths in a small ship affect everyone.

My feelers about a future in submarines brought news that the submarine service needed for a few ordnance engineers to look after the sophisticated weapon systems which would soon be introduced. Submariners prefer to trust their own, so the deal was to qualify as a Submarine Engineer Officer, serve for one commission as the marine engineer of a submarine and then revert to a specialist role, looking after the weapons of a squadron of submarines, conducting weapon trials, and similar tasks.

It sounded good. I believed in the operational value of submarines. Underwater weapons were about to enter a new era. Submarine pay would improve our finances, it would be like being one rank higher. I let it be known that I was interested and after an interview and medical I was in. We packed and moved back to Portsmouth.

Chapter 12

One Job in a Submarine

Most people assume that a submariner would have served in many submarines. It was not so for Ordnance Engineers. I have had to explain many times that one job as the Marine Engineer Officer of a submarine was our ration, after which we would be appointed to Submarine Squadron staffs or trials teams. But such explanations were far in the future when I joined the Engineer Officers' Training Course at HMS Dolphin in the autumn of 1954.

One O/E had done the course previously. This time there were three of us. The rest of the course were marine engineers starting their submarine careers, and three Royal Norwegian Navy engineers. We were all cadet entry Officers. That meant, we were told, that we would not be appointed to the smallest class of submarine, the 'S' boats which were the preserve of officers commissioned from the ranks of the Engine Room Artificers. We would only study the 'A' and 'T' classes of submarine. They lied of course. Two engineers were appointed to 'S' boats at the end of the course.

There was a saying at the time, 'If you're going to be buggered about, join the Submarine Service and have it done by professionals'. Notwithstanding the unexpected appointments to 'S' boats, the saying was a bit unfair. On major issues such as separation from families, the service was well ahead of the surface navy in the treatment of its people. Separations could be up to two and a half years in General Service. In submarines, the maximum was eight months.

Shorter separations were a good start. Other advantages were the nature of the service, the extra pay, the smaller ship's companies and their professional competence. Even 'small' General Service ships might have a crew of 200, a submarine typically about 60, every one of whom shared some responsibility for the safe operation of the boat. Top to bottom, everyone had to know their jobs, not least because there was still some measure of additional hazard in submarines, two having been sunk already in post-war accidents.

We soon saw a famous cartoon, drawn shortly after the introduction of submarines during the first decade of the century, A pukka army officer is being shown around a submarine. He gazes at the mass of pipes, valves and handwheels and remarks to the Lieutenant commanding it, 'I suppose you've got some kind of Sergeant wallah who understands all this kind of thing'. Submarine 'Sergeant wallahs' certainly understood their jobs but so did everyone else. One of the first things we were taught was never to believe any Commanding Officer who said, 'I don't know anything about engineering Chief', 'Chief' in this context being the customary title used by COs when talking to their engineer officers. It was good advice. And it was good to belong to a really professional service.

Technical skills were not paramount though. The primary criterion for selection for service in submarines was whether men could live harmoniously in the close confines of a boat. Even in a destroyer there was some room to escape the company of others. In Decoy for example, a mischievous officer caught a starfish while snorkelling. It was the colour of a beautiful Welsh Rarebit so he arranged for it to be served, live, as the Captain's Secretary's savoury course at dinner that night. The Secretary, nickname 'Bat' as in 'blind as', did not notice until the starfish waved a friendly limb. Then he knew he was the butt of a trick, chair thrown back, exit from Wardroom, escape to the upper deck or cabin until calmed down. In submarines, neither officers nor the troops had anywhere to go.

Equable temperaments were tried to the limit by the cramped living conditions. A space little bigger than a cabin in Decoy served as the Wardroom for the five officers even in the largest

'A' Class submarines. The ratings were even more cramped but at least everyone had his own bunk. Fortunately, 'hot bunking', though still part of the folklore, was very rare.

The living conditions were innocently summed up by a young stoker. During our training we each spent a week at sea in a boat, seeing how they operated and having a chance to talk to someone else's engineering team before we became responsible for our own. The stoker was not a volunteer but, unlike most non-volunteers, he did not believe the extra pay compensated for the living conditions. 'Take that last exercise, Sir', he said. 'Three weeks we were at sea. Three times I went to the bathroom to get a proper wash and it was occupied every time'. It's a story which makes the shower conscious submariners of my new country shudder.

Life amongst submariners ashore was a different matter. A US Navy Captain on the staff of the Flag Officer Submarines kindly invited us to a party and introduced us to a level of affluence we had never seen before. He and his wife not only had a refrigerator, an item which Lise and I, like many others, would not acquire for some years, they had a second one just for the mint juleps. It seemed materialistic and self indulgent at the time. Now that we have a separate fridge for wine and beer I'm not so sure.

Lise and I were able to compare notes with another O/E on the course, Mick, and his wife Vennie. We had a living room and bedroom in a house at Widley and shared the use of bathroom and kitchen with the owners, Barbara and Russell. Like me, Mick had been the first of his term to marry, but he and Vennie had been helped to buy a caravan in which, parked on Portsdown Hill, they lived a cramped but independent life with their two daughters. We were a bit envious. There was no one to help us financially.

The course was undemanding. The principles on which submarines operate are simple and with a couple of exceptions the rest was a matter of learning the practical details of the Admiralty and Vickers main engine designs, the auxiliary machinery, the various systems and the special equipments such as periscopes.

The most interesting exception was our training at the Royal Naval Physiological Laboratory on respiration under normal, pressurised and vacuum conditions, a subject with important implications for atmosphere control within our submarines, for which we would soon bear some responsibility. It was fascinating to get an insight into another professional world, especially one which included lots of jars of human remains from deaths in explosions and diving accidents.

Before visiting the laboratory we had practiced using the Davis Submarine Escape Apparatus, a device only suitable for escape from very shallow depths because it supplied oxygen, essential to life but toxic under pressure. At the physiological laboratory we learned about a new technique for 'free ascent' from sunken submarines hundreds of feet below the surface. After a final breath from an uncontaminated air bottle in the submarine the escapee would climb out of the flooded compartment and float up to the surface, breathing out to relieve the pressure of the expanding air in his lungs. We saw a film of a goat in a pressure chamber, fretful as the water was pumped in over his head, then relaxing and blowing bubbles unconcernedly as the pressure was reduced to simulate ascent through the water. Soon we would all be required to ascend 100 feet in the escape training tank being constructed in Dolphin. If a goat could do it, so could we.

My eye infection recurred and one Friday, I was whisked into the Haslar Naval Hospital, conveniently next door to Dolphin. Our landlady was a health visitor so we were living for the first time in a house with a telephone and Lise was amused the following Monday when the Senior Engineer of the Squadron called her. All he knew was that I had not turned up for instruction that morning and he had the unenviable task of trying to find out whether I had spent the weekend with my wife or, perhaps, with a girlfriend in Brighton. We felt sorry for whoever failed to tell him I was in hospital.

The minutes of fame said to be everyone's due have eluded me but I can claim to be unusual in one respect. There cannot have been many engineer officers who have studied Old Testament theology while doing their submarine training course. Under the supervision of a local minister I did a correspondence course organised by the Methodist Church. It was the first step towards a theological qualification and I was being encouraged to consider whether I had a vocation to become a minister.

Studying theology turned out to be a make or break affair. Extensive reading of the Old Testament and various commentaries on it were the basis of the study. I tried to use the same few brains that had been applied to engineering to generate honest responses based on analytical reading of, and reflection on, the set questions. All too often the work I submitted to my unseen tutor was returned with comments which implied that adherence to a 'party line' would be preferred to original thinking.

It was the beginning of a long attempt to reconcile Christianity, history and world affairs. I read the Bishop of Woolwich's book 'Honest to God' which implied that from the nineteen thirties some theologians had found it impossible to believe in the omnipresent, omniscient, omnipotent and loving God that was said to be at the heart of Christianity. Much of the evidence of history and contemporary life suggested they had good cause for their doubts. The party line response of the Methodists, like some other Christian churches, was that life without faith was unthinkable. That was clearly nonsense. My thinking had to accomodate all the evidence without qualification. It was a problem.

The course ended. We all passed our examinations though the Norwegians lived dangerously. When asked, 'Which design of main engine do you favour? Give reasons for your choice', They declined to favour either of those in British submarines, praising instead engines of ex-German U-boats now in service with their navy. It was not a popular response. The Royal Navy's submarine service had a party line too!

The Flag Officer Submarines gave us a farewell cocktail party as we prepared to leave for our next appointments. When we took our leave from the Admiral the cry was, 'Let's go to the club'. That referred to the Nuffield Officers' Club in Portsmouth, fifteen miles away. We were young, we were celebrating, it was long before the era of the breathalyser. Frankly, it was a race. As we passed through Fareham I realised how easily we could share Mike Hawthorn's fate, reduced speed, and drove as a responsible motorist should when 'having drink taken'.

My destination was the Third Submarine Squadron at Rothesay on the Isle of Bute, to serve as a 'spare crew engineer officer' until it pleased their Lordships to appoint me to a boat. The old car was sold. The reliability achieved by cars today was a long way off. We expected a breakdown during any journey of over two hundred miles. The old Lanchester could not be expected to survive a journey to Scotland without complaint. We took trains, spent Christmas 1954 with my parents, then I went ahead to find us a place to live.

A small flat was found quite easily, relations with the locals were quite harmonious, and life for us as a young married couple was fine. It was a different story for the unmarried young sailors for whom there were few facilities apart from sports grounds and pubs, and who were regarded with suspicion by the local parents of young girls and hostility by the local lads.

After three uneventful months in the spare crew I joined HMS Alcide, my most memorable appointment. Alcide's CO had commanded submarines since the last months of WW2 but had retained an easy going manner which made service under his command a pleasure. And, as so often happens ashore and afloat, when the man at the top is OK, everything else follows.

The 'A' class were the RN's largest submaines, built for the long haul of the Pacific war. Alcide was unmodernised, still had a 4 inch gun and wires from stem to tower to ward off mine cables. They don't build them like that anymore. They didn't even then! She was suffering, in the CO's words, '..... the material ravages of a long commission', and it showed. That was not surprising. My appointment followed the sensible idea that an engineer joining a boat just in time to become familiar with its defects before a refit, would be highly motivated to ensure that the boat was in good shape by the end of the refit because he would be responsible for running it during the next commission.

The wear and tear would have mattered little had we taken the boat to refit on schedule but plans change. Problems elsewhere caused Alcide's commission to be extended by six months. My job was to provide a care worn team with the motivation to keep her going until during those last months. They were such a good team, we did more than keep her going.

Our training class taught us not to contradict our CO if he says a periscope is defective in some way. Sometimes everyone's lives depend on his skill at interpreting what he sees through it, so don't argue. The lesson was reinforced when I joined Alcide. My predecessor said there was nothing wrong with the navigational periscope but the Captain believed there was so it had been removed from the boat and was being examined by the squadron's experts during our maintenance period. He departed. The experts found nothing wrong but we left it in their workshop for a few days before reinstaling it. The Captain said it was much better. Perchance, I had got off to a good start.

There is something distinctive about taking responsibility for a vital task for the first time. There were only three watchkeeping seaman officers in the boat, the First Lieutenant and two jumior *officers. They always appreciated an engineer who helped out occassionally and his help was virtually essential when 'snorting' for long periods. And in order to 'help out', practice was necessary.*

'Snorting' was running the boat at periscope depth with one or both the diesel engines sucking in outside air through the raised snort mast to propel the boat and/or charge the batteries. The top of the periscope was only a couple of feet above the water. Visibility was very limited, especially at night, and two officers were required when snorting. One kept a periscope watch while the other attended to 'the trim' and they changed over every ten minutes to ensure maximum concentration on the periscope.

Surprisingly, 'trimming' was the most onerous. Given good eyesight, good concentration and a strong sense of self preservation, periscope watchkeeping came easily. 'Trimming', keeping the submarine at neutral buoyancy by pumping water out of special tanks or flooding some in, and correcting the longitudinal balance of the boat by pumping water from forward to aft or vice versa, was as much an art as a science. Done badly while snorting, the speed of the boat could conceal several tons of negative buoyancy necessitating quick action when the engines were stopped. Done badly while trying to detect or track another submarine could necessitate running a pump, making unnecessary noise, and possibly revealing our existence to the enemy.

Trimming had to be learned on the job and it was a very public job. Everyone in the boat knew if an inexperienced officer was doing it badly. During my first watch, when a fine balance was required, the First Lieutenant wandered out from the wardroom and stood quietly near me. I could interpret his action as friendly moral support or a lack of confidence in my trimming. I have always hoped it was the former.

The submarine service was better organised than General Service. Maintenance periods were planned well in advance, an obvious advantage from the engineers' point of view. Planned leave periods could only be changed with the permission of the Flag Officer Submarines, good man management because no Submarine Squadron Captain would seek that permission without the strongest operational justification. It was a good organisation to have joined. But Alcide needed more than maintenance periods could provide.

The two eight cylinder, supercharged, 2,000 HP, Vickers diesel engines were running very raggedly. They seemed to be on their last legs and that gave me my first experience of an interaction between mind and body which recurred at times of stress throughout my life. When in my bunk, my head was on one side of a panel, the helmsman's feet six inches away on the other. The helmsman changed every twenty minutes and the course and engine revolutions were reported to the officer of the watch. I awoke every twenty minutes, listened to the report, and went back to sleep. I would never have made the kind of General who could sleep soundly after committing a quarter of a million men to battle and many of them to death.

When the refit was postponed we had to restore the reliability of the engines. Tests showed that the cylinders were all running at different pressures. It is one thing to do a valve grind and change the spark plugs of the family car's motor. It was another to ask a team who were going to sea at six each morning, exercising all day and returning at eight or nine in the evening, to spend much of the nights replacing the massive inlet, exhaust and fuel injector valves with spares from the depot ship. But that was the obvious first step and that is what they did over the next few weeks.

The performance of the engines improved greatly but I soon discovered that 'you can't win'. There was an expectation that the lubricating oil consumption of submarine engines should never exceed 9% of the fuel used. The lub oil to fuel ratios of Alcide's engines were poor before we worked on them. That was not surprising in view of the wear over her long commission. They were worse after we finished our improvement program.

My Engine Room Registers faithfully recorded the true figures. That was not popular. The registers were as sacred as a ship's Log Book and there was no question of recalling the moving finger once it had written. Though generally very professional, the engineering hierarchy of the submarine service had a few foibles and there was an expectation that everyone would conform to them. When the registers were submitted to the Squadron staff I was left in no doubt that everyone would have preferred fudged figures. No questions would have been asked. We would have been as solid as the staunchest unionists. But I had been stubborn and recorded the true figures. There was an embarrassment.

A bit of serendipity gave me the answer. I found all the Squadron's Registers in the Engineers' Office in the depot ship one evening. Smarting a bit from what I regarded as an unwarranted rebuke, I had no qualms about making quick notes of the fuel and oil consumptions of a comparable submarine for the number of miles steamed. The answer to my 'problem' fell out almost immediately. Now that Alcide's engines were running efficiently they were consuming about a third less fuel than those of the other boat. I kept my prying to myself. Honour was satisfied. The Squadron soon lost interest, there were always more important problems.

I soon encountered one. At a routine docking we tested the cooling water jackets around the pipes, each about fifteen inches in diameter, which carried the diesels' exhaust gases to the snort exhaust mast. A few drops of water appeared where they should not have been. Unless they could be written off as condensation, they had passed through piping designed to withstand the pressure at maximum diving depth. Repeating the test did not produce more drops but the Chief Mechanician and I had seen what we had seen. It was courage of convictions time. The boat's program was altered, our time in dock extended. Other boat's were reprogrammed to take over our tasks. Our exhausts were stripped out and removed to the depot ship. It took much time and effort.

In HMS Adamant's very capable workshops the jackets were removed from the exhaust pipes. Examination revealed a hairline crack three quarters of the way round the flange which connected one of the pipes to the submarine. It appeared that the original welding had never penetrated the pipe and flange correctly. It was not a nice defect to find. Had the crack become a catastrophic failure the consequences could have been very serious for the boat. I was pleased we took the drops of water seriously.

The extension of our time in dock provided another lesson in human nature. There was an unexpected opportunity to give half the crew an extra long weekend leave but we could not foresee any opportunity to give one to the other half. The ex-officio senior rating of the boat, the Coxswain, was asked to sound out opinion amongst the troops. Leave for half? Or leave for none? There was an overwhelming majority in favour of 'none'. Equal misery for all is a popular philosophy.

The experience of a RAF Coastal Command aircrew that we took to sea for a day in the Londonderry exercise areas was not miserable but it was rather uncomfortable. During the afternoon the hydraulic pressure controlling the after hydroplanes failed. When that happens, the planes fall to the 'Dive' position, the back end of the boat rises and down she goes at an unusual angle until brought under control. A handwheel driving the hydroplane shaft through a bicycle chain was quickly engaged. It was annoying that the failure had occurred but it was not a 'big deal'.

We levelled off at periscope depth and the Chief Mechanician and I were investigating the cause of the failure when the bicycle chain broke. Down went the planes to 'Dive' and down went the boat again. The Chief and I crouched under the torpedo tubes, clamped a stilson wrench on the appropriate shaft and passed it back and forth between us to wind the planes back to 'Rise'.

Incidents like this brought to our captain's face the sort of smile which means, 'I've seen it all before' and he allowed the officer of the watch to sort things out as best he could. In this case, the result was a submarine with its bow on the surface, its middle at periscope depth and its stern at a hundred feet. It also resulted in the aircrew, standing as best they could on the steeply sloping deck of the control room, exclaiming that they had never realised that our life was so uncomfortable. They thought we were kidding when we told them this was not an everyday routine.

Human behaviour is always a fascinating study and Alcide provided its share of examples, like the case of sailors not wanting beer. The Admiralty was experimenting with change. Beer in cans had just become available and Alcide was offered the opportunity to sell two cans a day to the sailors for a trial period. The Coxswain came to the engine room one day and asked if he could have a word with my senior ratings about the trial. 'I've asked all the other messes,' he began, 'and none of them wants beer onboard. You don't want it do you?' The Coxswain clearly wanted to avoid complications which might arise from beer onboard and had persuaded the Seamens', Stokers', and the Petty Officers' messes accordingly. My Chief Mechanician folded brawny arms and set the tone of the debate, 'We want it, don't we?' Coxswain's are key players in the life of every submarine but wise ones know the limits of their influence. Ours could not convert the Chief and his four artificers. He switched to plan 'B' and asked the Chief Mech to become the beer caterer, a reasonable request because the Chief was one of the few ratings who did not keep watches. It was agreed.

The First Lieutenant took a gloomy view of the trial, something was bound to go wrong. But the trial was on so he agreed the accounting procedures with the Chief Mech. 'Beer costs 10 pence a can from the depot ship canteen. We buy at tenpence, we sell at tenpence. We keep it simple and have no trouble'. And so it was. The sailors enjoyed their couple of beers each day, the trial was successful and beer is now a commonplace feature of shipboard life. There was never any trouble. 'x' cans of beer came aboard, 'x' tenpences went ashore to pay for them. The only unusual thing was that once a month, Chief Arthur would appear in the wardroom, deposit five cans of beer on the table and announce, 'Out of the profits, Gentlemen'. There are definitely some things we are not meant to know!

Not all life onboard went as smoothly as the beer experiment. Many readers will have heard or read of 'getting your own back', the consequence of pulling the wrong lever in the older submarine lavatories. No such problem in Alcide, it had a big tank to which all the 'heads' were connected, more or less like household WCs. The tankful could be conveniently discharged at sea using compressed air. Much better, unless, of course, you went to the loo at ten o'clock one morning in harbour, slipping quietly behind one of the Leading Stokers who was in the passage. I did not know he had been posted there to stop anyone attempting to use the heads. The system was being pressure tested and there was only the flap valve at the bottom of the pan between the contents of the tank and any contributor who pulled the lever. The inevitable happened. I will spare you the details. Suffice it to say that after eight baths in the depot ship I returned to the boat smelling like a human being once again.

At lunchtime when the rum ration was issued I was invited to the Artificers' Mess. There, the 'Outside Wrecker', the artificer responsible for all the systems outside the engine room and for *the alertness of the sentry, invited me to 'see off' his rum ration. Although sharing rum was illegal, the social code for doing so was understood throughout the navy. 'Sippers' was the merest wetting of the lips, just as well because one custom was for everyone in the mess to give sippers on anyone's birthday. 'Gulpers' was a significant swig, acknowledging a favour or something similar. 'See it off' was almost as rare as 'Splice the mainbrace'.*

In this case it signified a wish to 'settle out of court'. He need not have worried. My view was that I had contributed to the situation by slipping quietly behind the sentry, and that the Wrecker and his Mate had come off worse. I only had to clean myself. They had had to clean the submarine. We had all been punished enough already. It was the only time I was ever offered a whole tot. I appreciated the gesture, but gulpers and a chat were sufficient.

Much of the time we were the target for surface ships and aircraft practicing their trade. Pretty boring stuff. Then we were told to experiment by attacking a surface ship knowing only its sonar bearings from Alcide. We didn't know was how far away it was. That would not have mattered if we could have done the attacks from well below the surface but in order to analyse the attacks we had to be at periscope depth. An extra commanding officer onboard kept a continuous safety watch through the periscope, taking us down before the destroyer, nearer than we thought and steaming fast, rumbled overhead. That was not boring.

Routine was enlivened by a weekend in company with a couple of frigates at Blackpool, a place many people scorn. The visit proved to me that Blackpool was a very well organised city. After a civic dinner on the Saturday, the Lord Mayor's speech concluded, 'This dinner has been conducted with all the decorum due to a civic occasion but what happens afterwards is no concern of mine. I've got the Rolls outside. I'll take the COs in that and there's a bus for the rest of you with some of my blokes. We're going round the town, anywhere you like'. He meant it. If we said, 'Let's go backstage at that theatre', 'Mayor's party' was the word from our hosts to the stage-doorman and we were in. It was an interesting evening.

When the Captain of the senior frigate returned hospitality with a lunch on the Sunday, the party came to Alcide for a final drink. The mayor's opening question was how had our lads enjoyed the visit. The general opinion in Alcide was 'Very much indeed', the only disappointment being that Blackpool's football team had been playing away so they hadn't seen Stanley Matthews. 'Can I use a boat', asked the Director of Publicity and Entertainments. Half an hour later Stanley Matthews was onboard delighting the sailors with a chat and his autograph. Blackpool, like the Butlins I enjoyed in my childhood, is a serious business.

In addition to such weekends, every submarine could expect a one week foreign visit each year. We were offered one during our extension, to be followed by a month long exercise. The signal asking where we would like to go had a PS, 'Don't all say Copenhagen, Stockholm or Oslo'. Our Captain remembered his father had enjoyed visiting Horsens in Denmark in a minesweeper in 1931. We were at sea and knew nothing more about Horsens but asked to go there anyway. When we returned to harbour the navigator discovered that Horsens was approached through a narrow channel thirteen nautical miles long, dredged to about six inches deeper than our expected draught.

Captains who have seen it all are not deterred by such details and the Danish navy reported that the basin at the end of the channel was just wide enough to turn Alcide around. Backing out for thirteen miles would not have been a practical option. At seven o'clock one morning we were at the entrance to the channel, stored for the month-long exercise, with a Sub-

Lieutenant onboard for some 'small ship' experience, and ready to enjoy our 'showing the flag' week.

The Horsens pilot brought us smoothly up the channel and by nine o'clock we were secured in the basin and giving him the customary whisky. Scotch was still in very short supply in Denmark even ten years after the war so, there being no calls to be made so early, we gave him three or four whiskies which were much appreciated. His gratitude was shortlived. His face fell when he saw the Pilotage Certificate which our Captain had signed. Leaving technical definitions aside, the pilot's fees were based on the cargo carrying capacity of the vessel. Our submarine, however long and deep it was, was only rated at about 250 tons, a fraction of the pilot's expectation. I had filled in the correct tonnage but when the Captain said, 'Find a more suitable figure, Chief', a more suitable figure was soon found. It was probably the Suez canal tonnage or something similar. Exit happier pilot.

It was an excellent week. The people of Horsens were especially grateful that we had sought them out because, we were told, none of their Danish submarines had ever visited them. When we opened the ship to visitors, more than three thousand of them filed through. For our part, we enjoyed to the full their relaxed but responsible attitude to civic life and to entertaining, their smorgasbord style of food, and of course their schnapps. Drinking and driving was already a 'no-no', but when the cars were safely in the garage, their hospitality knew no bounds. It was an excellent preparation for a month at sea.

That month left a few memories beginning with the first dive. The Sub-Lieutenant was the Officer of the Watch on the bridge and therefore the last one down, or in his case, partially down. He carelessly allowed the belt of his oilskin to hang loose. The inevitable happened. The belt became trapped in the top hatch as he tried to shut it. The water poured down, the Sub was washed off the ladder and flapped away like a little cherub, suspended by the belt. Another wry smile from the Captain, and after letting the Sub get thoroughly soaked he ordered the boat to be surfaced. The cruellest word was from our mischievous Wykehamist navigator as the half drowned Sub climbed down into the Control Room, 'It was a good job you had your oilskin on wasn't it'.

The Sub's troubles had only just begun. He discovered he was seriously claustrophobic. He tried, as other officers have done, to tell himself that his fears were illogical, but, as he confided to each officer in turn, that didn't do any good. He became unable to interpret the routine noises of the submarine as anything other than impending doom. It was no good explaining to him for the tenth time that when the air compressor was running beneath the wardroom, the screaming noise every twenty minutes was just a drain being opened to blow any water out. He could no longer function rationally.

Unfortunately for the Sub, the wardroom depth gauge was only a few inches from his head as he lay in his bunk and he never slept for more than a few minutes before waking up to peer at it. Loss of sleep was bad enough but one night he awoke to find that the boat, at periscope depth a few minutes earlier, was now some hundreds of feet down and sinking slowly deeper. After his rush into the control room and agitated words to the officer of the watch, everyone knew about his problem. Characteristically, they just accepted it, there were no unkind remarks.

Why were we deep and sinking gently? After snorting at periscope depth to recharge the batteries we thought we might have been detected. We were operating against other submarines and quietness was of the essence. The rules of the exercise said we should operate some hundreds of feet down except when snorting at periscope depth. Between those depths were the operating zone for the opposing submarines and a separation layer for safety's sake. The rules also said we must signal our *presence when passing through the enemy's zone and the safety layer. No self respecting CO ever did. We slipped down as quietly as we could without worrying too much if we were a few tons negatively buoyant. The longer we could put off running the pumps the better our chance of hearing the enemy without being heard by him. The Sub need not have worried.*

That exercise began to teach me what fatigue was really like. When we kept two hour watches with four hours between them I found going on watch at four AM having come off at midnight, on again at ten AM and four PM, etc, exhausting. And I was only the stand-in for the bad bits. The seaman officers also had to keep the usual four hours on and eight off watches during the good bits and we all shared the extra burden of action stations which sometimes lasted for six hours as we attempted to sniff out an opposing submarine. The boat became the only reality, any other life was far away. We concentrated as hard as we could. I wonder how efficient we really were.

There was a postscript to the Sub's claustrophobia problem. After three weeks or so we rendezvoused with our depot ship in Iceland to refuel. The Sub was confident that he would be released from the submarine but after discussions with the Captain of the Squadron, our Captain told the Sub he would have to stay in the boat for the final week of the exercise. I'm not sure that decision achieved anything useful.

The closeness of life in a submarine and the professionalism of every member of the ship's company made life easy. Even the chores were easier. The Engineer Officer's chore was to be the wardroom wine caterer and the only difficult part of the job was working out officers' bills. In surface ships individual drinks were accounted for on chits and totalled by a steward. Alcide's wardroom was normally 'dry' at sea. Virtually all the drinking was done in harbour, often by the Duty Officers and friends they invited down to the boat while the rest of us were ashore. Getting them to keep even a rough record of consumption was difficult. Exasperated by my failure to get one officer to cooperate, I threatened to charge him for all drinks not accounted for by the rest of the team. He looked at me in wonder at my brilliance. 'What a great idea', he said, 'Would you mind?' It was Wykehamist Ian again.

A quiet lunchtime drink in Alcide's wardroom was the setting for the saddest event of those months. The submarine service had just changed its procedure for signalling that a submarine had failed to report surfacing safely. The new procedure involved two stages. 'Submiss' was the first. It usually meant that a submarine was having difficulty getting its surfacing signal through, but it served as a warning that search operations might soon be required. 'Subsunk' was positive confirmation that there had been a tragedy.

The signalman handed the Captain the simple signal, 'Subsunk Sidon. Alongside Maidstone'. We felt the usual human reaction of disbelief for a second or two, 'It can't be right. We haven't had a Submiss signal'. Details soon came through that the fuel and oxidant of an experimental torpedo had exploded in HMS Sidon sinking her alongside the depot ship. Those killed included the Squadron Ordnance Engineer. The sinking of a submarine, like the crashing of an aircraft, makes an impact because of its rarity. In 1955 the average time between accidental sinkings of RN submarines had been seven years. It's a pleasure to record that none has been sunk since then.

The extension of Alcide's commission had already taken six of the twenty four months I expected to be in the boat. Nevertheless, I had served my apprenticeship in submarines, learned to love the highly professional service to which I now belonged and the people who served in it. I was well pleased with life as the boat sailed up the Mersey on 17th October 1955 and the pilot slipped it neatly into the basin at Cammell Lairds. Six memorable months were behind me, a year of home life *during the extended refit lay ahead. I celebrated by shaving off my beard.*

By mid-afternoon, the formalities had been completed, the introductory and farewell lunchtime drinks had been taken, and the Captain, junior officers and most of the ship's company had departed. The First Lieutenant and I began to organise our team of sixteen ratings who would stay throughout the refit. Then home to the flat which Lise had found for us in Wallasey.

Chapter 13

A Soft Patch

The Admiralty recognised long ago that industries such as ship building and repairing cannot be switched off and on. Continuity of experience is essential, otherwise skills are lost and recovery takes years. Self evident? Perhaps, but not every government has learned the lesson. My submarine, HMS Alcide, was sent to Cammell Lairds at Birkenhead for a refit, rather than to one of the Royal Dockyards, to maintain their expertise.

Doubtless Cammells were pleased to have the contract but they didn't need it. The yard's shipbuilding and repairing order books were overflowing. The aircraft carrier HMS Ark Royal had recently been completed. Three refrigerated ships were being built for an American company, a submarine of the new Porpoise Class and a frigate for the Admiralty. Ships needing repairs were being sent away to European mainland ports because the yard was full. To that extent, those were good days for the industry. In other respects, as the First Lieutenant and I learned later, things were far from right.

Our role as ship's officer's during the refit was frustrating. Resident Admiralty Overseers at the yard were responsible for the refit. That was similar to the Merchant Navy practice of having Masters Ashore and Engineers Ashore representing their companies but the MN didn't leave the ship's engineers there as well. The Admiralty did, and although my training encouraged me to believe that 'only the best is good enough for the RN', I had to achieve it by influence, not authority.

Cammell's management's attitude towards naval officers was welcoming and friendly. The First Lieutenant and I became members of the Repair Manager's Mess and soon established friendly relations with the key players. The stage was set. If the official channels through the Admiralty Overseers were not working well, we could try to get work done by Cammells. If Cammells agreed with us they would try to persuade the Admiralty to pay for it or would hide the cost somewhere. The Overseers would try to restrict the work to whatever they thought necessary. It was an interesting system.

At first nothing happened, at least not to Alcide. Hydrogen released by the batteries of an operational submarine exploded and the boat was brought to Cammells for repairs. Work on Alcide was suspended for six weeks. I don't remember any of us complaining. Most of our small team settled into comfortable lodgings. We were content to enjoy the unexpected breather.

Lise had been living with my parents in Hull while I was at sea, until, that is, my father explained with some embarrassment that my mother, rather typically, was finding life with her two year old grandson 'too much of a strain'. Lise packed our belongings and moved to Wallasey. She walked for miles with Michael in his push chair exploring suitable areas, and within a few days, despite the reluctance of agents to let flats to couples with children, had found a downstairs flat in a fairly large terraced house in New Brighton. It was spacious, the furniture was especially comfortable, and there was a garden for Michael to play in. Though not self contained it was the best we had ever had, and having other people cross the hall was a small price to pay. Those others were the owner, who occasionally used his pied a terre in the attic, and the tenants of the upstairs flat, Aussies John and Thelma.

John was doing post-doctoral research at Liverpool University. Thelma, like Lise, fulfilled the role of wife and mother, in Thelma's case, of baby Timothy, too young to be a playmate for Michael. We became, and remain, friends and when we met again in Australia thirty years later, they revealed that they had regarded us as quite well off compared to themselves, and had looked forward hungrily to the evening meal we sometimes shared with them on Fridays. We had always looked on Australians as well-to-do and this must have been the first time anyone envied us. I wish we had known. It would have boosted our morale.

After the damaged submarine had been repaired Alcide was drydocked and the serious business of the refit began. The expression 'soft patch' was still used to describe the plate in the pressure hull through which the main engines and motors could be lifted out for overhauling. The term dated back to the days of rivetted submarine hulls when the 'soft patch' was secured with bolts instead of rivets so it could be removed easily. Our 'soft patch' was just a bit of the welded hull, cut open using oxy-aceteline torches. Work began.

Cammell Lairds was a traditional shipyard, 'us' versus 'them', workers versus management. Facilities for men to clean themselves before they left the yard for home were non-existent. The leaving procedure itself was a revelation. Until the exact instant of noon or five o'clock the area of the yard near the gates was deserted and the massive gates were closed. Only security staff could be seen. When the siren sounded, they opened the gates, jumped for cover, and thousands of workers rushed out. Rushed too fast sometimes. One man was said to have died when crowded off the platform onto the live rail of the local 'underground', a hundred yards from the works.

Experience revealed a lack of concern for the occupational health and safety of the workers. One concern which I shared was the terrible scaffolding used around the hull of Alcide. We walked and worked, high above the dock bottom, on two planks, side by side, with no handrails. The conditions endured by the men who chipped the old paint inside our tanks were beyond belief. It seemed that the top management believed the workers to be a class of people whose welfare didn't matter.

At first most of the work was removing machinery and taking it apart for inspection and we had an easy time. Work all morning, a couple of pints in the pub before lunch in the mess, a *couple of hours more in the office, and home. The routine left plenty of time and energy for other pursuits. At first I thought about playing rugby again but discovered that it was a much more serious business in that area, requiring skills beyond my level. So the memories are mainly of pleasant evenings when we could leave Michael with John and Thelma and enjoy the theatre, cinema or concerts.*

Some of those evenings were of truly memorable events. At an experimental concert the Liverpool Symphony Orchestra performed without a conductor and the resident conductor showed a great sense of humour by selling programs before settling to listen. During the very first night of Peter Ustinov's 'Romanof and Juliet', exposed to a tough north country audience before opening in the West End, we saw Ustinov walk to the side of the stage, lean against the scenery and put his head in his hands in despair. We learned it was almost his signature. Many other evenings were spent in a remarkable cinema in Wallasey.

The 'Continental' only seated about two hundred, and was run like a theatre with printed programs giving background information on the story, the director, and the actors and actresses. They served coffee in an interval, and generated such a pleasant atmosphere that people with cars responded to the management's suggestion that they stop at the bus stop and offer fellow patrons a lift home. There we learned a bit more about opera, laughed at poor old Fernandel, and learned how effective silence in a film could be, the twenty five minutes as the robbers patiently committed their theft in 'Riffifi'. An all time record, I believe.

Alcide's small company were remote from the mainstream of naval life. We first learned about pay rises from the newspapers, not from the navy. Once, that was an advantage. I saw the look on my Chief Mechanician's face as he read in the Telegraph that he was now earning over a thousand pounds a year, a magical milepost in those days. It was worth seeing.

The official Admiralty Fleet Orders did however bring the most historically important bit of news to us before the newspapers. Since the middle of the nineteenth century, engineers and other specialist officers had been subordinate, regardless of rank and seniority, to the 'Executive' officers. AFO 1/56 promulgated a General List Officer concept, the essence of which was that in future, although seagoing command would necessarily and rightly be reserved for 'Seaman' officers, a General List of most other officers would be eligible for non-specialist duties, including shore commands, according to their rank and seniority. The obvious, non-contentious, exceptions were doctors and dentists.

That AFO was intended to signal the end of discrimination against engineers and other specialist officers. It was intended to be a cause for rejoicing but the first reaction of many engineers was sadness and opposition. As a symbol of the new unity, the purple, white or green cloth between our gold stripes, which indicated our specialisations, was to be removed. I was very proud of that association of colour and profession, and wore it as long as I could get away with it, but I didn't share the reluctance of some the engineers to taking part in general duties such as Officer of the Day or conducting defaulters. As it happened, I didn't get involved in those for some years but when I did I found them fascinating. Perhaps it was that Whale Island training.

If any single event symbolised the cause of the decline of Britain's shipbuilding industry it would be the 'hole boring strike' at Cammell Lairds. The yard's methods were virtually unchanged from those of the thirties but the overflowing order book proved the yard was flourishing. Why change anything? Because like it or not, change was in the wind. For instance, a US company had specified that the refrigerated compartments of its three ships had to be lined with aluminium. Cammell's boilermakers and the sheet-metal workers both claimed an exclusive right to install the new material. At first it was just a demarcation dispute. Then the dispute became a strike. Weeks passed. Eventually all work at the yard was affected. Men were stood down. The unions remained intransigent. The yard shut down. We hung about. For months.

During the strike we arranged visits to local factories, beginning with the one which was repackaging our machinery spares in modern rustproofing, and then going on to general interest visits. The scenario may sound familiar to John Winton's readers, one of his books describes a factory visit to alleviate boredom during a strike.

No one seemed capable of breaking the deadlock, at least not until a tough little American representing the company buying the refrigerated ships visited the senior management. We heard that he had told them to get the workers back to work, somehow, or else! And somehow the dispute was resolved. Work resumed. Most of it was well understood routine but there were a few moments of drama and farce during the rest of the refit.

The Cammell Lairds fitters started work especially early one morning to align the propeller shafts which had just been reinstalled after repair. They had arranged with the Admiralty Overseers that we would all witness that the alignment was correct early in the afternoon and the couplings would then be bolted up. But, despite mutterings of 'It was alright this morning', the alignment was not correct. The yard's team set about restoring correct alignment and we agreed to check it the next afternoon. They completed their work that evening and rechecked it the next morning. It was wrong again. Then the penny dropped. For once, the sun was shining brightly, everyday. The hull of the submarine became banana shaped as the sun heated it, throwing the shaft alignment out. We agreed that the shafts would be aligned, and checked, at six in the morning. No problem.

Another problem was potentially more dramatic. After the main engines and motors had been replaced in the boat, a new plate had been welded into the 'soft patch' hole in the pressure hull. All the welding to be radiographed to verify its quality and where old and new welds met at the corners of the plate, half the film had to be of the old welds. The films showed that with trivial exceptions the new welding was good, but also that there were inclusions in all the old welding at the corners. Everyone agreed that Cammells would rework the defective bits. Which they did. But then, as before, half the radiography had to be on the new weld, half on the old. The new was ok, the old had inclusions. A final iteration gave the same result. We all agreed that Alcide's welding was no worse than it had ever been. It was the gamma ray photography which had improved since the boat was built in 1945. The Admiralty agreed we could leave well alone.

As the refit progressed personnel changed. A new First Lieutenant joined, a Chief Engine Room Artificer replaced the Chief Mechanician, and most important of all, in October 1956, our new Commanding Officer arrived. A Lancastrian known throughout the service as 'Ginge', his unfussy style of leadership reminded me of that which took Horace Law to the rank of Admiral and a Knighthood. Sadly the style did not do the same for Ginge, but no one could have been more welcome as the new CO.

The only time he ever appeared at a loss was when he wanted to meet the Admiralty civilian who had come to tune our new torpedo control system. We met in the pub at lunchtime and introduced the civilian who looked like a particularly respectable headmaster. After a pint or two, following our usual custom, the First Lietentant and I excused ourselves and went to lunch. We had to work in the afternoon, the boss didn't. At four o'clock Ginge came into the office, said 'Never leave me alone with that man again', sat down at a desk and slept for two hours. On waking he explained that after they had drunk eight pints of beer *without any food, they had walked back to the boat, where the man calmly carried on tuning where he left off, explaining as he did so that he preferred to finish his testing in the evenings when most of the workers had left and the boat was not crowded.*

We had been in dry-dock for eleven months, we could not progress until the boat was afloat again. Docking and undocking are never simple on that part of the Mersey. Tide levels are critical. Even so there would normally be a few days each month when Alcide could be undocked. The refit plan had taken that into account but the plan had been disrupted by the strike. This month there would only be one tide on one day on which there would be enough water over the sill of the dock.

That day began very early. After the Cammell Lairds team had checked that all the hull fittings were in place, we went through the boat and found there were still five holes. Time had been allowed for such discoveries and all was ready a couple of hours before high tide was due. The gates were opened and the rising tide began to fill the dock. The Captain, the Mersey Pilot, the Submarine Repair Manager, the First Lieutenant and I crowded the bridge. Most of the shores keeping the submarine upright had been removed. The moment of high tide came at noon and at four minutes past the boat shivered slightly and settled down again on the blocks. The wind was holding back the tide. The boat would be in dock for another month. Depressing and costly.

Depressingly slow or not, the work progressed and before Christmas additional ratings joined in readiness for the new commission. One of my new Engine Room Artificers tried to be a bit crafty. When he and I were walking back to the yard with my Chief ERA after we had all had a generous amount of Christmas cheer in the pub, he explained to me that he was an excellent and loyal member of the team but that he might occasionally disappear for twenty four hours or so. He implied that the Chief ERA would juggle the watchkeeping roster, he would square it with the other watchkeepers later, and no one would be any the wiser.

He was of course the naval version of an alcoholic, about thirtyeight years old, disrated from Chief ERA for drunkenness offences, who if allowed to do so would save his rum ration until he had enough for a blinder. I promised him two things. One, if he ever tried anything like that in my boat, I would charge him. Two, that I always remember when completely sober anything I say when I've had a few drinks. I learned later the Chief ERA was much relieved that his new boss wasn't going to fall for any line like that. It was a good Christmas.

Time had run out. Either I had to leave the boat early in the New Year or remain until the refit and subsequent trials were completed and boat worked up to a fully operational team. There was only one sensible decision. Although it was unusual and rather unfair to expect my successor to take over a boat which was still in pieces, at least he could oversee the last stages and be integrated into the new team right from the start. I had to go. Most disappointing. I only had seven months of operational running in my one and only boat. But I could now get on and work for the submarine service in my ordnance role.

Chapter 14

Damn the Torpedoes

The Royal Navy was in a bind. It had long believed, with considerable justification, that no one was in a better position to make correct operational decisions than the 'man on the spot'. It had implemented the doctrine by having the Commanders in Chief of Fleets afloat in their Flagships, supported by their staffs. It had been difficult to fit the C in C of the Home Fleet into HMS Indomitable in the early 1950s. By 1957 the last battleship had been scrapped and complex modern aircraft and their supporters filled the aircraft carriers. The only type of ship which could accommodate an Admiral and his staff was a depot ship. HMS Maidstone was chosen.

I was appointed Squadron Ordnance Engineer Officer to the Second Submarine Squadron, based on the Maidstone, after leaving Alcide in April 1957. Maidstone was well designed for her task with spacious accommodation for the officers, ample stores, and workshops for torpedoes, periscopes, sonar sets, machining, even a foundry. Given a reasonably sheltered mooring and willing hands, she could give her submarines good support.

There was no shortage of willing people. Even in the most disenchanted postwar times, the depot ships had managed to maintain a fine record of service to their squadrons. But these floating factories had to stay put to deliver the service. Maidstone had swung around her buoy in Portland Harbour for years, HMS Forth was secured in Msida Creek in Malta, HMS Adamant did not stray far from Rothesay and, later, Faslane. Now Maidstone was to conform to the Fleet pattern of three cruises a year, each of about three months.

At the personal level, the cruises would be more fun for officers and sailors alike, especially the visits to visit foreign *ports*. Depot ships always had the problem that life in harbour could be very boring for those not directly involved with the submarines. It was never easy to find a satisfactory compromise. Now, the roles were going to be reversed. Damn the torpedoes and stuff the submarines. We were to leave our boats boarded out with other squadrons or managing as best they could without us. Professionally, it was going to be a frustrating time for them and for the squadron staff.

'To hear is to obey'. Lise and I packed and moved south. We knew that some married quarters had been built in Portsmouth. Perhaps we would be spared trekking around the estate agents trying to find a place we could afford that would accept a family with a child as tenants. No such luck. We moved into a tiny house in Cosham for a few months, then moved again when a quarter became available. The married quarter was our tenth home since our marriage less than five years earlier.

We expected less moves in the years ahead but we had seen naval wives who chose to settle in one place grow apart from their husbands and get divorced. We believed in moving as often as necessary to maximise our time together. Renting furnished accommodation is always an expensive way to live, and even with the advantage of Submarine Pay, we could not save the money for a deposit on a house of our own. All the naval house owners we knew had access to family money. So we rented and moved often, waiting for better days.

Those better days were obviously coming, not just for service people but for the whole country. 1957 was the year Prime Minister Macmillan pointed out, with justification, that '..... most of our people have never had it so good'. The list of material goods which we, like many families, lacked when we married in 1952 included a car, washing machine, refrigerator, telephone, toaster, television, record player and lawn-mower. Since then we had bought and sold a few old cars and acquired a toaster in Scotland. Things were slowly improving and it was now time to think about buying the next item.

Second hand cars had become cheaper as production of new cars slowly increased and it was a good time to buy. Out we went. We looked at a few cars, then Lise pointed out that as she could not drive, our car would be unused for three quarters of the year. She would prefer something which would be of use every day while I was away. She was right of course. Having gone out to buy a car, we bought our first television set, a stylish piece of modern furniture with a record player at one end, a radio and four speakers at the other, and a television discretely hidden behind a sliding door in the middle. We bought a 'long playing' record to go with it, 'Carmen Jones', still giving pleasure forty years later even though it is only 'mono'. Stereo had not yet arrived at our end of the market.

The cruises which followed were most enjoyable provided we didn't get too frustrated at not doing our proper job. Foremost among many memories are the Queen's Review of the Home Fleet at Invergordon, the visit to the West Indies to celebrate the inauguration of the Confederation of the British West Indies, and visiting Helsinki to promote British trade with Finland.

One bit of old naval thinking is enshrined in a verse of 'The Laws of the Navy':

>   Dost thou deem that thy ship needs a-gilding,
>   And Their Lordships forebear to supply,
>   Dip thy hand in thy pocket and gild her,
>   There be those who have risen thereby.'

I loathe the implications of the verse, but would be the first to acknowledge that ceremonial occasions must be superbly stage managed. So when it was announced that the Queen would review the Home Fleet, I wanted to ensure that my Division would be conspicuously smart when they were inspected. It was not too difficult to arrange. They were all Chief Petty Officer or Petty Officer artificers and wore 'fore and aft' rig with jackets and trousers, shirts and ties. The focal point of the uniform was the white collar and black tie.

In one of those distinctions so common in British life, officers customarily wore stiff collars, ratings semi-stiff. I had several dozen stiff collars because I used to send them away for laundering. All I had to do was persuade my team to wear stiff collars for Royal Divisions. They all regarded stiff collars as uncomfortable but agreed that the general effect would be worthwhile. We were rewarded with the comment by the Commander as he followed the Royal party, 'A fine body of men!' He was right. They looked splendid. The modest price of laundering the gilding was well worth it.

Divisions was followed by a march past in single file, the only way possible onboard ship, but rare. I never saw it again in thirty one years. Ceremonial over, the order was given to 'Splice the main brace', for which the lads were duly thankful, and the Queen and Prince Phillip came to the Wardroom for a pre-lunch drink. On such occasions preplanning is necessary. The Mess President, who will necessarily be preoccupied with HM, asks some of the senior officers to assist him by looking after other members of the royal party. Other officers are warned that the key players will catch their eye when they are to come forward to be introduced, in my case to Prince Phillip. I can't remember the subject of our brief chat but that doesn't matter. My enduring happy memory of that lunchtime is of how natural it all was. There was the Queen, talking to some of her officers over a glass of champagne. We were her navy, we took no oaths to affirm our loyalty, we served at her pleasure. What could be simpler?

One of the best things about naval life is its variety. I've no idea whether the stiff collars gimmick put the idea into the Commander's head but I soon found myself asked to manage the ship's laundry. It was a reasonable request. With the submarines often far away, I was underemployed and the decrepit laundry machinery certainly needed an engineer's touch. One day helping to entertain royalty, another running a laundry. We operated on a quasi-commercial basis. The laundry crew of a Petty Officer and eight sailors were volunteers and I was allowed to pay them a bonus. Our prices had to cover the bonuses and all the detergents, starches and packing materials we used. We washed everything from dirty boiler suits to the Admiral's collars. The navy's laundry training was inadequate for anyone charged with the upkeep of the Admiral's smalls because unhappiness with his laundry could affect the health of my career more than anything I did with torpedoes. So I arranged a visit to Liners' Laundry Limited in Southampton.

As usual, it was fascinating to glimpse someone else's world. The firm had contracts to supply linen to Cunard and other liners whenever they docked in Southampton. The two working directors had evolved staff relations which made this possible, even if they wanted a team to work on Christmas Day. In one morning I found the answers to all my questions. I lunched with the directors after which I started making polite, 'Many thanks, most kind, must get out of your hair' noises. 'Have a whisky', was their response. Their explanation, 'We usually like to keep the afternoons for being sociable'. They had it made. They had up to date equipment, delivered the goods to the shipping lines, treated their staff well, and enjoyed themselves. There was a lot to be said for this laundry business.

Despite the age of the machinery, with care we could produce a proper finish on everything except stiff evening shirts. Having got the basics right, we branched out into good presentation with cardboard stiffeners to keep shirts neat inside their 'HMS Maidstone' bags. When the machines let us down, I employed some of the artificer apprentices we had onboard to hand finish shirts and collars in their off duty time, apprentices are always grateful for a bit of extra cash. I enjoyed running the laundry even though it brought problems at times. On the way to the West Indies for instance, the crew complained of the heat. I *stripped off and operated a steam press with a thermometer taped to my chest. It registered 140 degrees Fahrenheit. They had a case. Fortunately, we were able to improve the ventilation sufficiently. A bit of extra money and salt tablets, which were the 'in thing' at that time, did the rest.*

It was a pity about the stiff fronted evening shirts. No matter how hard we tried our machine would just not produce the required result. Having given up the machine, I experimented with hand finishing and am probably the only RN officer ever to go to an Ambassador's dinner party wearing a stiff shirt he ironed himself. It was fine but had taken me about two hours to achieve. Not a commercial proposition! Even at apprentices' pocket money rates.

Our cruise to the Caribbean was mainly to celebrate the inauguration of Confederation of the British West Indies. Sadly, it fell apart within a few years. The people in the bigger, better off entities did not enjoy contributing any of their modest wealth to smaller, poorer ones and there were the usual squabbles about the establishment of the capital. In which city, on which island? But that was in the future when we arrived in Kingston, Jamaica. Having a Commander in Chief aboard generally ensures a warm welcome. Kingston was no exception.

The first night set the scene for the visit. There was a reception at Government House, memorable for two incidents in particular. A photograph of two of us chatting to a couple of young women was published the next day. I was actually saying to one of them, 'Delighted to meet you. Your great uncle was a very good friend to me'. She was the only pretty eighteen year old to whom I could truthfully say that, Sarah Foot, daughter of the previous governor, who had been left behind for safety when her father and mother moved to troubled Cyprus. Fellow naval officers are hard to convince on occasions like that.

As always, Government House receptions were formal affairs. Those who were dining there after the reception wore tropical mess undress, complete with stiff white shirt and wing collar in the best 'dinner jacket in the jungle' tradition. Nothing could have been less suitable for tropical nights prior to the installation of air conditioning. It gave everyone a chance to keep a very British stiff upper lip and to pretend that it wasn't really hot. The wilting shirts and collars told a different story. The rest of us wore the tropical undress uniform known as 'ice cream suits', often disliked, but quite cool if worn without anything under the jacket.

Formality has its uses. The introductions of those days emphasised surnames and one couple reacted to mine. 'You must meet our Feasey', they said and introduced a retired army officer of some seventy summers who asked me what I knew of the family history. I told him I had heard a vague story that we were peasants who left Ireland seeking food and work in England during the potato famine. We split up into my north country group and an East Anglian group of which, I assumed, he must be a member. 'Oh I know all that', was his response, 'Don't you know how we got to Ireland in the first place? Years before that we were scullions in the English kings household, were caught thieving, and had to flee the country to avoid being hung'. I was rather sad when, years later, Donald Ward Feesey's research proved that both bits of the story were untrue.

Why sad? Not only was my real ancestry less dramatic, but I had amused myself telling Americans of my scullion ancestors. The story was good for a laugh in most British circles but Americans did not laugh. There was usually an embarrassed, 'That really is most . . . er . . . interesting'. I soon realised that I had never met an American who was descended from anything less than a Pilgrim father, an English peer or a Scottish laird. Even when author Haley went back six generations in his 'Roots', the only one he mentioned was Kunta Kinte, the great chief. I tested the response over and over again. No laughter. I'm glad to say that Aussies laugh .

The one submarine which had accompanied the fleet to the West Indies, HMS Turpin could not enjoy it to the full. Her CO and engineer officer were preoccupied with problems. Cracks had developed in Turpin's engine frames and she could not return safely across the Atlantic under her own power. And Commanders in Chief cannot wait for a single submarine's problems to be sorted out. Maidstone sailed leaving Turpin to wait for a tug to tow her home. If Turpin had been visiting Jamaica alone when the problem occurred, she would have had to wait for the tug. Nevertheless, leaving her there seemed to symbolise the unhappy situation the depot ship was in. I hope Turpin's crew found the six weeks wait a pleasant compensation.

The cruises often demonstrated the differences between showing the flag and the keeping submarines prepared for war. After lotus eating in tropical Jamaica we visited Halifax, Nova Scotia, still gripped by the cold of late winter, dirty snow piled along the streets. We were joined by another of our submarines and had an opportunity to replace torpedoes due for maintenance with a new batch. It was my turn to supervise the exchange, and if anything ever typified the dull reality of the support role it was standing on the depot ship's well deck for about four hours in the freezing drizzle of late Canadian winter. Anyone who has spent time in Halifax will know the feeling. I had never felt so cold.

Our visit to Helsinki was a different and quite glamourous occasion, a major promotion of British exports on the 'trade follows the flag' principle. The RAF provided the Red Arrows aerobatics squadron, the Army contributed the pipes and drums of the Argyle and Sutherland Highlanders, soon dubbed Argyle and Submarine Highlanders after taking up their accommodation in Maidstone, and a light fleet aircraft carrier was the other major naval unit.

The visit was later reported to have been very successful. As experienced at the time by someone low on the totem pole, it was certainly enjoyable. I was the token Lieutenant at a dinner given by the Commander in Chief of the Finnish Navy, and witnessed a rare sight. After the introductory drinks we sat down but nothing happened. There was clearly trouble in the kitchen. Our Admiral, Sir Jasper, perhaps the last of his kind, was one of the old school of impressive but idiosyncratic characters. After a few minutes he helped himself to some of the flowers, poured some water into his wineglass and began to eat and drink. By some magic of Sir Jasper's, his hosts appeared charmed and amused by the action. By some other magic, food and wine appeared very quickly! When the two Commanders in Chief departed after dinner, the remaining hosts insisted the rest of us sat down again and had another drink. The process was repeated when the Chiefs of Staff departed, then the Captains, then the Commanders. In the early hours a residue of Lieutenant Commanders and I were given a final round of after dinner drinks by our overwhelmingly kindly hosts who then took us to a club where we joined the Commanders in Chief, the Chiefs of Staff, etc. etc.

We raced the locals in their sailing boats. They introduced us to the enduring pleasure of the sauna. Miss Great Britain strutted her stuff, the RAF performed their aerobatics. We dressed up as pirates and gave parties for local children. The Marines and the Highlanders performed their martial music. The finale was a reception in the aircraft carrier. The aircraft were ranged on the flight deck and the hanger transformed to an English village. The large recess below the aircraft lift was flooded and became the village pond complete with a rotating mill wheel. Only live ducks were missing. At the end of the party the Royal Marine band stopped performing as a orchestra, changed into their splendid marching order, and reappeared on the aircraft lift as it was lowered halfway down to the hanger. Nature provided the final touch. Beyond the band, as we looked up through the lift opening there was the most beautiful balmy twilight. By the time the band had performed the evening hymn, *musical sunset and begun the national anthems, tears were plopping gently into the gin and tonic glasses. Showing the flag at its best!*

Romance blossoms during such visits. I was privileged to win the affections of the daughter of one of the British diplomatic families who entertained us so warmheartedly. Marion appeared indifferent to the difference between our ages. She was about eighteen years younger than my twenty eight and I was completely charmed by her. Never less so than when summoned from my breakfast on the day of departure, 'You are wanted at the gangway, Sir'. About two hundred people had come to see the ships depart, standing around a roped off area for the Ambassador and other VIPs. There in the middle of that area was my young friend, with flowers and a hug and a kiss for me. Lovely, though it was a rather public leave taking which raised a cheer from those watching.

The Admiralty management of its affairs was sometimes amateurish. One morning while Maidstone was in Portsmouth, we were told to assess the suitability of HMS Tyne, a destroyer depot ship, as the CinCs flagship and a submarine 'support ship', an expression which recognised that a ship designed specifically for supporting destroyers could not be a perfect 'depot ship' for submarines. I wasn't worried about definitions of support, what really hurt was that we had only about thirty minutes to assess Tyne's suitability before we had to commit ourselves to using her. That was too short a time by any standards. Fortunately, there didn't seem to be any major problems and the Admiralty made plans to update Maidstone to support the future nuclear submarines. We were to transfer to Tyne.

Dear old Maidstone had been in commission continuously since about 1938. One of the biggest practical problems was to account for all the stores and fittings involved in nearly twenty years of support operations. The navy's Supply Officers believed that if something was there twenty years ago it should be there now. The engineers who had been solving problems day by day for those twenty years had cared more about keeping submarines operational than about accounting. My small department had few problems so I agreed to join the Engineer Officers' watch keeping roster during the passage back across the Atlantic taking the place of the workshops officer to allow him more time to sort out his stores.

When I started watchkeeping again the Engineering Mechanics, as the Stokers were now called, seemed a sloppy lot. Perhaps they were. Or perhaps the Whale Island gunnery school had had too much effect on my behaviour. Perhaps I had forgotten some of the basics of tolerant behaviour in steamy machinery spaces. A cartoon soon appeared on the Engineers' Office notice board. I was depicted striding into a machinery space, my overalls tucked into the patent leather gaiters which are a tribal symbol of Gunnery Officers and Ordnance Engineers, and demanding a test sample of the distiled water, 'At the double'. It was a reminder not to become autocratic, if for no other reason than the ease with which 'the lads' can bring officers back to earth. I relaxed a bit the next time I did my rounds and we all enjoyed the homeward passage.

The home front was in pretty good order after we moved into a married quarter in Moortown Avenue. It was a new and very pleasant experience to have a well appointed, semi-detached, three bedroomed house to ourselves at an affordable rent. We always enjoyed our neighbours and soon became close friends of the Aussies Stewart and Pattie. We learned more about Australia. Pattie told us that only two kinds of cheese, 'mild' and 'mature', were sold where she lived in Frankston, close to Melbourne. Pattie had quite a bit to learn too. Lise took her to a shop in Southsea which never had less than ninety nine cheeses in stock. Despite the limited choice of cheeses, the more we learned about Australia, the more we liked it.

Cheese also featured in another example of the mutual education process. Lise looked after Stewart and Pattie's two sons while they toured Europe with another Aussie couple. They saved money by camping but camp sites with showers were rare in those days so hotels had to be afforded quite often. After one night in a hotel, the car was still filled with an unusual odour. When accusations of failing to shower had been rebutted, the trail led to a Camembert which they had bought as a present for us. 'They'll never eat that now', said the friends. 'They will', said the neighbours. They resolved the argument the usual Aussie way, betting on it. Our neighbours won. We loved the extra ripe Camembert.

Stewart and Pattie were rather competitive and one day they were arguing about who was the better driver. Quite unfairly, they appealed to their five year old son to give his opinion. After a few moments he delivered his verdict, 'Daddy is'. 'Why', asked the furious Pattie. 'Well, you only drive our car', said Ross, 'Daddy drives ours and tells everyone else how to drive theirs'. Out of the mouths of babes and all that. Stewart and Pattie are the only Aussie neighbours we have been unable to locate since becoming Aussies ourselves. Are you out there?

There were other developments. We acquired an extra family member, Raymond's son Roger. He had lived at the Holbrook Naval School since the death of his mother a few years earlier, but he turned sixteen in 1958 and had to leave. His father was overseas at the time so Lise agreed to provide a home for Roger. He was a pleasant young man and only caused me a problem when I thought that a mature chap of twenty eight should be better at cross country running that a sixteen year old. It took only one training session together to discover otherwise. A mile from home, I suggested that after running together thus far, we should now chose our own speed. He agreed amiably, shot off into the distance, and that was the last I saw of him until I reached home. Even kind young people can, unknowingly, be demoralising.

Lise too experienced Roger's amiable nature at its devastating worst. While Lise was out a stranger called and, asked, 'Is your mother in?' 'I hope you told them I'm too young to be your mother', said Lise when told of the incident. 'I didn't like to', was Roger's gentle response. Few parents can be as well prepared for the teenage years of their own children as those who have looked after a sixteen year old when they were twenty eight. Roger was good experience for us, though extra work for Lise, not always appreciated as much as it should have been by his father.

The cruises ticked by. The only major technical event during this period was the Squadron's acquisition of the navy's first homing torpedo, the Mark 20. For the first time our submarines would be properly equipped to fight other submarines. Only one submerged submarine has ever been sunk by another submerged submarine and that was only possible because both the German quarry and the British attacker were at shallow depths. There was no torpedo which could seek a deep prey. Now that was changing. The introduction was a low key affair. We received some torpedoes and the handbooks and taught ourselves to prepare the warshot and practice versions. There were no training courses to ensure that this new era started well. The Chief Artificer and I worked out how to service the weapons and taught the others. Fortunately it was not a very complicated torpedo.

A visit to Portsmouth by the USS Northampton created great interest. She was specifically designed as a headquarters ship, well equipped with the communications and other facilities to enable an Admiral to command his fleet in the traditional 'on the spot' mode. A Lieutenant from one of the shore establishments and I were appointed Liaison Officers for the visit. It was a fascinating time for we never knew whether the next invitation to have a cup of coffee would be the precursor to 'Where do I take this fabulous girl for the weekend?' or 'Where can I buy a Rolls Royce?'

It was not long before the Minister of Defence, Mr Duncan Sandys, and the First Sea Lord, Lord Louis Mountbatten, visited the ship to see for themselves how it operated. It was the only time I ever met Lord Louis and I wish I had something more to remember than his final brusque order to, 'Tell the Minister it's time to go'. The Minister had limped gamely around the ship all day and deserved the more diplomatic words I used to relay the message. The rest is history. The RN could not afford such a specialised ship and our Commander in Chief moved to the bunkers of Northwood in due course.

There were cocktail parties for the officers every night. Bill and I accompanied by our wives attended most of them, usually taking half a dozen American officers home for dinner afterwards. Although Lise and I were relatively well off now, we couldn't pay anyone to cook the dinners while Lise was at the parties. She solved that problem very simply by choosing a dish which could be simmering away until our return. The US officers loved her food, especially the thin slices of beautifully tender, fine grained meat in her delicious gravy. Only one asked what it was and when told was honest enough to say 'I wish you hadn't told me'. It was ox heart. We still love it.

An enterprising young Ensign had been given permission to take a car back to the States on the ship. I arranged for him to visit a Rolls Royce dealer in London and he bought a Phantom III circa 1935 for a few hundred pounds. When it was delivered to the jetty there was great interest in it. One debate was how many cylinders it would have, given that its engine capacity was 8,888cc. Some thought it would be a Vee-8, others a Vee-12. In fact it was a six cylinder engine, with a memorable bore of four and a half inches and a stroke of six and a half.

The new owner was unwilling to drive such a novel car on the wrong side of the road so I had my first and only drive in a Rolls, sitting upright on the chauffeur's uncomfortable seat. I had owned cars which predated the standardisation of controls, one even had the accelerator between the clutch and brake pedals, so having the gear and handbrake levers on my right was no problem. The other controls were in the usual places, mixture strength and ignition timing levers, for instance, being in the centre of the steering wheel. And there was one appealing oddity. I could imagine the chauffeur asking a technically interested master through the speaking tube 'Shall we have the magneto or the sparking coil or both today, Sir?'. I'm glad the American took it for granted that I could drive a Rolls.

The Captain and Officers of the Northampton planned a big farewell cocktail party at the Nuffield Officers' Club on the last night of their visit and a few days before the end the Captain sent for me. He was struggling with the invitation cards. Why he was writing them himself I never understood but I was there to help, not wonder. His problem was that our CinC had a peer on his staff, The Viscount Kelburn, and the Captain was trying not only to address the invitation correctly but to understand why one form was correct and another not.

He began by asking why Kelburn was sometimes referred to as Viscount and sometimes as Lord. I explained the specific ranks of the peerage and the use of the generic 'Lord'. Then we considered whether it was more important to be a peer or a captain in the navy. The Captain thought the address ought to be 'Viscount the Captain Kelburn' because, 'With all due respect, I should have thought it more important that he is a peer than a captain in the navy, so that should come first'. Ad libbing was called for. I argued that the rank as a peer and the family name were inseparable, therefore the naval rank had to come first. 'I think I understand now' said the Captain and with a flourish wrote 'Captain The Viscount Kelburn and Mrs Kelburn'. I put on *my most terribly British accent, 'Well actually, Sir, if you want to be completely correct, it isn't Mrs Kelburn'.*

There are many other memories of Maistone's cruises. They are mostly of social and ceremonial occasions such as the CinC's farewell dinner at sea one Saturday night with the Wardroom piano lashed tightly in a corner and the Royal Marine pianist lashed lightly to the piano, and the piping in of the port by the Pipe Major of the Argyle and Submarine Highlanders. Others are of visits to Stockholm and Copenhagen, where my tobacco factory manager host said 'Keep the box' when I appreciated the after dinner cigar he gave me from a box of fifty, and of teaching Lise the Limbo using the 'European cheat' of holding a partner's hand below the stick.

They were good times. But there was a tremendous waste of technical resources which should have been devoted to the upkeep of the submarine fleet. However, though I did not know it then, that was my last such experience. Not only did a lot of useful engineering work lie ahead, but when I would rejoin Maidstone four years later the climate in which we operated would have changed forever. I had seen my last of scrubbed teak and polished brightwork as the symbols of a comfortable naval life 'showing the flag' at the cost of neglecting preparedness for war.

Chapter 15

Some Real Work

Lise and I had been lucky again. My appointment to the Sea Trials Department of the Torpedo and Anti-submarine School at HMS Vernon did not involve packing. We could stay in our married quarter at Moortown Avenue. But that was as far as our luck went. During the first six years of our marriage our separations totalled two and a half years. That wasn't too bad by the standards of the day but we looked forward to my shore job in Vernon. Lise thought it was great when I was home soon after four o'clock on the first day, but was less impressed when told I was leaving in an hour for two weeks of trials in Scotland. It was characteristic of the management practices of the day that although my boss was one of the best, he never thought to write and forewarn us that I would be going away so soon. Absolute dedication was taken absolutely for granted.

The journeys to Arrochar at the head of Loch Long were tedious. We left Portsmouth at about five thirty in the evening to catch the seven thirty from Kings Cross which travelled up to Edinburgh, then crossed to Glascow and set out for the highlands, dropping us at about six thirty in the morning before completing the journey to Mallaig by ten thirty. It was the longest journey by a single train in the UK and it felt like it. Those were still the days of that curious British system of First Class and Third Class travel. A Second Class complete with comfortable two berth sleeping compartments had not yet replaced the ancient 'Third'. Our choice, Admiralty regulations said, was between sleeping as best we could in a First Class seat or dossing in what were known as the four berth 'cattle trucks'. We chose the seats, but it was a poor preparation for a fourteen hour day in Scotland after a days work in the south.

After the relaxed routines of Maidstone and Tyne there was no doubt that there was now real work ahead. Submarines fired torpedoes by admitting a charge of compressed air into the torpedo tube, then, when the torpedo was on its way, opening a valve to let the sea push the air back into the submarine to prevent it betraying the submarine's position. The air was followed by sufficient sea water to compensate for the negative buoyancy of the torpedo so that the submarine's trim was not disturbed. The amount of air depended on the submarine's depth. In older submarines, the pressure of air in the reservoir was controlled manually which was satisfactory when torpedoes could only be fired at shallow depths. Now an automatic system was required to allow deep running, anti-submarine torpedoes to be discharged at greater depths without changing the pressure in the firing reservoirs, because that made noise which might betray the submarine's position.

The new system was called the Dual Pressure Firing Gear. It was being installed in the old 'A' and 'T' class submarines when they were modernised and in the Porpoise Class submarines being built at Vickers, Cammell Lairds, and Scotts. After installation, limited tests could be done in the dockyard with the submarine on the surface by firing with the tubes full of water. The Sea Trials job which Robert, the first submarine O/E of the new school, was turning over to me, was to lead a team of ordnance artificers and complete the tuning of the system by fitting recording instruments and firing practice torpedoes over the designed depth range.

Torpedo trials are expensive and little else can be done during them so the work was intensive. The RN Torpedo Range at Arrochar in upper Loch Long was the base. Shallower firings were done on the range, deeper ones in the lower loch or Inchmarnock Water. On the first day 'watershots' were fired again to check that the calibration done in the dockyard had not altered. Pressures were recorded by reliable old Dobbie McInnes *instruments, designed for recording steam or Diesel engine cylinder pressures but modified to take the higher pressures of the compressed air. Timing was established by the vibrations of a tuning fork, the torpedo's movement by tying a wire to its tail and bringing the wire through a gland in the rear door of the torpedo tube to rotate a drum when the torpedo was fired. They don't make instruments like that anymore! Cleaning, calibrating and fitting to the tubes was labour intensive and firing up to twelve torpedoes a day kept everyone busy.*

We all lodged in the range workers' cottages a hundred yards from the submarine at the end of the pier. Some local pecking order determined who would take in the artificers and who would look after the officers but we all lived well. The wives of the range workers were kindly people and good cooks though they did have some peculiarities. A knock on the door of the cottage in the quiet of an evening sometimes indicated that salmon or venison was on offer at a shilling and sixpence a pound, about a tenth of the shops' price. Our landlady would buy venison but never salmon. Attempts to persuade her to do so brought a firm response in her rich, melodious accent, 'Fish is no food for a man. Thirty years I've been married and I've never given my man fish yet and I'm not going to start giving you young gentlemen fish now'. So no salmon, but it was nice to be thought a young gentleman.

I settled into the routine of the trials. The train north, hectic working days rounded off after our return to the jetty by an after dinner drink in the submarine's wardroom as we planned the next days program. I learned to enjoy whisky because it wasn't convenient to have more than one bottle circulating in the cramped conditions. There were visits to the Arrochar pub at the weekend to play darts with the crew of the boat and our trials team. We could drink there even on Sundays because the pub was a Sabbath day's journey from the range. Under Scottish law, we were bona fide travellers, eligible for refreshment. Hard work, enjoyable relaxation.

There were developments at home. Raymond had returned from overseas and Lise agreed to let him to move in with us, joining Roger. It was supposed to be a temporary move. Our family was growing rather too quickly but I was still rather taken with the idea of being part of a large family. That was no novelty for Lise, one of five children. However, the arrangement brought one unexpected advantage. Raymond, ever somewhat feckless, bought a new car then found he couldn't pay for it. We scraped the bottom of the barrel and took it off his hands. It turned out to be a good investment.

Raymond never did anything by halves and the car was a Standard Pennant, the top of the company's one litre range. Although the engine's valves had to be reground every 20,000 miles, common practice on many cars of those days, it served us for just under 100,000 miles. It was a pleasure to drive except when the brakes failed just after we had descended the hills into Carlisle. Unlike the dramatic scenes of the films, the car responded well to being slammed down into second gear and the ignition being switched off, which fortunately, unlike present day cars, did not lock the steering. An engine acting as an air compressor makes a good extra brake.

The Pennant had an overdrive system operated by a switch on the steering column which gave the car seven forward gears, all useful. The most popular one litre car had been, for many years, the Morris Minor. Their owners loved them even though they had a top speed around 55 mph, and they regarded Standards as second rate until a Pennant slipped into second overdrive after leaving the lights and left them far behind. There was another complication. Accustomed to Morris Minors doing about 55 mph, some motorists assumed that all small cars travelled equally slowly and crossed in front of Pennants which could cruise all day at 70 mph in top overdrive.

There was drama when we sold it to a fellow submariner years later. David telephoned me the day after taking delivery to say the car wouldn't start. and we arranged to examine it at lunchtime. It started perfectly for me, then refused to start for David. I demonstrated again: switch on, a bit of manual choke, a touch on the accelerator pedal, pull the starter knob and away she goes. Not for David. Ten starts for me, none for David. 'Go away', he said, 'I accept that you've sold me a working car'. I'm glad to say he soon learned the touch which started it every time.

Change was in the wind six months after I joined Vernon. Development of the Royal Navy's first nuclear propelled submarine, HMS Dreadnought, was beginning. It was to have radically different sonar and torpedo equipment which would be developed at the Admiralty Underwater Weapons Establishment created at Portland by integrating establishments hitherto dispersed at Havant, Bournemouth and Greenock with the Underwater Detection Establishment which was already at Portland.

Those R and D establishments were staffed by civilian officers of the Royal Naval Scientific Service, very loyal to the navy but often having limited experience of conditions at sea. Sometimes their brilliant concepts proved impossible to maintain at sea. The Stabilised Tachymetric Anti-aircraft Gun was the classic case, a sad outcome because a brilliant designer had given years of his life to the project. The Admiralty's answer was to appoint naval officers, usually ordnance engineers, to the design teams to 'breathe sea air over the projects'. They were to be known as 'Application Officers'. One was required by the team formed to design Dreadnought's torpedo loading equipment, torpedo tubes and firing gear, and to co-ordinate the layout of her 'front end.

At the same time the Dual Pressure Firing Gear was in trouble. Results were erratic and the design team were trying to *solve the problem at the same time as beginning the Dreadnought work. It was another reason to reinforce the team with an Application Officer. They seconded me to the Admiralty Underwater Launching Establishment in Bournemouth to get to know the team before we all moved to Portland in June 1959. More lodging during the weeks in Bournemouth, more looking for somewhere to live in Weymouth.*

It was worth the upheaval. I was now exposed to an entirely different environment. The scientists did not subscribe to the navy's 'Be loyal to your superiors regardless of their merits' code of conduct. They followed the academic tradition and could be scathing about their superiors, 'Old so and so hasn't had an original thought in the last ten years'. The Navy's teaching was clearly too narrow. There were other ways of doing things. I did not necessarily want to adopt those other ways but I did want to consider them. I had my chance and loved it. Many who contributed then to broadening my experience remain close friends.

When Lise moved to Weymouth we rented a place near the married quarters so that Michael, already changing schools for the first time at the age of six, would not have to change again when a quarter become available. We could only find a tiny one bedroomed flat in Lanehouse Rocks Road. It had to do. We thought that because it was so cramped, it would be the worst place we would ever rent. Little did we know.

My place at Vernon Sea Trials had been taken by Tom, who became another lifelong friend, and we shared one of the greatest engineering adventures of our careers. Despite the efforts of the design team, the Dual Pressure Firing Gear was still failing its trials and they were now preoccupied with building a full scale wooden mock-up of the front end of Dreadnought and installing a massive shore testing facility for her torpedo firing gear. They were so busy our masters took the unusual step of allocating a submarine for six weeks of trials and simply told Tom and I to do whatever we could to get the system working properly. Six weeks was generous, a typical trial was about ten days. We settled down at Arrochar to work as hard as we had ever done in our lives. Returning from the submarine to lodgings at about three in the morning would disturb our hosts so Tom and I had beds in our office in the range buildings.

The heart of the firing gear was its Impulse Cut-off Valve. The firing air bottle was always charged to the same high pressure and the valve had the task of deciding when enough air had been allowed into the tube to discharge the torpedo against the sea pressure at any given depth. In other words it had to solve the simple equation of a straight line $y = mx+c$ where 'y' represented the air required to fire the torpedo, 'mx' represented the sea water pressure, and 'c' represented the minimum air required to fire a torpedo on the surface. It didn't have many working parts. It was not obvious why the valve would not work consistently.

One problem was that the pressure at which the valve opened was too high to be recorded by the usual instruments. Instead, the pressure remaining after the firing was measured and subtraction was assumed to reveal the pressure at which the valve opened. We acquired a modified recorder and measured the real opening pressure. It revealed that 'c' was not constant. The valve had a nylon seat and its softness caused it to act like a second spring, modifying the effect of the main spring more as depth increased. We minimised this fault by using whitemetal valve seats instead of nylon and slowly began to get the system operating correctly.

We worked from eight AM until about three in the morning and slept in the office until seven. After a while two things happened. I began to have a recurring dream. My bedclothes were lighter than air and floated off me. I was supplied with those beautiful brass weights used on physical balances and spent the night trying to calculate how many weights would be required to keep the bedclothes down and where I should place them. I didn't feel very refreshed in the morning.

The other symptom of stress was more serious. After some weeks of maximum effort I called a halt at three AM. We resumed at eight and the first job was to strip one of the valves so I could examine its seat. The artificer and I were squashed up the side of the torpedo tube while he unscrewed the brass sleeve to get access to the interior parts. As he unscrewed the last turn, the sleeve, which probably weighed about five pounds, flew past his ear and mine, followed by all those interior parts. We had stripped the valve with some cubic feet of air at 1,500 pounds per square inch still in the system. I had not checked that the submarine's duty rating had drained the air off the system before going to his bunk. Like us, he had been 'bombed out'. Fortunately, no one was hurt. The Commanding Officer, the ultimate arbiter of the safety of any trial in his boat, told us that like it or not, we had to stop work at noon that day. We didn't argue. And since that dream and the fatigue-related incident I have always felt qualified to lay down the law on a 'Been there, done that' basis when my staff have wanted to work dangerously long hours.

Torpedo firing gears have an odd duty cycle. They may not do anything for several weeks but must be ready at any moment to generate about 1,200 HP for a few milliseconds, then stop and get ready for the next shot. And to cut a long story short, that was our undoing. We got the system working and it passed its trials which none had done before. We were the blue eyed boys. There were murmurs of possible recognition in the New Year. But there was one simple question to be answered. After he congratulated me, the Director General, Weapons, the greatly respected Rear Admiral Mike LeFanu asked, 'How long will the system stay in tune?' Thank goodness I gave the simplest possible answer, 'I don't know, Sir'. I knew the system stayed in tune if it was firing torpedoes each day but a few months of experience *after the trials showed that when it was not used regularly, the friction levels in the valve changed and the discharge velocities went out of tolerance. The system's problems were never solved by minor modifications. Major surgery proved necessary.*

Dreadnought's firing gear was quite another matter. The reactor and main machinery were being bought from the Americans, not so the torpedo equipment. In theory the team could take a 'clean sheet of paper' approach to the design. In practice, in addition to meeting the operational requirement for 'all depths' discharge, the tubes and firing gear had to be integrated with the domed front end of the pressure hull designed by the Royal Corps of Naval Constructors and with the massive hydrophone array designed by our sonar colleagues. It was a great challenge for the whole team.

The principle of the new design was clear. To make the system independent of the depth of the submarine, sea water would be used to discharge the torpedo. The pressure on its nose and tail would be balanced, and energy would only required to accelerate the the weapon and the accompanying water. It was called water ram discharge. High pressure air moved a piston along a cylinder inside the submarine. The piston rod passed through a gland in the pressure hull and a piston in a much larger cylinder squeezed sea water into the tube behind the torpedo. Very simple in principle. In practice the equipment was necessarily cumbersome because it had to accelerate a total mass equivalent to nearly three torpedoes. It was impossible to provide a firing ram for each tube and in practice two rams were needed to meet the requirement to fire salvos of torpedoes in quick succession. So much for principle, the rest was in the detail.

A wooden mock-up of the whole torpedo compartment and external structure was built and Admiral Jackie Fisher's wisdom from the turn of the century had not been forgotten. The sign in the lab which housed the mock-up reminded us of his belief that, 'The best scale for any experiment is twelve inches to the foot', wisdom which has stood the test of time. The mock-up enabled the best positions of all the systems and equipment to be identified, inside and outside the pressure hull. Almost all those positions were compromises but that's engineering!

It was not just a matter of finding the right positions for things. We ensured that every maintenance operation could be performed with space to swing the spanners, space to remove assemblies for repair. Some of the problems occurred simply because the draughtsmen had little experience of practical submarine maintenance, like one who asserted that an artificer would carry a gearbox weighing perhaps 50 pounds up to the depot ship workshops before stripping it to find a fault. I persuaded him to redesign the box so that its entrails could all be withdrawn from one end, enabling diagnosis to be done in situ. He invented the saying, 'Make it easy for Feasey'. I've never had any problem with that idea and I never enjoyed working with anyone more than with that team.

The amalgamation of the four research and development establishments was to encourage co-operation and also cross pollination. There was a real danger of isolated design teams becoming too set in their ways. For instance, a glance at the design of one valve in Dreadnought's torpedo firing gear showed that it had evolved from a design of the nineteen thirties, except that it now weighed about four hundred pounds instead of the original hundred. Weight saving is important in submarine design and our new division head decided to redesign the valve. One day he asked my opinion of a design sketched on a sheet of foolscap, paper little bigger than today's A4. I examined it quickly. The essential ingredients were there, a 3.5 inch valve with a profiled skirt, an air motor to open the valve, and a dashpot to limit the rate of opening. I had only one question, 'What's the scale?' The boss looked very, very pained and said, 'Full size'. Previously, he had worked in guided missiles. His design was probably fine for a missile with a working life of a few minutes and no humans onboard, but completely unsafe for a submarine equipment with a life of twenty or more years. Cross pollination did not always work as expected.

The detail work was fun but serious management problems also had to be solved. Tradesmen building ships and submarines in British yards tended to work on a 'First come, first served' basis or, to use the phrase of my new country, 'First in, best dressed'. If ventilation trunks were the first to be installed in a compartment they would run straight. Pipes and cables would be installed around them. I'm exaggerating a bit but not much. It was not the way to build a nuclear submarine, or any other modern vessel. Unless the old ways could be changed, our work on the mock-up would be wasted. These changes required greater co-ordination of contributions from designers and shipbuilders than ever before, but everyone wanted to make the project a success, not least because the US Navy's Admiral Rickover, the cantankerous 'father' of the nuclear submarine, was said to be certain we would make a mess of it. The prospects seemed good when the Admiralty appointed an 'overlord', the 'Dreadnought Project Executive' to provide the forceful management needed in the design offices and the building yard.

It was a good try by the standards of the day. Symbolism was invoked by stamping project papers with the image of an old fashioned flat iron, a silly choice but the message 'hot item, keep it moving' was well understood. Unfortunately, two other things were not. It was common practice to summon forty or more people to meetings. Mr Baker, the DPE, could be a tough chairman but even he couldn't make meetings of that size efficient. There was infighting between departments and the waste of time was enormous.

The DPE's organisation had been superimposed on the existing Admiralty structure. He was charged with the overall leadership of the project while the old structures were still in place. He had influence but not authority over specialist departments. If they disagreed with him he could not over-rule them. Things had changed, but not enough. However, capital 'M' Modern, capital 'M' Management, capital 'M' Methods, had been tried. A start had been made and it was good to have been a part of it.

It's also good to record that there was much more to life at AUWE than technicalities and management. There were some excellent management practices, for most of which the naval team set the tone. The establishment's leader at that time was a 'Captain Superintendent' and although the quality of the establishment's work depended a lot on his closest colleague the Chief Scientist, the motivation of the staff to serve the navy well depended primarily on the successive captains. The best of them devoted most office hours to what became known, decades later, as the technique of 'managing by walking around'. Paperwork was attended to later, much later.

There was a thriving Principal Scientific Officers' Mess at the Southwell establishment where our team worked and, to the chagrin of some of the junior scientists, all the naval officers were members, more or less on the grounds that they couldn't sit around in uniform eating sandwiches for lunch. It was good that we were members of the mess but the excuse was flimsy. Some of us made a point of lunching in the canteen frequently with people from all parts of the establishment, and at other times got out of uniform to take part in lunchtime sport.

Sport was not the earnest kind so common today but social sport. The girls of the typing pool and tracing office enjoyed thrashing the navy at netball, which we discovered was not always the genteel, non-contact sport we had previously thought. Another sport had to be found to save us too much humiliation and we were pleased when a manuscript was found describing the sport of 'Puddox', the forerunner of both cricket and baseball. The ancient game was immediately revived and proved popular not only with the players and the spectators but with the *members of the PSOs' mess when it provided an entertainment just outside the mess windows.*

Sexism was thriving at AUWE in the late 'fifties and it was mostly a one sided affair in which men, especially youngish naval men in uniform found out what it was like to be stared at as a sex object. It was generally accepted that no man ever entered the tracing office and became the focus of about sixty pairs of young female eyes without wondering whether his fly buttons or zip were in order. The typing pool had a similar effect. When I was about to move on, my old winger from the Vernon days came to take over. The ever youthful Tom's introduction to the typing pool was followed by a phone call from the Superintendent of Typists, 'My girls want to know three things. How old is he? Is he married? And can they have him for Christmas?' On hearing that he was only a couple of years younger than me, she remarked, 'Oh, that puts him more in my bracket doesn't it!'

The sexism may have been mainly one sided but it wasn't exclusively so. The mini-skirt, first sighted in the West Indies a few years earlier had made its way to Dorset, and any man would have to have had a heart of stone not to appreciate the sight of the hem of typist 'Big Lill's' mini threatening to dangle in the cup of coffee on a standard height desk. When film makers came to Portland to shoot scenes for Petticoat Pirates' and hired locals as extras, no one was surprised when Lill was chosen to show off her long legs in a wet suit as a 'frogwoman'. Lise, like most extras several inches shorter, spent the night rushing around one of the local frigates dressed as Wrens.

Many activities thrived in the establishment, football, darts, Christmas parties for the children, complete with some of the tallest pussy cats and teddy bears ever seen, and many others. I joined the rifle club and we competed regularly within the establishment and against other clubs. Most of our shooting was done with 0.22 rifles, but the navy had surplus 0.303 ammunition made during the war which we were could buy quite cheaply. So even wives who were not regular shots had a chance to experience the kick of a 0.303. Lise remembers it well. And there was a footnote to our purchase of the old ammunition. Our experts discovered that the grouping accuracy of the old stock was better than the recently manufactured lots. We didn't tell our naval rivals that.

The establishment was fortunate in having not only a senior management which recognised the value of social and sporting activities but also many talented people who were willing to organise and run them. Car treasure hunts were one of the most popular. Dorset is a wonderful county for such events, lots of tiny lanes with high banks at each side, steep hills, beautiful views, old buildings and, at the end of the hunt, many lovely old pubs in which to sort out what went wrong and to reconcile drivers and navigators. The hunts left many happy memories. Some were trivial like that of the retired Commander who was worried that his beloved Jaguar had to be put into first gear to climb a hill. He did not know that according to the Ordnance Survey map it was the steepest in Dorset, one in three and a half. But it isn't trivial that organiser Bill wrote a whole treasure hunt in verse, two lines of which remain in memory over thirty years later,

'Wipe your windscreen clear of midges,
See those pretty little bridges'.

Organising research and development is a complex matter and the record of development by in-house government development teams is not a happy one. The appalling story of the 'K' Class submarine development in the 'twenties is well known and Neville Shute's autobiography records the problems of the R101 airship in the 'thirties. Various government enquiries have revealed shortcomings in the case of post WW2 aircraft, missile and torpedo developments. But whatever the route to development, public sector or private, there is no doubt that any *organisation benefits by the kind of motivation and loyalty usually exhibited by the AUWE team at work and play.*

Sometimes, though, social activities can become too successful. The car treasure hunts led to a suggestion that we should get together with the Atomic Energy Authority's people at Winfrith, and the Army enthusiasts at Bovington to form a motor sport club. The idea was that the existing club covering the area, the Hants and Dorset Motor Club, was committed to 'serious' motor sport. We wanted something between that and the 'family' fun provided by the treasure hunts. The Woolbridge Motor Club was formed. Rallies were run on the public roads under rules laid down by the Royal Automobile Club. The maximum permitted average speed was 30 mph which may sound ridiculously low compared to the speeds of off road rallying today, but it was high enough for the Dorset lanes using the family cars of the 'fifties. It was fun while it lasted but it didn't last long. Within a couple of years 'serious' speedsters, who couldn't believe that we used the family transport for rallying, dominated the club. We less affluent rallyists organised our revenge before dropping out of the club.

The serious rallyists assumed, as they drove at high speed down narrow, winding Dorset lanes with the usual high bank at each side, that Farmer Giles would only be doing about 20 if he came, unseen, the other way. In planning our final rally, we merely arranged that in one tricky bit, the car coming the other way was another rally car. There was a certain amount of bank climbing and the fast men were far from pleased. It was not many years before cars had become so fast and specialised that rallying on the roads became merely drives between the 'special stages'. We may have been slow and careful but we were competitors, not spectators. We had the best of it.

The Royal Navy decreed that Lieutenants shall serve eight years in the rank before adding the Lieutenant Commander's 'half' stripe. It seemed a long time but in December 1960, having been of good behaviour, I was promoted. Automatic promotions do not have the impact of those earned by competition or selection, but are still very welcome. In my case, for two reasons. My father had reached his 65th birthday in 1959, having ended his working life as a Clerical Assistant in the Tax Office. He and my mother wanted to move south but houses there were much more expensive than those in Hull. My promotion provided the means of closing the gap. Lise and I agreed that we now had the chance to start saving while benefiting my parents at the same time. They sold the Lee Street house for about eleven hundred pounds, used five hundred of it as a deposit on a bungalow in Weymouth and we paid the eighteen hundred pound mortgage.

It was a new lease of life for them. They loved Weymouth, the climate was milder, they enjoyed being closer to us, and they had material benefits they had never had before, their first refrigerator and an early form of central heating in which a back boiler behind the living room fire supplied radiators in the two bedrooms and a towel rail in the bathroom through large bore convection pipes. They never moved again and although the purchase immobilised our slowly growing savings for seventeen years, we are glad we did it.

The other benefit of promotion was a great blessing. Lieutenant Commanders travelled First Class on the railways. The journeys to Arrochar were never so dreadful in the comfort of a First Class sleeper. And there was the added amusement on one occasion of being joined on the London to Portsmouth train by Rodney, who had been the Admiral's Flag Lieutenant in Maidstone. Only an ex-'Flags' could utter the reproachful words as he was sent off to the Second Class by the Ticket Inspector, 'I do think you might have told me you had a First Class ticket'.

There were other changes too after the half stripe was in place. The gap between workers like myself and the Commanders who held my future in their grasp narrowed. Sometimes *increased mutual confidence took a surprising form, never more so than when one of my bosses wondered whether, if the nuclear threat under which we had all lived for years ever seemed likely to escalate into imminent nuclear war, he might prefer to spend the last days with his family rather than where duty called. More food for thought.*

As the years passed the Dreadnought took shape and journeys to the building yard at Barrow became almost as common as journeys to Arrochar had been. Inevitably, there were problems during the building stages. Perhaps the most unusual was having to adapt the torpedo equipment to allow for the torpedo compartment being too long at the front end and, paradoxically, too short at the rear.

The front end of the pressure hull was an enormous forged dome. When the edge which was to be welded to the rest of the pressure hull was machined, solid metal was revealed two inches earlier than allowed for in the planning. It was decided to save time and money by leaving it, hence a front end longer than expected. The shorter than expected back end was the result of a late decision by the constructors that thick doubler plates had to be welded to the after bulkhead of the compartment to spread the thrust of our torpedo loading gear.

Our equipments were modified to match these new dimensions and my final journey to Barrow was to conduct the preliminary trials of the torpedo stowage and loading equipment. They went unremarkably well. I fared less well. The first battery driven recorders had become available and I decided to use one instead of a notebook. It just fitted in the pocket of my overalls and the microphone, about the size of a small apple, was clipped to a lapel. It had a recording capacity of one and a half hours because it used thin wire, not tape. That was the snag, literally. After appearing to record perfectly, the wire jammed and wouldn't rewind. No wonder that technology didn't survive long. It took half the night to reconstruct all the notes.

Work on torpedo equipment involves a lot of bending, stretching and reaching to see what's happening and one day my right knee locked. I couldn't get up after crouching to look under a torpedo. It was my introduction to the world of cartilage problems. Treatment was not urgent provided I accepted that the knee would lock every so often, and that if I was walking too fast at the time I would fall over.

Officers usually changed appointments every two years. From the beginning of the Vernon Sea Trials time to the end of my AUWE time, I had worked on the same equipments for four years. By the end of the time I knew my job. The Admiralty must have agreed. They sent me to the Third Submarine Squadron to help look after the Dreadnought when she joined the Porpoise and Oberon Class diesel electric boats of the squadron and the older boats working-up there after refits. Most satisfying!

Chapter 16

Third Division North Again

When a big organisation like the navy changes slowly it's easy to think that it isn't changing much at all. That's why it's necessary to review the past as accurately as one can to assess progress, though as Leslie Thomas wrote in his autobiography, 'You summon your past and it obediently, if reluctantly and vaguely, wanders back to you like an old dog'. When I look back at the Third Submarine Squadron to which Lise and I returned in August 1962, I realise a lot had changed, enough to mark the period as our first encounter with a new era.

The most obvious change was that the squadron had moved from Rothesay on the Isle of Bute to Faslane, a hamlet on the shore of the Gareloch, only seventeen miles as crows fly, but quite a different environment. Some, but not enough, married quarters had been built in the nearest town, Helensburgh, and until newcomers came to the top of the roster it was back to the old routine of finding rented accommodation wherever they could.

Lise and I were relatively lucky. We rented a cottage converted from outhouses at Shandon, less than a mile from Faslane. It had no damp course, the walls were soaked to three feet above the floor much of the time and water froze in glasses by bedsides. It had two baths. The one in the kitchen had a wooden cover as a working surface when it was not being used for washing clothes. The one in the bathroom sat in a slot in a concrete slab over the stream which ran under the house. The water cooled rapidly, and though we sat on towels to protect bottoms from the cold iron, baths were brief. Less lucky families had to go friends' houses to bath. Wellingtons were the correct footwear for leaving the cottage whether going shopping or to a ball, shoes were kept in the boot of the car, to be put on later.

Looking back, it's hard to understand why we put up with such conditions.

My job had changed in two significant ways. The ordnance and electrical engineering streams of the navy had been combined. I was no longer directly responsible to the Captain S/M but to the electrical engineer Commander at the head of a combined Weapons and Electrical Department. In practice, the change made little difference. I was the junior of two Lieutenant Commanders. The senior one, Leigh, was responsible for all the electrical aspects, I ran the ordnance team.

After working mainly with civilians for four years, Faslane brought my first exposure to the General List practices introduced in 1956. I joined the roster of Duty Lieutenant Commanders who were responsible for the ship and squadron when the Captain, Commander and Commander S/M were ashore. I was taught how the squadron would be told about the outbreak of world war three and what to do about it. I had to be firm with submarine Commanding Officers who thought the Wardroom bar should be reopened, in contravention of the mess rules, because they wanted a nightcap after returning from shore. Between those extremes, the most common duty was investigation of offences committed by sailors which were too serious to be dealt with by the Officer of the Day, followed, if there was a charge to answer, by prosecuting the case before the Commander the next morning.

Those disciplinary duties began badly. A new Discipline Act had replaced the old Naval Discipline Act during my years at AUWE. The old regime was characterised by the apochraphal story of the Commander who sentenced a defaulter to 14 days stoppage of leave, adding that, 'If there was any real evidence you'd committed the offence, I'd have doubled the punishment'. The new Act required a more rigorous approach to evidence, prosecution and punishment. The navy didn't train us in the new system. The 'in at the deep end' principle applied and one sailor got lucky. Knowing no better, my first case for the Commander lacked the detailed presentation required by the new system and he had to dismiss the charge. To his credit, he recognised that he should have checked that I was familiar with the new requirements before putting me on the roster. It did not take long to learn what was required.

Those investigations were very important because the 'crime' rate was high, a matter of great concern to the senior officers of the squadron. There were at least three underlying causal factors. First, the long standing problem of inequality of workloads in submarine depot ships. There was too little real work for many of the 'ship' ratings, because the ship spent almost all its time in harbour, compared to the high work load of the 'squadron' ratings, busy supporting the submarines. The old adage about idle hands always applies.

The second factor was the lack of social and recreational facilities for the young ratings. The Faslane facilities were Maidstone on its jetty, a floating dock, the facility for storing the High Test Peroxide for the experimental submarine, HMS Explorer, a fenced patch of cinders about a hundred yards square with a guard room, telephone exchange, some old WW2 military caravan bodies and various dumps of stores and empty crates. The lack of recreational facilities didn't matter to those with families in the area. We were pleased we could go home to them most nights. It was a different matter for our testosterone-charged, unmarried young sailors. There was nothing for them nearer than Helensburgh, five miles away. That might seem a trivial distance but sailors rarely had cars, public transport was inadequate, and there was not much to do except drink when they got there. Not surprisingly, there was plenty of crime, mostly petty, some serious.

As another learning experience, the crime was fascinating. Leaving aside incest for which there was no scope in the squadron, during two and a half years I investigated almost everything. The most serious was an alleged attempted murder, the most predictable was homosexual misconduct. The saddest was a smuggling charge. In order to ensure a quiet Christmas, the word was put about very strongly that smuggling liquor into the ship was 'off' that year. The word was effective. Two sailors decided they had better get rid of the liquor they had already brought onboard and were caught smuggling it out. They would never forget their attempt to beat the Christmas rush!

Two crimes tied for first place as the most unusual. The first arose from an audit of the Wardroom wine fund. David, the Spare Submarine CO of the squadron led a team of myself and a Lieutenant. Things did not quite tie up and David, whose meticulous thoroughness I always admired, ordered a check on the thousands of transfers from bar chits to the record books. It took a long time but we proved that the Leading Steward responsible for the bar and our Chief Steward had been milking the system of two bottles of spirits a day for at least a year. The Leading and Chief Stewards were charged and disrated. Two previous teams of auditing officers had not been thorough enough to detect the thefts.

We suspected there was more to the matter but couldn't prove anything until a Leading Patrolman, one of the ship's 'policemen', revealed that his boss, the Master at Arms, the ex-officio senior rating of the squadron, had connived at smuggling one bottle of the stolen liquor ashore for sale each day and distributing the other around the ship as the price of silence. Before I could conduct the initial investigation the Regulations had to be searched to find out who should march him up and charge him. Logically, the Queen's Regulations and Admiralty Instructions nominated the most senior Chief Petty Officer. He was an Engine Room Artificer with over twenty years seniority but he hadn't seen the light of day for most of that time, let alone been exposed to the complexities of the modern investigations. We used common sense, and the Spare Crew Coxswain, well *versed in the procedures, prepared the charges. When the case was tried by the Captain the Master at Arms was found guilty, disrated and discharged from the navy.*

The other case was bizarre. One morning the Chaplain was distressed to find that the ship's Chapel had been desecrated. The candles were broken, a dagger stuck into the altar, and a rosary and broken crucifix draped around it in a carefully arranged display. The Detective Sergeant from the Admiralty Constabulary at Rosyth, who was almost a resident, had his sources and soon identified the seventeen year old culprit. The books were consulted. The curious charge of 'an act in derogation of God's honour', which no one seemed ever to have understood, had been removed from the Act, but plenty of charges remained. There was little doubt the lad would admit the offence but he would not say why he did it. Getting carried away after reading too much Dennis Wheately was one possibility. Another was that he had joined one of the Black Magic circles which offered naked orgies, illegally, at about five pounds a head in those pre-permissive society days. But in either case, why would he not tell us?

Slowly, a picture of the sailor's activities was constructed. He was considered a young stud but even messmates were unaware that he was enjoying eight girlfriends, some older married women, some as young as himself. And there was the final clue. One of his youngest friends was a catholic lass who confessed to the Helensburgh parish priest. A priest must keep the secrets of the confessional but that did not stop him, in his role as Visiting Roman Catholic Chaplain to the squadron, giving our sailor hell, theologically speaking. Father Pat was a popular figure in the squadron but we all recognised how easily this formidable Irish priest, six foot three tall and as broad as the proverbial barn-door, could overwhelm the youngster, who then returned onboard and revenged himself by savaging the

Chapel. He got 14 days in the RN Detention Centre and quite a bit of sympathy.

Sometimes the traditional navy way of doing things provides a simple answer to a problem which could otherwise become serious. One Sunday afternoon the Chief Petty Officer on duty at the gate of the compound allowed a young naval wife to come in and the Officer of the Day let her get onboard the ship. Her husband was in the ship's cells charged with a serious offence. She didn't give a damn about that and said she would stay aboard the ship until he was released. The Daily Mirror loved such incidents but their style of publicity was often quite unfair. A publicity-free solution was required. The sailor was brought out of the cells and told he had ten minutes alone with his wife to tell her what was going on, and to persuade her to leave quietly. If he failed, two of his messmates would remove his wife from the ship, kicking and screaming and showing her knickers if that's the way she wanted it. They would put her outside the compound gate where she would be arrested by the local police if she attempted to re-enter. I've no idea what he said but she went quietly.

As is often the case, punishment for minor crimes by silly young sailors, though necessary, was not an answer to the problem. That required a more drastic step. Technically and operationally, the squadron was generally in good shape. Dreadnought had arrived and after completing her shipbuilder's trials had been accepted into service and joined the squadron. The nuclear monitoring which began with her arrival detected more radiation from the luminous paint on the precision pressure gauges in one of my workshops than from Dreadnought. There were many everyday problems but nothing to prevent the squadron making a significant change.

A new pattern of working was adopted. About once a month when the operational submarines departed for the week on Monday morning, Maidstone sailed and spent the week away *from Faslane, giving the ship's company practice in their job of running a ship at sea, and visiting some other port before returning to Faslane on Friday in time for the return of the boats. The first expedition was to Liverpool, then best known for a club called The Cavern at which the Beatles had made their name. No prizes for guessing how much that raised morale.*

When Maidstone was away, specialist officers and ratings were left behind to support submarines which were in harbour for maintenance. The old caravans in the compound were pressed into service for all sorts of purposes. The arrangements were crude but we made them work and we lived as best we could in the primitive conditions. One caravan, for example, was the cabin for the Officer in Charge while the ship was away. I did my turn and enjoyed the novelty of cooking my own supper on a gas ring. Would it ever happen in the Guards?

Introducing more variety into the routine did not bring the crime rate down to zero but once it seemed to have done so. After a visit to Belfast, the Officer of the Day reported that there hadn't even been any minor problems. I passed the good news to the Commander as we waited for 'Colours' at eight o'clock. No problems from the OOD, none from the medical side. It sounded too good to be true and it was. At five past eight, we learned that fourteen jars of rum had been stolen from the spirit room. We were almost relieved. We now knew the worst!

During those years the squadron did its best to get the correct balance between the exacting technical requirements of a modern navy and the needs of 'the troops'. I was not privy to the discussions with our Captain S/M which generated the new routine but I was well aware that the he, like all of us who were fathers of sons, had had to come to grips with the family aspects of the changing times. The Beatles' hair, which seemed so long then, was a symbol of those times and it aroused intensely antagonistic feelings in some parents, particularly fathers. One AUWE scientist insisted that his sixteen year old son kept to the 'short back and sides' custom so the son left home. Our Captain showed understanding of the changing attitudes of young men in his family and his official life. He was a good model in both roles.

I hoped the openness to new ideas was a sign that the navy was finally putting the days of 'appearances above all' behind it. Much had changed since the days in Decoy but you cannot please everyone. The navy's recruiters invited young men to 'Join Britain's Modern Navy'. A sailor in one of our rather squalid old submarines promptly put in a request to his CO to be allowed to do so and it was referred to the Captain S/M. The boss lost his sense of humour that time, perhaps because he always tried so sincerely to do his best for everyone and was hurt by the request. It wasn't the sailor's fault or the Captain's. The recruiters were doing the unforgivable, advertising something they could not always deliver.

Moving to a married quarter was a great relief. We were in a semi-detached house and our neighbours on the detached side, the Commander S/M of the Squadron, Peter and his wife Issy and their five sons became close friends. My boss Bill, his deputy Leigh, and their wives and children lived nearby. So did many other nice people. Most were just about as penniless as we were, even if they were Commanders with submarine pay. That didn't stop us enjoying life. Entertaining based on South African sherry and home brewed beer served us well.

Many of the locals were hospitable and that was sometimes a problem. Some, like the Teacher family of whisky fame. were seriously rich. Some had difficulty understanding why we couldn't just fly over to Belfast with them for a party. Others did their best to understand our limitations, like the wife who asked Issy how much her husband earned and on being told exclaimed, 'Issy, you poor darling. How do you manage?' I don't know what she answered but the words probably meant, 'Somehow'.

Helensburgh proved to be an exception to Scotland's proud tradition of good schooling and Michael began to worry that if we ever returned to the Weymouth school he would have been left behind by his peers. We had never considered boarding school but now it was clearly the answer. Two of the boys next door were already at Dauntsey's and Michael's contemporary David was to join them there as part of the eleven year old entry. Everything fell into place and Michael went with him. As far as we could tell he was happy to go. He remained at Dauntsey's for five years. Many of his contemporaries there remain friends and that's not a bad test of a school.

There were ups and downs in the work of the ordnance team. We introduced the RN's first wireguided torpedo, the Mark 23. The dispensing of the wire from the tail of the torpedo and from the submarine had given a great deal of trouble while I was at AUWE but modified equipment was increasingly reliable. It was a tremendous pleasure to be aboard submarines when the COs first practiced attacking with the weapon and realised how much more freedom they had now that they could alter each weapon's course and depth while it was on its way to the target. Sometimes it was like being on a submarine road to Damascus.

We prepared hundreds of the old Mark 8 anti-surface ship torpedoes, some as part of the war stock carried by the submarines, others practice versions. Our losses of practice weapons became a headache. Five per cent was usual. We lost up to fifteen per cent. Until, that is, my Chief Artificer and I discovered that, hitherto unknown to us, we had one member of the team who talked to the torpedoes as he prepared them for running. We never found out exactly what he told them but after he was removed, our losses fell dramatically.

Sometimes the job was stressful and I learned more about the effects of stress. My opposite number in the marine engineering department had a heart attack and his place was taken by an officer who had just left the Services' Mental

Hospital at Netley after recovering from a nervous breakdown. Suitably late one evening the Engineer Officer of one of the submarines and I primed the newcomer with whisky and he told us his tale. He was happy to do so because, as we knew, the primary teaching of the psychiatrists was always to 'go forth and tell every one all about it'.

Nothing dramatic happened, our new colleague told us, as he progressed from happily doing his job to being convinced that he couldn't do it any longer and that he must ask to be relieved. Each of the symptoms was insignificant in isolation from the others. His first example was an inability to get to sleep at night because his mind refused to stop churning over his problems. 'Got that', said Bill and I. Number two was waking up several times during the night with the brain still worrying away. 'Got that too', we said. We found that we both had ten of his eleven symptoms of a nervous breakdown. The only difference was that we saw our troubles as finite. Some would go away as circumstances changed. We might get help from somewhere with others. Our Netley graduate had been unable to see any light at the end of the tunnel. It was a good lesson to learn. We can withstand high stress for a limited time, without counselling and psychiatrists, provided we can see beyond our troubles.

Once we became involved in a tragic affair. The batteries which powered our Mark 20 and 23 torpedoes and the RAF and Fleet Air Arm's Mark 30 involved potentially dangerous chemistry. The electrolyte was isolated from the cells until the weapon was launched and monitoring systems provided a warning if premature mixing occurred accidentally. When warnings sound, people are often tempted to assume that the monitoring system is faulty. And when a submarine returned to Maidstone one evening with a problem and we began to remove the battery from the torpedo on the open well-deck, everyone treated it as an after dinner floor show. At least, they did until they realised that I wasn't joking. Then we had the deck to ourselves. That incident ended quietly. The standard procedures had proved satisfactory.

Some of the weapons staff at the RAF station at Kinloss were carrying out their standard procures for preparing Mark 30 torpedoes but they were not so lucky. An explosion brought down the thirty ton concrete roof of their workshop and they were killed. I was on leave and my Sub-Lieutenant was sent to assist with the investigation. I was not a party to all the details of the case but after becoming aware of some controversy about the role the battery electrolyte might have played we did a little experiment in the HTP depot laboratory.

We took a small piece of a thin insulating material used near the battery terminals, placed a drop of the electrolyte on it and allowed it to dry. The plan was to heat it gently under controlled conditions to see what happened but there was no need to do so. I merely held it a couple of inches above the lab's central heating radiator. The dry spot began to sputter like a tiny firework and then the material burst into flame. Whatever the exact cause of the Kinloss accident, there was no doubt that the potential for an accident existed if drops of electrolyte were spilled on the insulator during the preparation process.

There were other, less dramatic problems. We could never get enough spares for some unreliable equipments and when official channels had failed, I wrote a 'demi-official' letter to the Ordnance Engineer on the Staff of the Flag Officer Submarines making it quite clear that we were not getting the support we needed. It was returned with a covering note which said, 'I am returning your letter which I hope you will agree, on reflection, should never have been sent by an officer in your position to one in mine'. Naturally, my boss was informed and had to chide me for the incident. I expected no less, but was pleased when he later wrote in a report on my performance, 'Does not suffer fools gladly'. Could any Yorkshireman wish for more?

The time in Maidstone was marked by another change. Smoking, a habit since teenage, encouraged by the navy's duty free tobacco rations, had to be given up. The evidence was clear enough for any reasonable person, but how? I managed a year. Then some technical problem got the better of me and I started again. Then two years. Then a night job in the floating dock.

A submarine was to sail for the United States at nine on a Monday morning but while they were at sea the previous Saturday a young officer had failed to do a check correctly. A stainless steel cage housing sonar equipment had been crushed by the pressure of the sea. The boat returned to Faslane, entered our floating dock, and was high and dry around five o'clock on the Sunday afternoon. My marine engineering colleague responsible for nuclear aspects had some lovely new power tools, perfect for a job like this. By three in the morning, the ultra hard stainless steel had blunted them all. My team had done all they could. Further progress depended on a calculated risk. That was my department. 'Chief, give me a cigarette please'. We then bent rules, got the job done. The sub sailed on time, my career was safe for the time being. But I was a smoker again.

All the challenges were made bearable and often enjoyable by the quality of the officers and ratings of the Weapons and Electrical team. We had problems like the man who talked to torpedoes, but overall they were excellent. This had a particular significance for me when the other Lieutenant Commander left and I became the boss's Deputy. It made little difference except when the boss was sick or on leave. Then I had to be the department's interface with the Captain and others on all electrical matters affecting the ship and the squadron. Without a loyal team it could have been a nightmare because I had not been 'cross-trained' in electrical engineering. With such a good team it was a pleasure to sit in the department's driving seat for a while. And even when the boss wasn't away, there was one gesture which I found quite touching. Changing times had reduced the formality between members of the department. My two junior officers on the weapons team still used the formal 'Sir' but I was 'Geoff' to those of the electrical side of the house. Until I became the Deputy that is. From then on, I was greeted with 'Good morning, Sir'. Just once a day. More than one 'Sir' might have given me an exaggerated view of my own importance, one was just right for showing loyal support. I appreciated the gesture.

There were occasional sour moments. One was being told to take the salute at a Remembrance Day parade at some small town. All the local towns asked for a naval officer to attend their parades and the Captain and most of the Commanders were already committed. I believed the correct thing was to explain and say to the town, as the old naval phrase has it, 'Much regret unable' but the Captain would have none of it. I had to go. Having a much younger officer with a chest bare of medals take the salutes of veterans with row upon row of them would have been bad enough but I knew that people often assumed I was old enough to have served in WW2 and my lack of medals would have been a bit puzzling. The Provost and the senior ex-officers lunching after the parade were pleasant but I found it an embarrassing experience.

Sour experiences were far outweighed by the good ones. One of the best was spending a day at sea in Dreadnought during her trials, a chance to see how the equipment we had designed at AUWE had turned out. Quite a lot of naval engineers deride shore jobs saying they much prefer to serve in a ship. There are certainly a number of advantages in being afloat. The equipment has usually been designed by someone else and if 'they' have made a hash of the design it is easy to send a complaint up the line. In R and D establishments you are the end of the line. If a naval application officer doesn't help the civilians to do a good job, he only has himself to blame when problems occur at sea. I *was relieved to find that the torpedo equipment of Dreadnought worked reasonably well.*

Overall things were going very well. I knew my technical speciality as well as anyone in the service, enjoyed the new broader duties resulting from the General List reforms and my role as Deputy Head of the department. I was working in a good team, well led at department and Squadron levels, Michael was settling into school, my parents into their new life in Weymouth. We were even beginning to pick up some of the threads of the fragmentary Feasey family life. One of my nieces had joined the army and was serving nearby. Private Elizabeth Feasey enjoyed the attentiveness of the young stewards when she had dinner in the Wardroom one evening.

Two other bits of my life had been sorted out. I had attempted to paint and although I knew painters should record the way light falls on their subjects, I could not free myself from the conviction that my subject was a construction of so many lines, planes and intersections. I tried to paint them all in great detail. Hopeless. The answer was simple, take to carving instead. In that medium, all the worker has to do is carve a shape which looks good when the light falls naturally on it. I found that much easier and it was the beginning of an enduring interest.

The minor infirmity which began when my cartilage became damaged during Dreadnought's harbour trials was sorted out. There was no collaboration between the local hospitals and the navy so I travelled down to the Royal Naval Hospital at Haslar in Hampshire for the operation. When I asked the orthopedic surgeon how soon I would be back in Scotland with my family. 'Operation tomorrow, three weeks strict bed, a week to mobilise and then you can go home', was the answer. I thought he was joking but he wasn't. He believed that keeping patients in bed for three weeks was the best way of reducing infection after cartilage operations. The only thing worse than three weeks of bedpans was bending the knee again after all that inactivity! My operation was most successful and I ran my last 440 yards race for the departmental team a few months after the operation, but I doubt whether such a costly regime was justified, even then.

Lise and I had been married for ten years when we arrived at Faslane and we had developed a way of life which has changed little over the years. My job was to earn our living, Lise's to look after the family. The reality was not quite as traditionalist as it might sound. If I had any of the old fashioned illusions about the man being the 'head of the family', Lise would have been speedily dissipated them. We were a partnership of two individuals, one small symbol of which was my practice of breaking with British tradition and always writing to her as Mrs MLS Feasey, not GC.

After her early experiences of the 'plummiest' types of naval wives, some of whom would complain loudly if a 'junior' wife failed to attribute to them status according to their husbands' ranks, Lise insisted on simply being herself. She treated everyone the same natural courtesy and consideration, and had a happy knack of getting on well with people at all levels and all ages. But Lise was reminded that service life is different when we resumed naval life at Faslane after years with the civilians. She was a bit surprised when the wife of one of the squadron's senior officers sought her advice on how to make contact with the younger wives. And she was certainly surprised when the young wives of my torpedo officer 'customers' stood up when she first went to coffee with them. She liked the young wives but did not spare any of them who moped when their husbands were at sea, and it became the custom for some of them to say, 'I'm feeling sad. I'll go and get myself told off by Lise'.

When things are going so well it often means it is time to move on. In November 1964, after two years and a quarter years in the squadron, it was my turn to move south and try to become an Electrical Officer.

Boy
meets

Girl

Lise and Michael 1953

One of our Old Cars

HMS Alcide 1955
They don't make them like that anymore.

Or like that
HMS Zest 1966

Royal Review of the Home Fleet 1957

Looking Serious at a Friend's Wedding

Chapter 17

'Greenie'

One thing is quite certain regarding the education of engineers: nations and organisations are better served by variety. It is wrong to put all the eggs in one basket. The Royal Navy half grasped that wisdom when the Electrical Branch was established in 1947. Instead of introducing electrical engineering at the Royal Naval Engineering College, electrical officers did the Mechanical Sciences Tripos at Cambridge. It would have been wiser to send a proportion of all engineers to Cambridge. So many Cambridge educated electrical officers received offers they could not refuse, the navy had to convert mechanical engineers to 'Greenies' to fill the gaps.

Ordnance engineers were the obvious choice because weapon control engineering involved electrics and electronics and we were half way there already. Even so, conversion involved six and a half months of theoretical and general studies to make us acceptable to the learned institutions associated with our new disciplines, followed by briefing on specific equipments in the ships to which we would be appointed as Weapons and Electrical Officers.

The training was done at HMS Collinwood, the navy's Electrical School at Fareham in Hampshire. Lise and I were not qualified for a married quarter because we might not be there long enough. We were lucky to be able to rent a friend's house until he returned from Faslane and then lived over the chemist's shop in Titchfield. We certainly got variety in our living conditions while serving the RN.

There were six General List Lieutenant Commanders on our course, one who had recently put up his 'half' stripe, the rest of us having a few 'years in'. We were joined by eight graduate-entry Supplementary List Sub-Lieutenants who had joined the navy only a few weeks earlier. It was not like going back to engineering college. Collingwood trained everyone electrical, from junior ratings to senior officers. And Collingwood treated all trainees alike in two important respects.

Training classes, no matter how senior, were all required to parade and march past at the weekly 'Divisions'. If some of the officers' class were recent recruits who could not yet march very well, the class would be told to 'Go round again'. This involved waiting over an hour until the most junior class had marched past. After one foul up I 'read the horoscope' of one Sub for not heeding words I whispered to him as we approached the saluting base. At the bar that evening, I learned, he asked another Sub, 'Who's that grey bearded old Lieutenant Commander? He was very rude to me after Divisions today'. After explaining who I was, Alec went on to say, 'And if you ever get us 'sent around' again, I'll be bloody rude to you too'. I thought Alec a good advertisement for the Supplementary List entrants. And I believe it was good for the junior ratings to see that officers' training classes went through the same hoops.

The other Collingwood belief was that no one would study seriously unless they were examined every week. They were probably right. Most of us 'olds' found it difficult to get back to the mathematical basis of the subjects and found some electrical concepts difficult if there were no obvious analogies in mechanical engineering. It was a problem for the Instructor Officers, especially one who taught electronics with the fervour of a Welsh evangelist. 'How can we go on if you can't even understand what we've done so far', he lamented. We had to go on regardless and all came right in the end. We found there was a lag of about three weeks between first hearing about a difficult concept and finally understanding it. That wasn't too bad!

During our time at Collingwood Churchill died. It was an occasion for reflection on his life and the times through which he had lived. Whatever his shortcomings there was no doubt that he was a courageous and immensely talented man. The navy shared the duty of guarding his catafalque and a Lieutenant Commander of 'distinctive appearance' was required. My beard against Mike's impressive six feet four inches. He won. Pity, I would have felt honoured to be part of the old man's last public moments.

Towards the end, our Admiralty appointer sent the six 'oldies' a list of appointments and invited us to suggest who should go where. Five were jobs as 'Head of Department'. The sixth, as a 'Deputy Head', went automatically to our junior member. Then the other four argued that I was the only one who, if appointed to the aging frigate, HMS Zest, would be going to a younger ship than his last one. I had no answer to that. Zest was mine. We completed our conversion and were 'Greenies'.

It's an ill wind and all that. The navy's shortage of Electrical Officers provided me with a toe in the electrical and electronic fields which was to prove decisive years later when I sought a civilian job for the first time in thirty seven years. And the course provided Lise and I with two more cherished friends, one of the Subs, Peter, who served twice more at Collingwood, the last time as Captain, and his wife, Barbara.

Zest was in the Far East and I flew to Singapore to join her in September 1965. Or at least, I tried to. She proved elusive. I left England at 1000 on a Wednesday courtesy of RAF Transport Command and after a long diversion to Tehran for repairs arrived at Changi around midnight local time on the Friday. The 'Confrontation' between Malaysia and Indonesia was in full swing so not only was Zest not in Singapore but no one would tell me where she was. Instead I received a sealed envelope with orders to deliver about thirty sailors to their ships or the barracks in a waiting bus. At two AM, a second message at the barracks Wardroom told me a car would take me back to Changi at four. There, a third envelope said have breakfast and join a flight to Labuan, an island off the coast of Malaysian Borneo, at seven. My mood was not the best when I arrived at the British army headquarters on Labuan in middle of Saturday morning and I told the Corporal in the tiny reception office not to give me any more sealed envelopes because I was too tired to go anywhere. Like every good NCO he had a ready answer, 'They don't think you are half important enough to go anywhere until Monday, Sir. You are to spend the weekend in the mess here'. Still no Zest.

On Monday morning I dressed in my long white uniform, normally reserved for ceremonial occasions. We had to wear uniform, they said, so that if the plane came down in Indonesia the locals would not have an excuse to shoot us as spies. The usual naval shorts and short sleeved shirt offered little protection in case of fire and were unacceptable. So on with the 'ice cream suit' and sit in a narrow canvas seat in a transport aircraft with the chain holding down the cargo between my legs and a monstrous crate six inches from my face. A good time to keep the upper lip stiff.

Zest was waiting when we arrived at Tawau, a small port to the north of Malaysia's land border with Indonesia. The welcome was warm from the Captain, the recently joined First Lieutenant and my predecessor, a bit wary from the remainder. Not only had it been a long commission but the previous First Lieutenant had been on intimate terms with some young sailors. Discipline had been chaotic and the morale of the other officers rock bottom. Ships' companies are complex organisms but by the time officers become Heads of Departments or Commanding Officers they should understand them well. If the second in command is flawed, everything depends on the Captain. In Zest, Fido was a pleasure to work for. He handled Zest with great skill, reminding her that she had been born a destroyer and was still a powerful ship, but he had been given the command after years in aviation. He had not had a chance to develop the feeling for a ship's company and he paid the price. He was not promoted further. It was another unwise and unfair aspect of the navy's policies.

With Robert, the new 'Jim', as the key player, matters soon improved. We had a clear role and that always helps. There had been a barter trade along the coast for centuries and the locals were not going to stop just because their countries were at odds with each other. For obvious reasons, the coastal vessels travelled at night. It was our job to stop and search them to ensure they were not smuggling arms and explosives. The task was small but there was some risk for the boarding party. A Midshipman had been killed recently leading a similar examination near Singapore.

Working at night allowed us to enjoy some of the most perfect afternoons snorkelling, once even sharing the water with a pair of six foot turtles engaged in foreplay just off the beach of a tiny island, uninhabited since the Japanese left at the end of the war. In another place the shelving beach became a cliff about twenty yards off shore. The depth of the clear water increased from ten to about a thousand feet. Snorkelling there felt like being Superman flying off the top of a tall building.

The army had a more boring time of it. If memory serves correctly, the Second Battalion of the Scots Guards guarded that sector of the land frontier. We did our best for them, practicing our bombardment role, on which they could call if things turned nasty, so that they did at least hear a bit of gunfire occasionally. In return their Royal Artillery bombardment liaison officer took three of us for a swim. We took sub-machine guns in a Land Rover and drove for miles through jungle until we came to a beautiful pool, complete with lianas, perfect for playing Tarzan. We hung our guns on a branch and swam. I have often wondered whether we were in Malaysia or Indonesia. Then back to the Mess for tea, under canvas but complete with mess silver. They knew how to make themselves comfortable.

When we qualified for some rest and recreation we had a week in Hong Kong. In seventeen years I had never been east of Helsinki. Now I had my chance to learn a bit about Hong Kong and explored it, often on my own because the other officers had little interest in seeing how the locals lived. Sometimes I thought they might be wiser than I was. One night I strayed into a narrow street off the beaten track and had to dodge a bucket of slops poured from a third floor window. I shall never know whether it was a political statement or routine disposal.

Some of the other scenes I witnessed in Hong Kong impressed me. Students sitting in the gutters at the side of some streets were doing their homework for their 'A' level examinations. People were using old tin cans to make intricate parts for toy cars and similar products in mini-factories created out of passages between alley walls six feet apart. Those and similar impressions convinced me that if the Chinese nation had similar determination and energy, and if they ever decided to take over the world, there would be very little we could do about it. And such industrious people might deserve their success.

When Mr Ian Smith unilaterally declared Rhodesia's independence, part of the British government's response was to send the aircraft carrier, HMS Eagle, currently in Singapore to lie off Beira. Within hours Zest's maintenance period had been terminated and our return to UK brought forward. This allowed us to precede the carrier through the straits to ensure there were no Indonesian missile launching boats lurking there, waiting to attack the carrier as she passed. We did our job then returned to England and a well earned refit in Devonport Dockyard.

Refitting a vessel over twenty years old can be a difficult process. Zest was no exception. The survey of the hull was rather like the radiographing of Alcide's patch, it was difficult to know when to stop replacing plates as the various tests really only proved that Zest was past her use-by date. The dockyard experts were not happy with the situation and sought a decision from the

Admiralty. The response included the sentence, 'It is accepted that Zest will be at some risk during her last commission'. The Marine Engineer and I made sure we kept copies of that signal.

It was not just a matter of the vulnerability of the hull. There were repeated problems as we tried to get the gunnery system through its post refit trials. Fortunately my new captain, Graham, was an experienced small ship officer and a patient man. Hence his memorable response when Lise asked him whether the ship would be at sea for more trials the next day, 'Don't ask me, ask Geoff'. Eventually we had to ask the Rear Admiral responsible for refits to accept the best results we could get from Zest's old systems. He wanted a briefing before agreeing and I trotted off to see him in Portsmouth. He approved the concessions and then we chatted. The Admiral was rejoicing that day. The inability of the Royal Dockyards to complete refits on time was notorious, but the Rosyth yard had finished a refit 'only two weeks late'. 'If they can do that twice more', he said, 'I'll cut the length of refits by two weeks'. This confirmed my suspicion that some senior officers used the 'double cross' method of management. If a loyal team are trying hard to achieve targets, moving the goalposts has always seemed to me a good way to lose goodwill, ruin motivation, and degrade results.

Having Michael settled at Dauntsey's allowed us to choose the time of our move from Titchfield to Plymouth without considering school terms so Lise remained in Titchfield until a quarter became available in Plymstock. I commuted at the weekends. The time of arrival home on Friday was variable but the drive westward became a finely tuned procedure. A friend kindly lent me his Mini-van so that it would be exercised while he was overseas. It was a good vehicle for the two hundred mile drive along the old winding roads, leaving Titchfield at ten on the Sunday night and arriving in the Devonport barracks at two. The Mini enjoyed the exercise. Minis are fun.

A new Ship's Company was built up during the refit and I was reminded me how naval concepts of age were influenced by the eligibility of ratings for a pension at forty. By that age most of them had had enough, took their pensions and departed. At thirty six I was easily the oldest in the Wardroom and I felt it. Those changing times were at it again. Some of the younger officers actually wanted music broadcast in the mess at breakfast time. Shock horror! And, unlike my early days, there was a tendency to expect the mess to be run as a democracy. Deference to the oldest member was not to be taken for granted.

There was an interesting footnote to the post refit trials. One requirement was to do two hours at full power. Zest had more engine power than a modern supertanker, so full power, normally reserved for emergencies, was quite dramatic. The weather in the Channel was rough so we did the trial going downwind to minimise the stresses on the hull. For one and three quarter hours the trial went well. A lot of rudder was needed to keep the ship on course but the Coxswain could cope with that. Until, that is, the rudder jammed seventeen degrees from the midship position. Zest heeled outwards, her stern went down until part of the upper deck was under water, and she shook as if it were trying to rid herself of the engines causing the distress. The situation could have been eased at any time by slowing the ship, but that would mean repeating the trial. We circled, dramatically, for the remaining fifteen minutes. There's an order, 'Clear lower deck', which brings all ratings onto the upper deck except those on duty below. It would have been superfluous that day. After our return to harbour a pair of dockyard worker's overalls were found inside one of the steering machinery rams. No wonder the Royal Dockyards were distrusted to the point of hatred.

After the post refit trials came 'Work-up', six weeks at Portland under the oversight of the Flag Officer Sea Training and his staff. During these weeks we were to be exercised in everything that could be asked of us ashore and afloat, and marked on our performance. It was a dreaded process, not least because the program was deliberately designed to work everyone to the point of exhaustion just so that we all knew what it felt like. It was a good thing to do, otherwise how would recent recruits know that their dinners would not always be ready at noon and a working day might be twenty hours long?

Fun it was not, but I got help with my biggest problem. My Chief Artificer and I were converts from ordnance engineering, apprentices in our new field. The department needed an experienced electrical rating. My earlier complaints had been ignored but when FOST and his staff spoke, things happened. A Chief who had rejoined the navy some years after being pensioned off was drafted to the ship. Four rows of medal ribbons testified to his experience. He was a mixed blessing. During his first week in the ship he upset the Captain, most officers, his 'winger' the Chief Electrician, and a good many others. Ten years earlier I might have wondered what to say to him. Now, although ten years younger that he was, I was not inclined to mince my words. I called him to my cabin, told him we were going to take stock of his first week, and began with the words, 'Chief, you are a cantankerous old sod'. He beamed with pleasure and I realised it had been his life's ambition to be a cantankerous old sod.. Now he had made it. I tried another tack and we got along well enough during our eight months together. I often had cause to be grateful for his experience and workmanship, if not for his interpersonal and social skills.

Even though there are few things that the FOST staff have not seen before, Zest managed to provide a new and unwelcome experience. We practiced fuelling at sea, steaming along parallel to and a hundred feet away from a tanker with hoses connecting the two ships. It calls for the 'first team' and great alertness at the best of times. Our gyro compass managed to topple slowly while we were fuelling. The repeater tape by which the Coxswain was steering the ship slowly ticked across. In trying to hold the required course, he gently turned the ship towards the tanker. 'It was', the Commander Sea Training said later, 'the only time I ever gave a direct order while on the bridge of someone else's ship'. He had been the first to appreciate that the gyro had failed and there was no time for the courtesies. He gave the orders which averted a collision. The fuelling rig was torn apart as we pulled away. The dockyard overhauled the gyro a second time!

Despite such problems, we passed our Admiral's Inspection and were ready for Zest's first assignment of her last commission, eight months in the West Indies. She could be productive while I was away. When Michael first went to boarding school we had rejoiced in our term time freedom but later we began to feel, 'It's not the same without a child about the house, is it'? There was little chance of 'blue baby' complications so many years after Michael's birth, and even if there were, remedial actions had improved greatly since the early fifties. Becoming pregnant was so easy we wondered what might have happened had we let nature take its course during the past thirteen years. Lise was set to be productive.

Zest's duties in the West Indies were to provide approved help to friendly Caribbean Governments and to show a naval presence around the British West Indies. First we showed our faces to our boss the Senior Naval Officer West Indies in Bermuda and were briefed by our predecessors on the station as they paused during their return to the UK. We also enjoyed the kind local hospitality. This included my first attempt at water skiing, and a Bermuda Brunch given by SNOWI's Staff Officer, Hugh, at which his gorgeous three year old daughter, having helped herself to the 'cold tomato soup', asked if she could have a second helping because she liked it so much. Bermuda Brunch is a traditional meal of codfish accompanied by Bloody Marys!

On another occasion there was the preserved tail of an enormous fish in our host's drawing room. It must have been five *feet from tip to tip and a foot thick at the base of the tail. Introductions over, his wife disappeared to the kitchen and the obvious conversational opening was to ask if the tail was from our host's best catch. 'No', he explained, 'It was my wife's'. She had caught the nine hundred pound tunny off Bridlington, the heaviest fish ever caught by a woman, when she was eighteen years old. What a thing to have to explain to every visitor.*

One 'bread and butter' job in the Bahamas was to check uninhabited islands for Cuban refugees. President Fidel Castro's policy allowed Cubans to leave provided they didn't take anything valuable with them, and the US kept the door open to all who could get away. Many left in leaky old boats which got them to nearby Bahamian islands and then sank. We arranged for them to be collected by the US Coastguard, an organisation for which we soon developed a great respect.

Other duties were less mundane, like keeping the power station running at Nassau. During pre-election tension the power workers went on strike and Zest was sent to help maintain the supply. When we arrived there was no alongside berth available: the authorities didn't want to disrupt the cruise ship visits. Instead they wanted Zest to anchor and send a team ashore by boat. A party of electricians with no armed back-up available would not have been a wise move. Putting armed Royal Marines ashore with the electricians would have been inflammatory. A team of armed electricians would have been inflammatory and downright dangerous. All sailors are trained in small arms but are usually more than a bit rusty! Our Captain called on the Governor, an alongside berth was cleared for us.

Our Royal Marine Detachment could remain onboard, ready and itching to get into some action. They were denied the chance this time. Some of my team went to help the power station management keep supplies going. The strikers tried to trip the generators by throwing wire bolas across the overhead power lines to overload the machines. That was easily foiled. The adjustable time delays of the safety trips were wound out to maximum and the bolas burnt out before the machines tripped. The strike ended within a couple of days. Zest became an unpleasant reminder of the tense situation, and we were sent away. We had intended to spend Christmas there but had to change to Plan B.

Despite the above experience, Nassau was usually very hospitable. One night our host was celebrating. He was an accountant and had been setting up a deal for an ultra-rich American tax exile client. The only remaining obstacle was a small bank which opposed the deal. Our host had been given the final instruction he needed, 'Buy the Goddam bank'. Contrary to popular belief, accountants can be amused and we helped him celebrate with a meal of, at his recommendation, crayfish. When a vast wooden platter with sixteen crayfish tails arranged around it was brought to the table I thought it was to be shared by the party. That was not the Nassau way. It was placed in front of me. Everyone who ordered crayfish was served with sixteen. It was a memorable occasion.

Wives, left at home to look after the family, do not always realise how many brain cells their husbands sacrifice at cocktail parties, lunches and dinners during diplomatic visits like Zest's to the capital of the Dominican Republic, Santo Domingo. Twenty thousand US Marines had invaded the country a couple of years earlier to prop up a faltering regime. Although they had been withdrawn, bullet scars on every building remained and armed soldiers on almost every corner testified to continuing tension. Our firing of a twenty one gun salute to the nation, as required by protocol, had been well publicised lest some locals believed the revolution was on again and rushed to the barricades. We had been sent to break diplomatic ice and to foster a belief that normality had been restored. During the five days we were there all our meals except breakfasts were taken on the hoof at one diplomatic occasion after another. It was worth it. We stayed long enough to get the message some of the local people wanted us to take away, *'Please let everyone know that we who want to overthrow our corrupt government are not all communists!.*

Diplomatic niceties came into play again when we visited Venezuela. The British Naval Attache in Caracas briefed me that I would be invited to spend a day at sea in the Venezuelan Navy's only submarine. Subsequently, at some party, I would be asked by the American Naval Attache how efficiently the Venezuelan Navy operated the submarine. I was to give him my opinion. It all happened. I spent a day at sea in the boat, became an Honorary Submariner of the Venezuelan Navy, and was taken aside at a cocktail party by the US Naval Attache. After hearing my report, he thanked me warmly, ending with the words, *'I know we sold them the boat, I know we refit it for them. But we don't actually like to go to sea in it.'* There's only one answer to that, *'Thanks a lot, Sir!'*

Venezuela and Key West, at the tip of Florida, provided the evidence for Feasey's Law of Laundries which states that *'Democracy is incompatible with good laundering'*. Zest's laundry facilities were vestigial and we had to use local laundries to preserve the immaculate appearance expected of the RN. Venezuela was on the brink of a revolution. We were told that five per cent of the people owned ninety five per cent of the wealth. The poor devils at the bottom of the heap produced immaculate laundry, for a pittance. In Key West, which was the nearest thing we had to a home base, our white mess jackets looked as though the local laundry had put them through the flatwork ironer and they charged an arm and a leg. I rest my case.

Key West is remembered for much more than the poor quality of the laundry. It was the home of a friend from Faslane days, Mike, now on the staff of the US Navy's Anti-Submarine School, and his wife Ann. Their warm welcome was a real treat.

Less welcome was the spectacle of two of my fellow officers at one of Mike and Ann's parties dragging an embarrassed woman across the room, announcing, 'This lady says she wants to paint you'. She explained that she was a serious artist preparing for an exhibition and wanted a variety of subjects. Despite the unlikelihood of Lise believing a word of a story like that and given that Ann confirmed what Marian had said, we agreed she would take some photographs and paint from those.

Taking photographs is one thing, picking me up at the ship on Sunday afternoon in a red sports car to do so is another. It enhances an officer's reputation with the lads but that kind of reputation is a dubious asset. However, the deed was done and the picture was painted. I never saw it before we returned to the UK but many months later I was part of an Admiralty team at a NATO meeting in Brussels. Marian's husband Bob, a submarine CO now serving with the London outpost of the US Office of Naval Research, was there. After I returned to AUWE a package arrived with a note, 'Marian and I thought you would like to have this'. The painting has a place of honour in our home. The small world was finally made smaller still. Lise and I said thank you for the painting by inviting Bob and Marian to the Summer Ball at HMS Osprey. 'Bet you didn't believe the story when you first heard it', said Marian. No prizes for guessing Lise's answer.

My father died while I was in the West Indies. He awoke after an afternoon nap, told my mother he'd get up for tea, and died peacefully while she was making it. Lise was told and she telephoned the naval welfare people in Devonport to ask about the arrangements for getting me home to take charge of the funeral arrangements and sort out my father's affairs. She remembers the response. They said if I had been a rating it would have been OK but because I was an officer they didn't think it would be possible. There may be some occasions, even in peacetime, when officers cannot be spared from their duties but it's a pretty thin excuse. If an officer has a heart attack or gets sick, ways of managing have to be found. I dare say the welfare people got a bit of an earful from Lise who was definitely not impressed with their logic.

My Captain's view was that any well organised department can manage without its boss for a week without difficulty. My flight home was arranged from our next call, San Juan in Puerto Rico. There was a slight hitch on the way home. When RN ships visit foreign ports everything is arranged through diplomatic channels and neither officers nor ratings use passports. So if one of them walks ashore in a US affiliated territory like Puerto Rico and flies to New York on the way to UK, there is nothing in his passport to say how he got into the US. So why should the US authorities let him out? After midnight arguments they decided I was telling the truth and let me board the plane for home.

Lise had more excitement driving from Plymouth to my mother's house in Weymouth than I had flying the Atlantic. The bonnet hinges fractured and if the catches at the front had not held, the bonnet would have flown up against the screen. Lise completed the journey with the bonnet tied down with the belt of her raincoat. Pregnant or not, naval wives could cope with anything,

A simple cremation was arranged which Raymond, Clifford and I attended. The simplicity was appropriate for my father was a simple man. Sometimes his innocence protected him from the harsher realities of life. He had often tried writing stories and when the standard cliches of rejection slips told him the editors had found the work 'interesting' he was convinced of their sincerity. I prefer to remember him for two more worthy characteristics. He taught us by example to be punctiliously honest. It would be unthinkable, for instance, for him to get off a tram or bus without placing an uncollected fare in the 'honesty box' on the platform. But perhaps his most touching act was to apologise to me when I was sixteen because he did not *understand enough, academically or about 'the system', to help me realise my ambitions. A simple man but a good one.*

When I rejoined the ship it was ringing with a jingle, 'God Bless Bim on Independence Day'. 'Bim' was Barbados. Zest was there to support the Queen's representatives, the Duke and Duchess of Kent, at the island's independence celebrations. Happy though the atmosphere was, I resisted invitations to go ashore after a sixteen hour flight. But ashore partying at night or not, we all enjoyed the gentle charm of the Duchess when the Kents came aboard for a lunchtime drink the next day.

In most of the islands the transition to independence was a gracious procedure, often symbolised by an invitation to the Colonial Governor, often a white Brit, to remain as the first Governor General for the first six months or so. But it was not an invariable practice for Governors or officials. One island could not wait to get rid of the white Chief of Police. The colony became independent at midnight, Zest removed him from the island one minute later, complete with his dogs, safely housed in a strong kennel our shipwright built for them. They were that kind of dogs, he was that kind of Chief of Police.

A independence story told by a Trinidadian politician was rather sad. During the years preceding independence political agitators were so convincing when they told people they had been working for the white man, that some assumed they would never have to work again when the white man yielded power to the locals. They had a rude awakening.

While operating in the Bahamas we usually had a local policeman living onboard to provide certain powers of arrest. One was remembered for his skill at fishing. The ship was anchored in a hundred feet of clear water, the shoals of fish could be clearly seen turning lazily, grandfather always safely in the middle. Most of us had bought good sea-fishing gear at the US Navy's PX store in Key West. Our policeman bought one hook and some line at our canteen, begged one piece of bait from the galley, and in a two hour competition, won all the prizes, heaviest fish, most fish, heaviest catch. We caught the young fish who rashly darted out to investigate the offered food. Only the policeman knew how to persuade granddad that there was no hook in the bait.

Another policeman taught us a different lesson. Although junior sailors could buy a beer ration each day and the senior ratings had beer bars in their messes someone always wants more. There were signs that spirits were being smuggled aboard. But by whom and where were they hidden? Experienced officers should know their people and their ship well enough to answer those questions pretty quickly but for some days we were foxed. We questioned suspects and searched all the hiding places we could think of but found nothing. Key senior ratings hinted that discipline threatened to get out of hand but they probably exaggerated a bit because they enjoyed our puzzlement. Eventually the penny dropped. There was one place we hadn't looked, one person we had assumed to be above suspicion. Our Bahamian policeman was invited to open his suitcase. And there it was. Goodbye.

Policemen selling illicit liquor leave a bad impression but police duties, properly handled, can create goodwill. One of our Sub-Lieutenants showed how it should be done. Trevor was in charge of a boarding party taking an American fishing boat, arrested for poaching in Bahamian waters, into Nassau and was abused over the radio by the skipper's wife. A few weeks later the skipper brought his wife down to Key West one Sunday afternoon to show her that Trevor was a regular guy, 'just doing his job'. Being British, we gave them afternoon tea and a agreeable time was had by all, though there was an unpleasant postscript to the visit. The skipper named a rival fishing boat and hinted where and when we might find it poaching. Preoccupied with other tasks, we never used the information but weeks later we read in a local paper that fishermen had been killed in a gun battle between the rival boats. No wonder the skipper's wife had been tense when her husband was arrested, and charmed when she realised how gently the Brits did their policing.

Social life sometimes brought more potential headaches than our police work. We spent Christmas at Freeport on Grand Bahama Island where many people ensured that everyone enjoyed it as much as possible. I have particularly pleasant memories of the kindness of Jack Hayward and his family. Jack had become a public figure for his gifts to buy Lundy Island for the British National Trust and to bring the hulk of the SS Great Britain home from the Falklands for restoration. No problems there.

Then we had a break from Caribbean duties and visited New Orleans. I loved jazz until Dizzy Gillespie made it too complicated and was happy to spend my evenings at the Preservation Hall listening to the aged musicians who gave birth to jazz. It was an unprepossessing hall, rough wooden benches, entry only a dollar. By midnight the tourists with little interest in jazz had all gone. The remaining audience was appreciative and two or three hours of real jazz began.

The social problem was that three of our sailors and our Ghanaian Navy Midshipman were black. In one incident, a Leading Electrical Mechanic ordered three beers in a bar. One was for a young, well educated Radio Mechanic, a pleasant young man known to everyone as Coco. The bartender poured the beers, took the money and then intervened when one was passed to Coco. He was not allowed to drink in a 'white' bar. They contented themselves with telling him what he could do with his beer and left immediately. Good for them.

Midshipman Joe fared only a little better in the Wardroom. After a cocktail party one of the local belles invited 'all' the young officers to party at her house and was embarrassed when she realised that 'all' included Joe. I don't know how the party went but the girl told me a couple of days later what a strange experience it had been for her. As she said, if you have been brought up to believe that you will never, ever, meet a black person as a social equal, it is a bit difficult to make the necessary adjustment in one night. It would take a bit of getting used to. But at least she was willing to try. Good for her.

Those examples were from private situations. Things became more official towards the end of our visit. A dance was being arranged for the whole Ship's Company. Over the morning coffee our US Navy Liaison Officer had the difficult task of discretely telling our First Lieutenant that it would be better if he stopped our 'coloured' ratings going to the dance because it might cause embarrassment. The Liaison Officer was sent away to pass the word to the organisers that our black ratings could please themselves whether they went to the dance and that if any of the locals felt they might be embarrassed by their attendance they might wish to stay at home. I heard it was a good dance but the word had got out and none of our black sailors went. A pity, but at least they were free to choose for themselves.

There were other manifestations of inequality in the churches. I had been considering my beliefs for many years now and although I still attended church it did not help to see the segregation of black and white in the US and Caribbean churches. But far more important was recognition of the paradox of believing that an omnipotent, omnipresent and omniscient god could also be the Christians' 'loving god' and still tolerate man's inhumanity to man as demonstrated throughout history. A vengeful Old Testament god seemed equally unlikely. And it was obvious that many people attending Christian churches had never heard of the vicarious atonement, let alone considered whether they really believed it was a credible doctrine. And an increasing number of theologians now seemed to share my conclusion that a supernatural God didn't exist. I still recognised that many Christian churchgoers were very good people, but the time had come to declare myself, as I remain, an 'Honest to God' atheist.

Technically, those months in the West Indies were an interesting study in the terminal unreliability of aged equipment. Of the major systems only the boilers and steam turbines seemed immune. They had been 'over designed' in the pre-war tradition of British marine engineering and they lasted well. Not so my electrical equipment. The insulation readings of the main generators were below standard. The echo-sounder was reluctant to tell the Navigator when the depth of the water was changing rapidly from a thousand feet to forty, a matter of some importance to him. At least one of our seventy odd ventilation fan motors would burst into flames each week. It was a battle to keep Zest effective.

My department's equipment was the most sensitive to what by naval standards was extreme age, but we did not have a monopoly. At sea, early one Sunday morning, I pottered around the ship looking for trouble. One boiler was shut down so the unoccupied boiler room was an obvious place to check. As I climbed down into it I saw the most beautiful ray of sunlight shining in the bilge. A corroded plate had succumbed and the water flowing through the one inch hole was acting as an optical conduit for the sunshine.

Our Captain came in for his share of the problems of keeping an elderly ship in tip top condition. After we had been on station for several months the Admiral commanding the Home Fleet's small ships arrived and reproached him because our ship was not freshly painted. Fortunately, Graham was able to point out to the Admiral that during some weeks of minor crises which involved frequent races from one end of the Caribbean to the other, we had steamed further than his Flotilla, which had merely crossed the Atlantic. In due course, I'm glad to say, the boss got his fourth stripe, and later, his Flag.

Keeping Zest going was good experience and a perfect opportunity to consolidate my practical electronics skills but it was wearying. My successor joined in Bermuda as the ship returned to the UK, took over the department a few days later and I became a passenger. For the first time in my life I asked the doc for a sleeping pill. It was a disappointing experience. Sleep still eluded me. But it didn't matter, a few days later we were back in Devonport and I was meeting my six weeks old son, Peter. Lise had indeed been productive while I had been away. She had some support from Michael during the school holidays. He had been pleased at the idea of having a sibling after so long as an only child, and commented after being told of the pregnancy, 'I know all about it. We did "the female" last term'. But in addition to all the normal problems of pregnancy, at birth Peter had proved to be a 'breach' presentation and a caesarian operation was required with all the consequential weakness and longer recovery time. There was of course support from kind friends, particularly Issy, our friend from Faslane days, and Diana, the wife of Zest's Royal Marine officer. It's well known that naval wives can cope with anything, but that experience stretched Lise's close to its limit. I think she was glad to have me home.

Chapter 18

Training and Torpedoes

There's a sailors' song which begins:
'Oh I wonder, yes I wonder,
Did the Jaunty make a blunder,
When he made this draft chit out to me?'

A prosaic translation would be, 'Did the authorities get it right when they appointed me to my next job?' I had been appointed to the Flag Officer Sea Training's staff at Portland, the nearest thing the navy had to 'an elite', apart from the submarine service of course. The staff, many of them ready for promotion to higher ranks, contributed to the efficiency of all the Royal Navy's destroyers and frigates and some NATO navies' ships.

Why had I been appointed to this company? My card must have been marked during Zest's work-up as suitable for the training team. Although I had spent more years in ship appointments than many officers and felt well equipped to help ships with their organisational and human problems, I had been involved with submarine weaponry for ten of the previous thirteen years and knew nothing about the missiles and computerised information systems which had been introduced into the new surface ships. Should I challenge the appointment? Technical arguments suggested that I should. My organisational experience indicated that there was no reason to do so. As usual, I decided that 'they knew best'. It was the worst decision I ever made.

Lise and I were able to move into a naval flat after a couple of weeks in private accommodation. That was a big benefit because the pace of life on the staff was furious and wives had to organise homes, visits to boarding schools, etc, unaided.

The FOST Weapons and Electrical team's working day began in the office at seven. Those of us who were 'sea-riders' were briefed on any repairs which had been done overnight by the shore party, and exchanged information on the plans for the day. At seven thirty the staff boat took us out to our respective ships which then sailed for the exercise areas. The working day ended between seven PM and one AM the next day. On Saturday mornings we wrote our reports on the past week. Our first priority was to discover major weaknesses which required drastic action. Even Commanding Officers were subjected to critical examination of their strengths and weaknesses.

We were there to help ships become efficient in everything they did: basic organisation and administration, anti-surface ship and anti-submarine operations, air defence, refuelling at sea, helicopter operations, transfers between ships using jackstays, damage control, fire fighting, defence against nuclear and biological warfare, aid to civil powers ashore. The ships' teams had an ambivalent attitude to the sea-riders. Mostly they appreciated our help, but setting and monitoring exercises was the primary method of training and they knew that at any moment we might announce that a fire was raging somewhere in the ship or some similar tribulation. And the exercises could be very realistic. Connecting 440 volt emergency power cables, sometimes live, in a smoke filled compartment was a new experience for many. It concentrated minds wonderfully, ours no less than theirs.

Made deliberately exhausting so that everyone knew what exhaustion felt like, the exercises tested the sea-riders more severely than the crews of visiting ships. They only had to do one successful work up, we merely moved on to the next ship. Sleep became a desirable priority and occasionally, after completing our exercises in a ship which was not returning to harbour for several hours, we were winched out by a Wessex helicopter, grateful for a quick ride back to base. At other times a jackstay transfer to another ship offered an earlier return to harbour and home. Interesting ways to travel.

It soon became clear that although some of the officers in the ships were friends, opportunities to entertain them at home would be rare. I asked an experienced sea-rider how anyone found the time and energy for a social life. 'You don't', was his answer, 'In this job you'll be lucky if you can find the energy for a sex life'. Increasing familiarity with the exercises and the ships' systems helped but the job was never easy as my last day as a sea-rider showed.

In June 1968, on the recommendation of my Captain in Zest, I was promoted to Commander, a very happy event. Officers were usually reappointed soon after promotion but no replacement was available until November, so it was arranged that the other Lieutenant Commander WE and I would exchange jobs. David was a 'born and bred', surface ships electrical officer so there wasn't much I could teach him about the job. Nevertheless we arranged to spend one day at sea together in HMS Hampshire as part of the handover. By 1700 all the exercises in which we were directly involved had been completed but a major engine room exercise was about to begin so we went 'walk-about', looking for trouble. We visited the electrical switchboards. The electrical distribution system was broken down into sections so that damage in one area could not overload the whole system. Generators driven by steam-turbines, diesel engines and a gas-turbine were all on load. The electrical system appeared well prepared for anything that might happen.

The 'happening' was a sea-rider starting the exercise by shutting a steam valve on one of the boilers to simulate damage. An oil pump lubricating the massive gearing which connected one set of main turbines to its propeller shaft lost power. The gearing could not survive without continuous lubrication but an automatic electrical switch sensed the loss and switched on another pump. Unfortunately, one switch out of several hundred on the electrical switchboards was in the wrong position, and David and I hadn't noticed. Instead of supplying electricity to the alternative pump from a diesel or gas turbine driven generator, the switch tried to supply it from a steam driven generator which had already stopped. Oil pressure was lost. The marine engineering rules for that event were quite clear. The turbines had to be shut down even if it meant having the ship towed back to harbour. Big nausea.

The responsibilities for problems in ships working up were clearly defined. We did all we could to prevent accidents of any kind but the responsibility remained with the ship's team. So in theory, David and I were blameless. That fact neither prevented us kicking ourselves nor altered the old philosophy described in two of the better lines of the 'Laws of the Navy'. Apropos courts martial, the old wisdom ran:

'Tis well thou hast been acquitted,
Twere best thou hadst never been tried'.

It would undoubtedly have been better if we had spotted the switching error, alerted the ship's staff, and prevented the accident.

The shore support role was sometimes as strenuous as sea-riding. Two or three times a week, my team and I would be recalled because a ship was returning with a problem which had to be solved, if humanly possible, before the start of exercises the next day. Those recalls marked the last time my Yorkshire stubbornness resisted the stinginess of the Admiralty.

After my promotion Lise and I moved into a Commander's married quarter a few yards from our previous flat. It was a pleasant, almost new house, with four bedrooms instead of the three granted to a Lieutenant Commander, plus a study. And the designer had not repeated the mistake made in some of the older Commanders' quarters which were built without a serving hatch because someone thought Commanders' wives would have maids to serve the food. Fat chance.! The aberration this time was that the married quarters had no telephones. It sounds incredible from the perspective of life in Canberra in 1998 that any of us lived without a phone as late as 1968 but that's the way it was. Furthermore, the Admiralty would not pay for the installation of a telephone to facilitate the recall of officers. An answer I shared with other officers was simple, 'If they want me they can send a car for me'. And, at a cost much greater than that of installing a phone, they did. On one occasion the car recalling me overtook me on the Chesil Beach as I drove home and was waiting when I arrived.

In an interesting job it's best to put up with the annoyances for the sake of the rewards. And there were many. We did work-ups in the first of each of two new classes of Federal German Navy ships, the Bayern and the Koeln, and in the Royal Netherlands Navy's British built Leander Class frigates. We responded to a request from a US Navy destroyer for help with her gunnery computer. There was much to learn from all of them.

The German ships were particularly impressive in several features of their design. Their watertight doors, which were easily closed by a single handwheel, made our doors with eight user-unfriendly clips seem very clumsy. More importantly, whenever possible they converted electrical supplies to the various special voltages and frequencies for weapons and other equipments in the compartments where they were required. This was fundamentally different to the RN design practice of centralising converted supplies with a consequential risk of losing them all to a lucky enemy shot. Often, when the Germans ran an emergency 440 volts, 3 phase supply, they were back in business.

The Dutch gunnery system in the Netherlands Navy's Leander Class frigates used digital computation resulting in a compact, reliable system, which on the available evidence performed as well as our more complex 'Medium Range System 3'. Their system could be operated by a Petty Officer after half *an hour of training, ours required three operators and far more training. My boss, who had been associated with the design of MRS 3, didn't like it at all! There were teething troubles with the British designed gun turrets and it was interesting to see that the Netherlands Navy sent a Chief Petty Officer to Barrow to negotiate solutions with Vickers, the manufacturer. It was a good example for us in the RN. The best of our Chiefs were itching to be given more responsibility.*

My experience with the US destroyer combined amusement with sadness. She arrived about eleven PM and I decided to see the problem for myself. I couldn't have been more warmly received, 'Gee it's most kind of you Commander to come yourself, personally, in person'. The CO's refrain was echoed by the Executive Officer and the Gunnery Officer. They all followed the greeting by expressing their belief that if only the Assistant Gunnery Officer and his Chief Petty Officer were more motivated they would have the problem solved before morning. The young Ensign and the departmental Chief were a bit depressed when I met them. Pressure had been applied.

Their Mark 1 gunnery system mechanical computer comprised about a cubic yard of shafts, gears, integrators, cams, and other mechanical devices. Six gear wheel teeth had broken off and gone walk-about somewhere in the interior. An hour studying the excellent manual confirmed that even if a replacement section were immediately available it would take at least half a day to install it and make the necessary seventy two adjustments. There should be a sign on Senior Officers' desks' reminding them that 'Nothing is impossible to the person who doesn't have to do it'. It is easy for those who do not understand modern systems to make impossible demands on their staff. Patient application by competent practitioners is required, not wishful thinking by seniors with inadequate knowledge. The days of simply pulling harder on a rope are long gone. But I'm sure that didn't stop the American CO feeling disappointed by my visit.

On the family front, we needed an economical way of visiting Lise's home in Germany with eighteen month old Peter and fifteen year old Michael. The answer was to buy an elderly Volkswagen motor caravan and a tent for Michael to sleep in. We could cope with the cramped conditions quite happily. We enjoyed the ease with which we could park and be settled for a drink, a meal or sleep within minutes. It was the start of an affection for motor caravans which remains with us, but that was the last holiday as a family. The next year Michael paid his first solo visit to Germany. He camped in the orchard of a friend of Lise's whose son Herman, a little older than Michael and the owner of a small BMW, had lived with us for some weeks in Scotland and knew Michael quite well, So Michael not only had a friend with 'wheels' and local knowledge, but also the support of his very tolerant grandmother, Minna Honig, to whose house he could retreat when disaster struck his tent in bad weather. As far as we know he had an enjoyable introduction to life as an independent young adult.

In November 1968, I said goodbye to the FOST organisation and to the 'dyed in the wool' department head whose dislike of ex-ordnance engineers was widely known. He was intolerant of my lack of surface ship knowledge and I was lucky that he had been powerless to prevent my promotion. My successor, another ex-ordnance engineer, was not lucky and was not promoted. There have been many worse systems for reporting on staff than the one used by the Admiralty, but it was very susceptible to the idiosyncrasies of senior officers.

Taking up my next appointment at AUWE was like coming home. Although the Chief Scientist now presided over the establishment instead of a Captain Superintendent and there were other changes, the essence of the place had not altered. Most of my scientist friends were still there. Technically, it was a *different story. The challenges were much greater.* I took over the 'desk' responsible for the management of the submarine launched torpedoes which were already in service and for the introduction, when its development was completed, of the navy's first torpedo designed to attack nuclear submarines, the Mark 24. The in-service torpedoes were the 'bread and butter' job. The Torpedo Officers of submarines, the squadron staffs, and the civilians in the armament depots all had ideas for improvements but, however good the ideas, money to implement them was limited. Fortunately a well understood procedure allowed them all to contribute to decisions on how best to spend it.

Maurice, a Senior Draughtsman assisted me in the in-service task. He and his peers were some of the loyalest fellows you could ever meet. They had usually started as trade apprentices, been selected for better things in the drawing office, and twenty years on were very experienced para-professionals. But they had one fault. From the best of motives, they had become part of a civil service culture which had 'never making a mistake' as its highest ideal. Maurice would have felt he had let me down if any action of his had erred so he tended to refer everything to me for decision. My predecessors might never have been aware of the trait because for decades they had only one torpedo to worry about. Now we had three torpedoes in service and one, far more complex, to introduce. The leisurely days were over. The answer was obvious. Maurice was authorised to decide many matters relating to the in-service torpedoes and to sign them off on behalf of 'The Director General Weapons'. As far as I could tell, he loved it. Delegation had actually happened for once. I had more time for the new torpedo.

The development of the Mark 24 torpedo was a Pandora's Box of horrors. There was a suspicion that unwelcome evidence had been concealed by reporting development trials as successful if the objectives of the trials had been achieved, even though significant shortcomings in other aspects of the development had been revealed. And there was a lot of tension between the civilian project team and John, the Commander of a Torpedo Trials Unit which had been set up at Coulport on Loch Long to do the trials on which the torpedo would be accepted by the navy.

Within days of joining I was off to visit John at Coulport as part of a team led by the Chief Scientist and the Director of Underwater Weapons, a naval captain, John's boss and mine. The Chief Scientist was supported by the Head of the Heavy Torpedo Division and the Mark 24 Torpedo Project Leader. I never saw any paperwork for the visit but the objective was well understood. John said that the torpedo was nowhere near ready for acceptance trials. The project team said it was and they wanted the Chief Scientist to persuade the Director to sack John. The excursion led to the right conclusion, our Director resisted the civilians' pressure and experience proved that John was right. In fact, John's biggest problem was that his forecasts of doom were always right. He was sometimes very unpopular!

During the next few years the Mark 24 project and the Mark 31 air launched torpedo project came unravelled and they were swept up in the far reaching changes whose moment had come. The Rayner Report of April 1971 laid the basis for the establishment of the Defence Procurement Organisation. There were Parliamentary enquiries to establish what had gone wrong with the torpedo projects. A Torpedo Project Executive was appointed to manage the projects using techniques pioneered by the Dreadnought Project Executive and improved by the Polaris Project Executive. Finally the completion of development of the weapons was put out to contract, to Marconi in the case of the Mark 24. They were stirring times to be in the business.

It is easy to decide to contract development work out to industry and there are some advantages in doing so. The flexibility of the private sector was, and remains, its most important advantage. In his autobiography, 'Slide Rule', Nevil Shute particularly appreciated the willingness of commercial developers to abandon bad lines of development to avoid 'throwing good money after bad', whereas a government team was warned, 'We can't change our minds now. Public money has been spent'. Equally important, three decades later, was the way Marconi could expand a torpedo project team from one person to three hundred in eighteen months and disband most of it equally quickly when its task was done.

Many new management processes had to be explored, and problems solved, to reconcile commercial development with government accountability. How does a government remain an 'informed customer' without doing some in-house development? How do engineers get administrators and lawyers to recognise that it is impossible to write a perfect specification? How can governments and industries develop the mutual confidence which enables projects to proceed harmoniously and without recourse to law when problems arise? And how can governments be satisfied that contractors have met specified requirements? Performance and reliability are not easily demonstrated if the product is to sink nuclear submarines or something equally difficult. These remain perennial problems which still challenge us to find the best practical solutions. Taxpayers should beware of anyone who claims to have a perfect answer and of inexperienced executives who do not recognise the difficulties.

Much new technical ground had to be broken by the Mark 24 program. A tracking range on which the performance of firing submarines, torpedoes and their targets could be recorded and analysed was needed. The project for the development of a British Underwater Tracking and Evaluation Centre, BUTEC for short, was born. Analysis of the performance of practice versions of the Mark 24 torpedo would be virtually impossible without the assistance of the device which was now beginning to make its presence felt throughout the weapons field, the digital computer.

This is a good point at which to pay my tribute to my immediate boss of those days. There was no one else in the navy quite like him. Some of the stories may be apocryphal like the one about him meeting a young officer at the intersection of two of the paths between the buildings at the Admiralty's technical headquarters at Bath. They talked technicalities for twenty minutes, then Peter asked, 'Before you go, which direction did I come from?' 'That way, Sir'. 'Oh good, that means I've had lunch.' Apocryphal yes, but not far from the essence. As a Captain appointed as the Deputy Director of Underwater Weapons, Peter cared little for his administrative role. Instead, he became the driving force behind the development of the tracking range and the analysis centre.

He gave the work a degree of attention few could have matched. For example, when he found that the best available computer for analysis of torpedo exercises had inadequate memory for the task, he visited the computer designer to 'find out how it really works', so that he could get more out of it than the manufacturer promised to ordinary users. I calculated that at commercial rates his output of computer programs would have earned fifty seven thousand pounds in a year. A Captain's salary was less than a quarter of that.

I was well aware that I was a run of the mill officer already moving towards the 'managing engineer' role appropriate to those less gifted than Peter so I did some of the admin to let him get on with the work he loved. He disliked wasting time and had little interest in the commonplace small talk of social life. When he came to lunchtime drinks at our house one Sunday, he and his daughter and a son had, within minutes, broken away into an esoteric conversation which seemed to be about the torsional vibrations in Pratt and Whitney radial aircraft engines circa 1935.

A family dedicated to such cerebral stuff needs one member with both feet firmly on the ground. And that was of course Peter's wife, Ann, who supported him in many ways and in the course of looking after the family became wise in the ways of the young. Our son Michael was introducing Lise and I to the perturbations of teenage years. Thoroughly frustrated one day, I wandered along to Ann's house, told her my troubles and asked, 'When do sons become reasonable human beings?' After a moment of thought she replied, 'Judging by my lot, I can't hold out any hope before they're twenty three'. Experience has proved that to be pretty accurate, but parents of very young children do not find it a comforting thought!

One thing was quite sure, the AUWE work was a return to normality after the frenetic pace of Sea Training. There was time for recreation. Some activities were a matter of economic necessity like overhauling a very cheap old car, first for Lise to use and then to be given to Michael when he could drive. It was a worthy addition to the oddities we had owned over the years. This one was a Standard 10 which had no clutch pedal. The gear lever had a small switch on it which had to be depressed to disengage a solenoid operated clutch acting in series with a centrifugal clutch. The idea never became popular.

There was time to explore woodwork further. When we lived in Helensburgh we had been attracted to the beauty of the driftwood found during Sunday afternoon walks along the side of Loch Long, and had soon developed the techniques for improving on nature without seeming to have altered the wood. Then we lusted after an expensive coffee table with one natural 'sculptured' edge. I discovered that one of the old cabinet makers had large, interesting boards, set aside by his father twenty five years earlier, which would never warp again. I made our table for about twenty five pounds.

The table had been followed by carving a modern chess set of my own design and I was hooked. The main Weymouth project was a model Georgian house for a goddaughter. It remains at her parents' home waiting for another generation to play with it, one of the few surviving pieces of work from those days. That is the price paid for a wandering naval life and emigration.

Good things come to an end, sometimes a rude end. The Admiralty could never quite get its act together. The foolishness of moving officers every couple of years without good reason had been recognised. It was obviously better to leave me in my job at AUWE for three years than to move me earlier but I had already been in a Commander's quarter for some months before I joined AUWE. We therefore fell foul of the Admiralty rule which said that we could only occupy a married quarter for three years. Given that there were rarely enough quarters to meet the demand, it was a fair rule, but that was cold comfort when it meant leaving our home some months before my time in Weymouth was up.

Fortunately we knew that my next appointment would be in Bath. There were no quarters there but we were able to rent 'Church House' in Wellow, just outside Bath, from an officer serving overseas. Our Volkswagen campervan was put to good use. Outside the back gate of AUWE there was a little-used lane and the remains of some hard standing for wartime huts, a tap and a lavatory. I camped in the van during the week and drove home at the weekends. The saddest thought is that the allowances paid for separating from one's family and commuting weekly made all the difference between financial struggle and modest comfort. It remained so to the end of my time in the RN.

Chapter 19

Bottom-up Study Management

The Chief Scientist (Royal Navy) wanted to develop the most beneficial research program to be done prior to building a new class of submarines in the nineteen nineties. Should the limited resources be used to develop a more powerful nuclear reactor to increase the speed of the submarines? Or a new steel to allow them to go deeper? Or longer range detection systems? Or longer range weapons? And so on. Each expert advised that all the available money should be spent on his speciality. That was nothing new. What was new, was that CS(RN) wanted analytical study techniques to be applied, so that the funds could be allocated on a more rational basis than response to the lobbying of vested interests. In 1969 he set up a study, the biggest ever undertaken in the RN. More than twenty authorities were to identify the technological possibilities in each area, study how they might be applied in future submarine designs, cost them, and then assess their effectiveness in roles postulated by the experts on submarine operations.

Eighteen months later, all the questions asked at the beginning of the study had spawned new questions. The study was diverging. Management procedures to force the study to converge on useful answers had to be developed. I was appointed 'Program Manager' and a Constructor Officer, Chris, became the 'Technical Co-ordinator'. Based at the Admiralty offices at Foxhill in Bath, my job was to get the study finished on time, his to ensure compatibility between the 'Material' and 'Operational' sides of the study.

When given desks in a dusty store room, the message appeared to be that we were not welcome but we made a start and were soon given a reasonable office. An Assistant Program Manager and a clerical assistant were appointed to help us.

Chris was a delightful person to work with. That meant a lot because we were the most junior people in the study. We had to persuade scientists, constructors, engineers and operational analysts, all of them senior in rank and status to us, to do their bit and deliver on time despite their many other commitments and our lack of any authority over them.

Almost every scientist complained that science couldn't be done to a time scale. But we were not looking for new science. We knew that the experts could give us the projections we needed, but only they knew how quickly they could be produced. A naive approach brought results. 'When will you be able to give me the answers?' 'I can't possibly tell you that'. 'Well, I assume it won't be tomorrow?' 'Of course not'. 'But you could certainly do it within six months?' Reluctantly, 'Yes'. 'Right, then there's some point in between which you think is the most likely time. Tell me when that is'. It was tedious for both parties but persistence worked.

I devised suitably concise paperwork to define tasks and facilitate reporting to the top management, but the real work was persuading people to contribute their bit on time. Some authorities were in the London area, the rest mainly at Bath and Portland and there was a lot of travelling. Round and round we went. Our initial objective was to complete the study by the end of 1972, but a resource review proved that the study resources were inadequate and the timescale was extended by three months. Completion was defined as the delivery of an Executive Summary to the Chief Scientist so that he and his Admiralty Board colleagues could study them. We made it, just.

I travelled to London late one evening with a briefcase full of the highly classified and sensitive summaries which the Soviet Navy would have loved to see. Until Sub-Lieutenant Bingham sold classified NATO material the loyalty of naval officers was assumed to be absolute. We were simply the Queen's Navy and didn't even sign the Official Secrets Act. Although much had changed I was pleased it was still taken for granted that I would not copy the FGS Study Report and sell it to the Russians.

Interwoven with work on the study were a lot of changes in our personal affairs. We enjoyed living in Church House at Wellow. Although the kitchen arrangements were rudimentary, cold and often damp, the rest of the house was spacious and even a bit gracious. The gardens were full of apple trees and roses. As usual we brewed our own beer and Michael, now eighteen and living at home, turned the rose petals into some of the finest, light, dry wine we had ever tasted. Wellow was a sociable village, home to more artists, craft-workers and Admiralty civilians than agricultural workers, with a pub in which snuff boxes circulated every ten minutes. I enjoyed the snuff, which mitigated the effects of not smoking, until I read about the incidence of cancer of the nose and sinuses after long term use of snuff, and began to observe some of the village users more closely. The snuff box had to be relegated, like the cigar clipper, to an ornament.

We were really quite comfortable but stability, like perfection, is not to be found in this world. House prices were increasing at a rate far outstripping inflation. We heard sad reports of naval families who, having sold their houses when appointed overseas, returned to discover that they could not afford the deposit on another house. Sooner or later the navy would say goodbye to us and we would need a house. We had a good income but no savings, no 'expectations' and a mortgage to pay on my mother's bungalow. Something extraordinary was called for.

I took a day off and tramped around Bath from nine in the morning to four in the afternoon. By that time I had negotiated two mortgages to buy a house at Gurney Slade, one for ninety per cent of the cost, the other for ten. It was the best day's work I ever did for my family.

Gurney Slade, seventeen miles south of Bath, was still a working village devoted to quarrying and agriculture. The people had retained some of the best 'old fashioned' values and practices. For example, the builder said 'I loikes to look a man in the eye, agree a price, and stick to it', he didn't 'hold with' gazumphing, He was as good as his word, though when the house was finished and was already worth more than the eight and a quarter thousand pounds we were paying for it, he offered us a thousand pounds extra if we wanted to sell it back to him.

The house, the garden and starting life in the village gave us particular pleasure because they co-incided with our twentieth wedding anniversary. We had lovely neighbours, Lesley and Mike, in our house's twin. We could manage the mortgages. We had never had it so good.

The only question was, 'Were the locals friendly?'. They were obviously prepared to be, because Mike and I were asked to join the Gymkhana Committee. We recognised a test question and agreed instantly, leaving our ignorance of horses to be dealt with later. The first committee meeting was fun. The others were getting stuck into the nitty gritty detail straight away but we asked if they would first tell us their objective in having a gymkhana. They hadn't thought about it. They had always had a gymkhana. We suggested three possible objectives: equine sports for the horsey, a fete for all the village, or to raise funds for the church roof. The answer was 'A bit of all three'. Mike, an insurance company executive, asked, 'In that case, how much money do you want to make for the church roof?' More thought. 'A bit more than last year'. We enjoyed teasing them but the questions provided the basis for some improvements. One of the little side-show games they 'always had' was capable, flat out, of raising about sixty pence an hour. It was dropped.

Given my lack of horse sense, I was put in charge of the 'Clear Round' ring on the day. That was a brilliant money maker. Young riders could win rosettes merely by completing a simple circuit of low jumps without any faults. It cost the parents of some determined but inferior riders a small fortune before the cherished prize was achieved. Some children were not content unless they had more rosettes than their friends. And each rosette cost a small fraction of the entry fee. Brilliant.

We had never before lived a real village life and it was great. There were two pubs, one on the main road to Bristol for passers by, and one, sometimes referred to as the 'Town Hall', tucked away down a lane. For the first time, a pub became part of our life. If anything needed fixing, like a dry stone retaining wall washed away by a storm, the 'Town Hall' was the place to find out who fixed what. Lise was even happy to go there on her own, a rare compliment. One of us would often stroll down there around half past nine in the evening while the other kept an ear open for Peter, then four or five years old. In a village like that we could not merely be consumers. Lise was soon helping with the playgroup which Peter attended and subsequently assisted at the school when he moved there.

Many fond memories remain, some of lessons learned. Never have a teenage son and an off-white carpet, never dig too deep even in about eight feet of fine soil, lest strange, ghostly white weeds emerge from long hibernation. Never be afraid of putting oneself in debt to others by accepting help. The locals offered all sorts of help and we accepted the lot, the loan of a special tool to do a job, advice about the garden, a supply of pea sticks. There are always ways of repaying kindness.

Michael was less pleased with Gurney Slade life. He hoped to find work in Bath but also felt that the seventeen mile separation from friends now living there was ruining his social life. He plucked up courage to suggest to Lise that he should move in with Bill and Harry in their flat in Bath. Parents rarely make much of an impression on teenage sons but we think Lise scored that day. Michael, expecting several reasons why he should not leave the nest, was told, 'What a good idea, we'll help you pack'. There was more to the response than he knew. We knew we would only be able to remain in the house for sixteen months. I was to be appointed to a job in Malta, accompanied by Lise and Peter. Michael, now eighteen, would not be allowed to work there and had to stay behind. We hoped that living with friends in Bath for a few months before we left would smooth his introduction to the next phase of his life.

For our part we could not have been more pleased. My mother was settled in Weymouth. Her anti-social nature made her likely to refuse help which her neighbours and our friends Bill and Marjorie would have been happy to supply but we just had to say that was her problem not ours. The timing was excellent from Peter's point of view, he was still young enough to be moved without problems. The only pity was that we could not get sufficient rent for the house to balance the books. It had to be sold but that didn't matter too much. After sixteen months the house was worth nearly twice as much as we paid for it, the escalation of house prices was slowing, and we had the makings of a stake.

We had open house at the Town Hall to say goodbye to all the kind people who had welcomed us to their community. It was a bit sad, not least because there was at least one person whose intense Somerset accent we had not been able to understand completely in all the times we had enjoyed his company.

Chapter 20

Plans and Administration in Malta

When you arrive in a strange place at midnight there is nothing better than a welcome from a friend. Michael, the eldest son of our Faslane neighbours, now a Lieutenant serving as the Admiral's Assistant Secretary, met us and took us to his flat for a nightcap before delivering us to our hotel. The drink was welcome, his anecdote less so. His flat had, he told us. like many others, a large cockroach population until a few days earlier. He had been puzzled by their sudden absence until he discovered that a scorpion had moved in. Welcome to Malta.

Malta: just over three hundred square kilometres of limestone forming the two main islands of Malta and Gozo, inhabited since ancient times, cleared of venomous snakes by Saint Paul when he was shipwrecked there, given to the Knights of Saint John of Jerusalem in 1530, invested by Sulieman the Magnificent in the Great Siege of 1565, invaded by Napoleon in 1798, rescued by Nelson, and confirmed British in 1814 by ' ...the Love of the Maltese and the Voice of Europe.' Awarded the George Cross in April 1942 for heroism during World War 2. Independent since 1964, Malta was a constitutional monarchy within the Commonwealth with a population of about 340,000 when Lise, Peter and I arrived in August 1973.

Lise and I were there because a rift had developed in 1971 between the British government and Malta's temperamental Prime Minister, Dom Mintoff. He wanted more money for the facilities used by the British, the UK did not wish to pay. Tensions increased and the dependents of the servicemen in Malta were hastily ordered back to Britain.

The British services were in Malta as part of the North Atlantic Treaty Organisation. NATO relied on the availability of port, airfield, communications and logistic facilities in Malta. A

Royal Marine Commando Group was stationed there to reinforce NATO's southern flank if the need arose. It would take years to replace those facilities by others in a more stable polity. Furthermore it was vital that Mintoff should not evict the British Services from Malta and then attempt to recoup the consequential financial losses by inviting the Warsaw Pact countries in. There was quite enough Russian activity in the Mediterranean to keep NATO surveillance forces busy without giving them a base right in the middle of the Med from which to operate.

Many Maltese were displeased when the rift threatened the continued presence of the British. Their reasons ranged from the business interests of the bar and brothel keepers, through the desire of Maltese society hostesses to have British naval officers at their parties, to the recognition by hard nosed Maltese government economists that the British services provided about a third of the government's annual income and employed over 2,000 Maltese civilians and naval ratings. The RAF operated the island's civil airport and air traffic control system. Many Maltese people just simply liked the British. Others recognised that the alternative to renting facilities to the British would be increased income tax, anathema to most Maltese.

It made good sense when an 'Agreement with respect to the Use of Military Facilities in Malta' was signed by Dom Mintoff and Lord Carrington on the 26 March 1972. The facilities were extensive. Over 2,400 acres of lands and buildings included the Admiral's headquarters at Lascaris, facilities for the navy and the RM Commando, communication stations, a power station, stores depots and fuel installations, Admiralty police facilities, and all the infrastructure required by the dependents: quarters, schools, medical and dental clinics, a hospital, even a beach facility.

Problems began to occur soon after the signing of the Agreement. The Service units began to settle in as though they were going to be in Malta for another hundred and seventy years. Not only did they want to replace equipment which had been hastily removed for withdrawal but they wanted it improved. Every unit had ideas which could have absorbed all the money available for maintenance and improvements. Other problems involved the British Services' rights to land and property. Under the Agreement these rights were based on the customary Deposited Plans drawn up by those good friends of engineers, the surveyors. Unfortunately, such plans are two-dimensional and Malta's soft limestone had been tunnelled over centuries of war and peace into a three dimensional problem. Who had the right to control access to tunnels which started outside Service properties and then went underneath them? A good question, especially if the tunnels passed close to sensitive communications or similar facilities.

There were many other kinds of problems. The navy was to administer the army units and the Royal Marine Commando Group. The latter task might seem routine given the long association of the 'Royals' and the navy, but in fact the Commando Groups had only ever been administered by the army or their own RM command, and some believed they had often played both ends against the middle to get their own way. To say the least, the marines and the army units had their own ideas about how things should be done and didn't always like the navy's ways..

The man facing these problems was the Rear Admiral responsible as Flag Officer, Malta for the naval facilities and associated civilian support, and as Commander British Forces, Malta for co-ordination with the Air Commodore commanding the RAF units to ensure a united front in their relations with the British High Commission and the Maltese Government. The only Commander on the Admiral's staff at his Lascaris headquarters, the Staff Officer Operations, was fully committed and could not cope with the new problems. Extra help was needed, someone who could become an absorbent filling in the multilayered sandwich: Admiral / naval, RM and army units / the RAF / the British High Commission / the Maltese Government. A diplomatic operator with brilliant liaison and planning skills was obviously needed.. None was available. The Admiral got a thick skinned Yorkshire-born engineer instead.

There was no married quarter available for Lise and I but we were not worried by that. Although we had invested most of the proceeds of the sale of our Gurney Slade house, we were determined to enjoy to the full what would almost certainly be our only overseas job together. The allowances for service in Malta helped and we were soon installed in the Villa Camasen at Tal Ibbrag at the eastern end of the Madliena ridge. It was a rich Brit's holiday home but his family now disliked going to 'the same old place' every holiday. He would have liked to sell it but not while prices were depressed by the tension between Britain and Malta. As the estate agents would say, the spacious hall led to equally spacious drawing and dining rooms with marble floors throughout and Casa Pupo rugs scattered here and there. A marble staircase led to three air-conditioned bedrooms and two large bathrooms, one en suite with the master bedroom, both with sunken baths.

We had a view of the sea beyond the Royal Marines' St Andrews Barracks at the back of the house. At the front there was a view across a valley of terraced fields, the nearest of which was sometimes used to grow night-scented stocks. A few yards away was a swimming pool shared with three other British families from nearby houses, two retired couples and a civilian meteorological officer accompanied by his wife and six year old daughter and visited by their two older daughters during their boarding school holidays. We had facilities, we made friends, seven year old Peter even had a ready made girl friend. Things were getting better all the time.

It was the first time I had had an appointment completely divorced from engineering. The work was challenging and *fascinating, the more so because it was different to anything I had done before. One of my earliest tasks illustrates the point. Anyone who has read accounts of naval life between the two World Wars will know how important a part polo played in the life of the rising naval officer, especially in Malta. Shortly before I arrived, Lord Louis Mountbatten had visited Malta and told the Admiral, 'You must get polo going again quickly'. The idea was absurd but Rear Admiral's do not wish to jeopardise further preferment by neglecting the wishes of great and powerful men. A delicate draft was needed. I cannot remember the exact words of the letter which the Admiral sent to the Ministry of Defence. No matter. Nothing more was heard about polo.*

It was downhill after that, even when faced with the classic question by the Surgeon Captain in charge of the Naval Hospital and its Maternity Unit, 'How can you put a price on a baby's life?' He had been seeking funding for new accommodation about a hundred yards nearer to the Maternity Unit so that the Registrar would not arrive breathless. I remember that answer clearly: 'I've no idea, sir, but it's something every administration has to do arbitrarily when it decides whether to spend 'x' pounds or 'y' pounds on hospital facilities'.

The easiest of all was refusing the Colonel of the Commando Unit a substantial sum to build a wall to improve the security of the barracks complex, even though he had won the support of the Superintendent of our Admiralty Police Force. I didn't control the funds the units were seeking, I was there to recommend approval or rejection to the Admiral, and when I rejected proposals the officers in charge of units often exercised their right of appeal to the Admiral. Fortunately, he and I shared the view that the 1979 withdrawal was 'practically tomorrow' so serious investment in long term works was not justified, and he usually agreed my reasoning and conclusions. He certainly did in the Commando case.

There were hundreds of cases like that and I was privileged to gain more insights into the work of other professions. For instance, in one school the arrival of a new Head Teacher would be followed by a request for the removal of an internal wall to establish a big hall. In another school, the request might be to partition an existing hall to provide two classrooms. I had to learn that there might be valid reasons for both proposals. Sometimes it merely meant that the new Heads and their staffs had worked out different ways of doing things. Fortunately, the gentle Malta stone and the skill of the Maltese masons on our Property Services Agency staff made both proposals affordable.

We had to ensure there were no breaches of the Agreement by our personnel or their dependents. Most of them were pleased to be in Malta and it was rarely difficult to explain to them why they must conform. The only difficult case involved the wife of an army officer. The Agreement prohibited 'dependents' working in Malta and she was certainly a dependent for the purposes of the Agreement. Nevertheless, she pressed her case that she must work to maintain her skills as a doctor. I don't think she liked the rather unorthodox solution: unpaid work at the Maltese Government hospital. The hospital's management did not complain about a breach of the Agreement.

Preventing breaches of the Agreement by the Maltese sometimes called for a theatrical approach. The Chinese were going to construct a dry dock for 200,000 ton ships as an aid project and the Maltese were responsible for excavating the great recess in the rock. Fuel pipelines to our nearby berthing facility ran close to the site and some of our sports pitches were alongside it, albeit separated a vertical rock face some tens of feet high. In their characteristic enthusiasm for explosions well known to every visitor to Malta at Festa time, the Maltese were using such large blasting charges that they threatened to shatter our pipelines. The first countermeasure was a deliberate 'pompous British' showpiece. I was driven to the site to warn the

Maltese supervisor of the blasting that, *'If the blasting damages the pipelines we will hold you personally responsible for a breach of the Agreement between our respective countries.'* Then quickly back to the office for the telephone call from the British High Commission, *'We've had the Minister on the line .. ..'.* Lines of communication in Malta are short.

In such situations, however strong the position in law, it's better to find a practical solution which makes angry confrontations unnecessary. Especially so in the political climate of Malta at that time. Being *'in the right'* would not have been much use if a dissatisfied Minister for Buildings and Works complained to his Prime Minister. Mintoff's usual response was to telephone ministers in London. Not surprisingly, they expected us to find local solutions to what were to them *'storms in a teacup'*. Fortunately, there was a good solution to the blasting problem. One of our Property Services Agency experts was a civil engineer experienced in blasting techniques. David realised the Maltese were using excessively large charges, and after discussions they adopted new practices which reduced their blasting costs by a third. What a pity the expression *'Win-win'* would not be coined for another fifteen years or so.

The Admiral always took a strong line on the maintenance of our rights under the Agreement, sometimes to the puzzlement of the High Commissioner and his staff. They often seemed to believe that nothing was sufficiently important to risk *'rocking the boat'* because the outcome of some greater issue might be prejudiced. As far as we were concerned there was no greater issue. Certainly there were no long term naval and military issues: 1979 would be the end. In the Admiral's view nothing should prevent us insisting emphatically that the Maltese kept their part of the bargain to the letter. Sometimes this puzzled the High Commissioner. Early one Saturday morning, as I joined the staff in his office to brief him before we went to see the Minister about some problem, he went so far as to ask, rather wearily,

'What's the Admiral up to?' I hope he didn't expect a reply. Tired of naval intransigence or not, he made life easy for me. 'When we meet the Minister, I'll do a brief introduction, you take over and do all the rest unless it turns 'political', in which case I'll take over'. Couldn't ask for more than that.

During the over-enthusiastic blasting, rocks big enough to kill were hurled up onto our sports pitches high above the dock site. Our Sports Officer, being a thoroughly nice Brit, agreed with the Maltese blasting controllers that they would sound a siren in time to allow the pitches to be cleared before detonation. Admirals can be nice, but they are not always so, and ours went through the roof when he heard about this arrangement. My next tasks were to tell the Sports Officer what he had done wrong and that sports were to continue without hindrance, and to remind the Maltese authorities that we could use our facilities 24 hours a day if we wished, that they must therefore do their blasting when we were not playing games, and that they must clear up any fall-out from their operations. It was not the sort of tough line the High Commission liked to support. Fortunately, the improved blasting operations adopted to safeguard the fuel lines didn't throw rocks onto our playing fields and that problem was solved.

Planning the naval, Royal Marine and army aspects of the 1979 withdrawal was a great pleasure. The final date was fixed, 31 March 1979. The only other requirement was in the Agreement: '.......and the discharge of such (Maltese civilian and naval) personnel shall be in accordance with arrangements agreed between the Government of Malta and the Government of the United Kingdom'. Opportunities to start such an interesting task with a clean sheet of paper, a clear objective, and so few constraints are rare.

The 'arrangements agreed between the governments' had already been settled. The run-down of Maltese personnel would occur over the last two years of the Agreement. The officials in London and Valetta who agreed it forgot to specify whether the run-down should be spread evenly over those two years but there was little defence against the reasonable Maltese view that dismissals should be evenly spread and after a bit of quibbling the point was conceded. With that settled I could start work.

The key to the planning was our dependence on local staff for almost everything. The Maltese staff accounted, buttled, cooked, cleaned, clerked, concreted, drove, dug, gardened and much more. There were few letters of the alphabet which did not provide an initial for their activities. It soon became clear that an evenly spread run-down could only be achieved by sending home most of the Commando Group and their families during April 1977. That released enough Maltese staff to provide the flexibility needed to fit in all the rest, finishing with the ceremonial departure of the Admiral, accompanied by some of his staff and safeguarded by the Internal Security Company of Royal Marines, on the last day. Having been exposed by Michael to much Monty Python, I called the draft 'Feasey's Big Red Plan'. After clearance by the Admiral, it was sent to the Ministry of Defence in London. Then the trouble started. The ministry realised that someone had blundered. The 'rent' for the facilities, paid by Britain on behalf of NATO, was 14 million pounds from the first full year of the Agreement to the last. It was now being pointed out that the facilities they were getting for the money would reduce to virtually nothing during the last two years because of the dependence on Maltese labour. The MOD was not amused, NATO was not amused. The messenger was not popular.

Reconsider was the order. Variations on the plan were drafted. Each was rejected. That was not surprising because apart from that financial problem the first plan was the optimum one. The matter was still not resolved when I left Malta at the end of 1995. Two years later Lise and I returned to the island for a holiday. My successor in the appointment told me that Plan 8 had been approved. It was, he said apologetically, Plan 1 with cosmetic alterations and a new cover. He was later awarded the

OBE for his efforts. As a well known Australian is reputed to have said, ' Such is life'.

There was much else to make this the most diverse appointment of my 31 years in the RN. Military services often take a leading role if their nationals have to be evacuated in the event of civil disturbances. Contingency plans are prepared and updated whenever necessary as the political circumstances or the available resources change. Malta was well placed to play a part in the plans for many Mediterranean and African countries.

One of the plans was implemented when Turkish troops invaded Cyprus but our role was minimal, until, that is, the Commando Group was ordered to Cyprus to help keep the uneasy peace. With the exception of an internal security company, the group had been away in Canada for two months doing cold climate training. They were now returning in their Commando Carrier, HMS Hermes, and were about 24 hours away from being reunited with their families in Malta when they received their orders. The ship would close the island for some essential helicopter transfers and would then proceed to Cyprus.

When plans become operations, planners must take a back seat. This was the Staff Officer Operations' moment. Ideally, there would be little to do once orders for the operation have been given. In practice there are always problems. A sick Commando is best landed for hospital treatment. A US marine officer attached to the Commando for training must be sent ashore for diplomatic reasons, however much he would like to join in the operation. SOO had his moment while I hung around to learn how things went. Perhaps the most important feedback was that although morale plummeted when the marines learned that they wouldn't be at home with their families that night, it climbed to a higher level than before as Malta slipped below the horizon and the prospect of action lay ahead.

Once we had to do an unusual plan at short notice. After the price of oil rose dramatically in 1974, the Maltese government tried to find some cheap fuel somewhere. While they were shopping around stocks ran down and around noon one day we learned that the island's buses would stop the next day. Once again we were reminded of our vulnerability. Many British personnel and virtually all the Maltese staff used buses to get to work. SOO and I, with the help of the Intelligence Officer, had to decide priorities for staffing operational and logistic facilities, mobilise our transport resources, and develop a plan for getting essential people to work.

I learned new lessons every day in Malta. That day was no exception. At about half past six in the evening the Intelligence Officer suggested we stop work. He got a very hard look from his boss, the Staff Officer Operations. Then he told us he had had a tip that a tanker might arrive sometime 'in the next few days', and having just looked out of the window, he had seen one steaming up the harbour. We never had to use that plan. And we were reminded to lift our heads from the weather forecast occasionally to look out of the window to see if it is raining. It might be asked 'Why didn't the SOI tell us about the tanker tip earlier? There are two reasons. The tip might have been wrong. Wrong tips are not good for IOs careers. The second reason was more subtle. Even if the tip was basically correct, the Maltese sense of time often differed from ours.

The classic example is probably apocryphal but it illustrates the point. A British professor visiting the Royal University of Malta asked his Maltese colleague if there was a Maltese word conveying the concept of 'manana'. 'We have several' was the answer, 'but, frankly, none of them conveys the same sense of urgency'. My experience was not exactly like the professor's but there was an elasticity which made planning difficult. When the Maltese staff had completed some important piece of work on our facilities, I would arrange for the Admiral to visit the site, inspect the work and commend the workers. But when would the work be complete? 'Next week, Senhur' was the usual answer. I soon learned that it meant, 'Sometime in the next few weeks' and that I must inspect the work myself before putting a visit in the boss's program.

The tasks and experiences which came my way could hardly have been more varied. I flew in a Nimrod maritime patrol aircraft, enjoyable even though the crew were not very forthcoming about their equipment and techniques until I volunteered to cook the steaks for our lunch. My technical knowledge was only used once. A torpedo had been reported floating to the south of the island. It was a threat to fishing boats and the Maltese authorities asked us to remove it. The RAF Search and Rescue Unit were ready and willing provided someone could assure them that it wouldn't go bang. I was the obvious choice.

The weather was foul and, as I had learned at Dartmouth, seagoing in small craft is different. It was an 'interesting' ride. The crew were accustomed to braving very bad weather in their small but powerful launch. I had been behind desks for years. There might have been some surreptitious gloating if the RN rep had succumbed to seasickness while they gave every appearance of enjoying being bounced about. We shall never know. I survived without sickness. The torpedo was a practice version and there was no security issue involved but it could easily have damaged a boat. We improvised a way of towing it to a buoy in the harbour and, with difficulty, secured it there to await calmer conditions. Not well enough it seems. The storm continued and it was gone the next day.

I even had an experience as a film censor. We had the right to show any films we liked in the Services' cinemas, but some of films available to us were banned by the Roman Catholic Church in Malta and some Maltese staff had access to our cinemas. If the Church or the politicians wanted to stir up trouble, they might accuse us of importing corruption. Discretion was always appropriate but when the film 'The Clockwork Orange' arrived the Admiral became particularly concerned. I knew the book was quite frightening in its portrayal of possible events but it was definitely a 'serious' book. I had not seen the film. The Admiral would have liked to return the film to the UK without allowing it to be screened but he was made aware that banning the film would be a very unpopular, and in many opinions unjustifiable, decision. So, before deciding, he sent me to review the film, accompanied by a WRNS officer and the Intelligence Officer.

Nine o'clock Monday morning, three of us in a cinema with a choice of three hundred seats. A couple of hours later, a disappointed Admiral. We were unanimous that although the film was 'strong stuff', and some people might wish they had not gone to see it, it was neither immoral nor pornographic and should be shown. When the others had left, the Admiral pounded my ear. I had obviously failed to give a strong moral lead to the others. As he saw it, society had to make a stand against the sort of behaviour portrayed in the film. 'That's exactly what Anthony Burgess thought', I responded. 'Who's he?' Then I had my revenge for the ear pounding. 'He wrote a book warning us of the problem', I said. 'He called it "The Clockwork Orange". They made it into a film'.

Lise and I enjoyed the most active social life we had ever led. We were lucky enough to share in a number of interwoven social circles: the diplomatic circuit, the Services, Maltese society, the business circle, the civil aviation circle, the British settlers. Two or three cocktail parties a night followed by a dinner was not unusual. We gave the usual Sunday lunchtime parties when ships visited Malta and thanks to the splendid work of the Lascaris mess staff, whom we could engage for special occasions, we gave pool parties, usually for sixty to seventy people.

It was so unlike our usual existence. Lise actually confessed to feeling a bit guilty at times. She became close friends with the wives of the deputies to the British High Commissioner and the

American Ambassador. On Monday mornings they played Mah Jong, usually at their well staffed residences while, back at the Villa Camasen, our maid cleaned the house and did the washing. At other times we had the pleasure of meeting people far removed from our usual circle. John Wayne's son Patrick rented one of the houses next to the pool while in Malta with his wife and two children to make the film 'Sinbad and the Eye of the Tiger'. They came to our parties, we learned how exhausting film making can be, and I taught the children to carve the soft Maltese stone. Frankie Howard and his friends lived nearby when in Malta but theirs appeared to be a lonely life.

Family and friends benefited from our social life. We received news of Michael's intention to marry a girl called Ros. Instead of returning to UK for their low key wedding, we treated them to a honeymoon holiday in Malta at Christmas in 1973. We loved Ros at first sight and they were acknowledged by our friends to be a very handsome young couple at all the parties. We invited Caroline, a newly arrived Third Officer WRNS to stay with us and that was the start of another friendship. It was a splendid Christmas, repeated the following year when Michael and Ros returned with their young son, James. We were grandparents at forty four.

During the second visit one young bachelor Lieutenant serving in a visiting ship under Mike, a mischievous friend of ours, thought he was in like the proverbial Flynn when his boss asked him to show Michael and Ros around the ship, because, as Mike whispered to Ros when they were leaving to begin the tour, 'He thinks Michael is your brother'. The tour was completed with the wedding ring firmly behind Ros' back. Only when we were all having a drink in the Wardroom afterwards did the conversation reveal that although I was called Dad by Ros, I wasn't her father. Perhaps young officers should expect such tricks when their engineer boss has a doctorate in applied psychology.

The social life provided some beneficial shock treatment for my oldest friend, Clive, a contemporary of high school days, separated for several years and working hard to bring up his son while coping with his work as a chemistry lecturer. The contrast between our lifestyle and his own was sufficient to kick-start his social life when he returned to the UK. After all, why should the Feasey's have all the fun. Not that parties were fun for everyone. Clive witnessed one of the last examples of the old school's ways of doing things. The Matron of the naval hospital was leaving and gave the usual drinks party for about a hundred people, many of whom heard the public reprimand she gave to a young Surgeon Lieutenant who came without a tie. That party wasn't much fun for him.

Not all visits had happy outcomes. We were delighted to be visited by a Weymouth dentist friend, Ian, convalescing after a serious operation, and his wife Pam, though very sad that he succumbed to a brain tumour after a second operation only a few years later. Another visitor during our time in Malta was Raymond and his second wife, Florence. Raymond was his usual self, living in open-handed style and being good company until he ran out of money. For old times sake we were happy to lend him some while they were in Malta but it became clear after their return to UK that he was capable not only of living above his income but, given the chance, living above ours. Stern measures were called for and we never saw him again.

We would not have wished an intense social life to last for ever. Quite the opposite. There seems nothing so awful as a lifelong exposure to diplomatic cocktail parties. But with the variety we had, it was great fun while it lasted. And it amused us how envious the Admiral was of our pool, a feature his otherwise very desirable residence, the Villa Portelli with its staff of twenty eight, lacked. The lack of a pool meant denied him personal experience of one of the most unusual and in its way saddest incidents to occur while we were in the island.

Fresh water was very scarce. The average annual rainfall of about twelve inches just met most needs but in 1974 the rainfall fell short of the average. Importing water in tankers was expensive and someone had a bright idea which the Prime Minister approved. All the fresh water in the swimming pools would be collected and used for irrigation. Swimming pool owners, who were mainly British, would be given sea water instead. Why sad? Because some of the Maltese workers dumped the fresh water from our pools into the sea before filling their tanks with salt water. Either no one had told them where to deliver the fresh water or the supervision was so lax that lazy workers beat the system. And in the long term there was worse to come.

It was Mintoff's policy to encourage tourism and as might be expected the largest swimming pools were those at the hotels. Tourists always use lots of fresh water, but never more than when they swim in salt water pools several times a day and shower with fresh water after each swim. To keep up with demand, the extraction rate from the aquifer below the island was increased, the sea water followed the fresh through the porous rock, and the salinity of the available water increased. It was unpleasant when we left Malta in 1975 and when we returned in 1977 we learned that the island was now dependent on desalination plants for its fresh water, and the economy now depended on tourists bringing in enough money to pay their fuel bill. Had Mintoff not disliked the British so much, he could have invited more British retirees to live in Malta, bringing in specified amounts of money each year, using less water and other resources, and providing employment for domestic staff and service industries all the year round. It would have been a better option than seasonal tourists dependent upon cheap air travel.

There were many things to do other than parties. One of the most interesting was to join the Maltese Geographical Society's monthly walks which explored all parts of the island and whose members were only too willing to share their expert knowledge of Malta's history, flora and geology with us. One contact led to a particularly interesting experience. Most of Malta is covered with thin soil on soft globigerina limestone but in a few areas a hard corraline limestone layer is exposed and there are pairs of ruts in its surface, sometimes a foot deep. They are generally described in the textbooks and spoken of locally as 'the cart ruts or tracks' and it is believed that they are very ancient. Von Danniken speculated that they might have been made by the landing gear of alien craft.

A retired US ambassador living in Malta invited me to help him with an experiment which supported a more down to earth explanation. During walks, he had found many pieces of hard limestone about the size of a large man's hand. They were always cut, or perhaps worn, to the same angles at one end. He hypothesized that they were stone runners for wheel-less carts. The angles of those stones, measurements of the ruts and the stature of typical Maltese people suggested the proportions for a cart that could be made of poles lashed together, with the stone runners bound to vertical bearers supporting a load platform, and drawn by two men pushing against a cross bar at the front..

A cart was constructed and one Sunday morning a couple of stocky young Maltese men pulled their equally stocky sister along many of the cart ruts near Naxxar Gap. The remarkable discovery was not that it was possible to pull the cart along, but the ease with which it tolerated the unevenness of the tracks. Such carts would undoubtedly have been a practical proposition for transporting loads much heavier than a man could carry. One cargo was probably salt from the evaporation pits near the sea being taken to the inland villages. Once alerted to the shape of the stone runners I discovered more of them scattered about the countryside. Other researchers are said to have done similar experiments. But there is nothing like seeing for oneself.

Life on the staff in Malta was generally harmonious but one incident left a sour memory. The President of the Admiral's staff mess is normally the senior Commander at the headquarters, regardless of specialisation. In that way it differs from the Presidency of the Wardroom mess of a ship, which is always the Executive Officer, regardless of seniority. When I joined, although I was the senior Commander, the Admiral asked me to forgo the privilege in order to concentrate on my other exacting tasks. I agreed to postpone taking over the Presidency for six months but the Admiral later claimed that no set time had been agreed and refused to allow me to take over the presidency. Once again I had been too easily persuaded to do as I was asked and I have little doubt that the Admiral's reason was his personal belief that only seaman officers should take such roles. It may have been one of the last examples of discrimination against engineers which was supposed to have ended with the introduction of the General List concept in 1956.

It was now 1974, but Admirals get reappointed like everyone else and I served the next Admiral as President of the Staff Mess, a congenial conglomerate of eight naval, three WRNS, one Army and one RAF officer, and about 35 Admiralty and MOD civilians. It was a great pleasure, even on occasions such as the Ladies Night dinner to mark the departure of a WRNS officer who, having enjoyed her time in Malta to the utmost, finished her farewell speech with the time honoured words, 'Thank you for having me!'.

In Malta it seemed entirely natural to put a lot of effort into fancy dress parties. Everyone enjoyed those few moments at the beginning when friends were trying to work out who was hidden behind a particular disguise. In our small community we knew one another very well and really effective disguises had to be developed. Lise had to conceal her blond hair and I my grey beard, otherwise it would have been too easy for friends to recognise us. Lise became a 'black mammy' with the traditional bandana over her hair and I turned into a black bearded Indian with a thousand carat diamond in my turban. As we drove slowly to the party overtaking motorists nearly crashed slowed down to get a better view of us. There were no black people in Malta at the time.

Had there been any prizes for the most puzzling fancy dress, I would have awarded one to the Instructor Captain who ran our schools and his wife. At a St Valentine's Day Massacre party, the most convincing 'hood' arrived, wearing a tuxedo, carrying the customary violin case, and accompanied by his glamorous blonde moll, 'Gloria'. I welcomed them to the mess trying to work out who they were. Fortunately I didn't get familiar with 'Gloria'. His wife, the hood, might not have liked it.

Towards the end of our time, we experienced Malta's transition from monarchy to republic. I have no idea why Mintoff chose that particular time to make the break but it was remarkably easy to achieve. The Constitution of Malta had entrenched clauses, which could only be changed by a two thirds majority in Parliament and a referendum, and ordinary clauses which could be changed by a simple majority in Parliament. Would you believe that the clause which stated 'The Constitution is superior to Parliament' was not entrenched? It was reversed by Parliament, therefore everything else could be changed and Malta became a republic. My new country is agonising over whether to become a republic, and if so, what form it should take. Many believe that the change is inevitable. Lise and I hope it will be as trouble free as Malta's. The only discernible change during my time was the formality of the High Commissioner becoming the Queen's representative because the Governor General became the President. The rest was business as usual.

All good things come to an end. Our farewells lasted six of the most hectic weeks of our life at the end of which, in October 1975, we were poured onto the ferry to Sicily and started the journey home.

Chapter 21

Dead Centre and Dead End

There was no need to hurry back from Malta to the UK. I had worked for over two years without a holiday and earned eleven weeks leave, the longest Lise and I could ever expect to enjoy. And we had good reasons to enjoy ourselves. Both the Admirals I had served in Malta had recommended me for promotion. I had expressed a preference for Joint Service work and my next appointment, to the Directorate of Systems Co-ordination, would bring experience on the Central Defence staff in London. A married quarter would be available at Hendon soon after we arrived. A friend in Weymouth had a harbour-front house which we could use until we moved to London. We had money in the bank. We had no worries. There was no hurry.

It was too good to last and it didn't. When we got back to the UK my prospective Director, an Air Commodore, asked me to forgo my leave because my services were urgently required. The tri-service team of engineers in which I would be working needed their naval member. Could I join immediately? Even I had more sense than that and a compromise was reached. I would take five weeks leave, defer the rest and join early in December. We changed our plans and moved to Hendon as soon as a quarter was ready.

The quarters had been built to the 'New London Standard'. That meant 'a terraced house with a postage stamp sized garden, in which every room was smaller than in previous designs, with no separate dining room and no study'. Incredibly, the central heating system had been installed on the upper floor and a fan worked overtime trying to blow hot air downstairs and keep some there. The houses sat in a sea of mud and although we were warmly received by our naval neighbours, they were very depressed by the dismal surroundings. So were we. Instantly! However, we had a base and I was ready to start work.

During our telephone negotiations the Air Commodore had implied that the directorate's work was so important that he wanted me to forego the remainder of my leave altogether, rather than taking it at some mutually convenient future date. Perhaps I was lucky to get the appointment, especially as I had never done a staff course. But it was strange that neither I nor my friends knew what the directorate was supposed to do. Perhaps it was a bit spooky?

The location of the directorate's offices added to the impression that it might be part of the intelligence empire. At the back of the Abbey National Building Society's office in the Strand was the sort of door you see at the emergency exits behind cinemas. No 'Department of Defence' sign, no 'Government Property Keep out', just a concrete staircase. It led to quite pleasant offices on the two upper floors where I found the office I would share with my Army and RAF colleagues, and met my predecessor.

The rot set in quickly after that. The Air Commodore told me how important the Directorate's work was. My predecessor and my new colleagues told me there was virtually nothing to do. I couldn't ask my immediate boss, a Group Captain, for his view. There was so little to do he just didn't come to work until Friday that week. I had never seen anything like it. When I finally met him, he explained the rationale. The Directorate existed to seek reductions in defence expenditure through rationalisation of stores holdings and engineering functions. Rationalisation was simply defined as 'the elimination of unnecessary duplication of resources'. It was occasionally a political hot potato and our top brass liked to be able to tell the Minister that, 'We have a team of clever chaps continually looking for economies through rationalisation'. The Minister could pass it on to Parliament and that should make everyone happy. When I found how little there *was to do it didn't make me happy, either as a tax-payer or an under-employed officer.*

The life was very pleasant in a lazy sort of way. Sharing a tri-service office was a good way of learning more about the other two services. My first RAF colleague had started his career as an apprentice in 1935 and was able to tell us a lot about the way air force attitudes had changed over the years. My REME colleague and I compared the strengths and weaknesses of our services' respective systems for reporting on and promoting officers. We studied the rationale behind current practices. But there was no denying the basic truth, there was little in common between the needs of the services. For instance, the rotary balancing machines in the Royal Dockyards could handle fifteen ton rotors, those of the RAF about sixty pounds. No 'unnecessary duplication' there. The only significant area for rationalisation was aviation. All three services operated fixed and rotary wing aircraft but those high level responsibilities were far beyond our influence.

Others also felt that resources were being wasted. The Rear Admiral on the Steering Group which oversaw the directorate's work used memorable words, 'The ground of rationalisation has now been worked over so thoroughly that the crop has been harvested and only the most unrewarding gleaning remains, which is certainly not worth the hire of the labourers'. My first year in the job was almost up when that was written. The new leader of the engineering team, a Colonel this time, had had time to discover the score. I told the others I proposed to ask to be relieved of my appointment. They did not join my protest. Soldier John depended on his service allowances to keep his children at boarding school. Air Force John displayed no wish to stir the pot. I was on my own.

Officers with a more patient approach to office politics would have spent time lobbying potential supporters outside the Directorate. I didn't. My letter requested that I be relieved of my appointment and proposed that the post be left vacant until there was full time employment for a future incumbent. The letter is still a good record of the unpalatable facts. I reminded the Air Commodore of the words of the previous and present leaders of the engineering team that the decline in workload would soon require a revision of the team's mandate or reduction to one Grade 1 officer. I sent a copy to the Rear Admiral for his information, knowing that he would implacably oppose any expansion of the Central Staff mandate, and that reduction to one officer, which my analysis showed was quite reasonable, was the only sensible answer.

The Colonel's response on behalf of the Air Commodore was of the 'I don't wish to know that' category but they didn't let me leave the stage. He referred to my work as Secretary of the Defence Engineering Terminology Committee, which was deliberating at tedious and costly length definitions of terms like Reliability and Maintainability, as potentially 'long and onerous'. There was much in similar vein. My views on the division of officers, managers and all kinds of bosses into 'empire builders' and 'hatchet men' were confirmed. And my guess that about nineteen out of twenty were builders and 'turf protectors' didn't seem too far out. It still doesn't.

Although there was little prospect of early release from the Directorate, it was time to take stock of my career and our family life. The navy had introduced a 'horoscope reading' scheme in which Commanders could receive an estimate of their chances of promotion from the Captain responsible for their appointments. The idea had been received cynically by everyone I knew. We expected weasely words rather than an honest and open assessment. That is how we expected representatives of the Admiralty to behave. We were wrong.

My 'appointer', Chris, referred to the Admiral's luke warm report at the end of my time on his Sea Training staff and remarked there was still doubt about whether that appointment should ever have been made. Despite the succession of 'Recommendeds' from subsequent masters I was only half way up the list of engineering Commanders who were suitable for promotion and only the top third would be promoted. Unless there was 'a bloody war or a sickly season' my prospects were nil. I was annoyed that the appointment to FOST's staff had gone ahead if my submarine background created doubts about my suitability. It had virtually put me out of the running for promotion to Captain within four months of being promoted Commander. If only I had known! However, I appreciated Chris' frankness. That part of his work cannot have been pleasant.

Taking stock on the home front was the next task. We had never loved London and Hendon did not make the heart grow fonder. The old Hendon airfield had been divided into four parts. One was local authority housing, mostly flats of the sort which figure largely in the television series 'The Bill', not least because the local authorities were said to have dumped their 'hard cases' there. Another part had been developed as high density private housing. The third was the married quarters estate. The fourth remained RAF territory. They interacted in various ways.

Peter had a few shocks when we returned to the UK. He had little experience of the constraints of big city life, and a school which included all the local thugs was no fun. The children had to remove their outdoor footwear in school so that any kickings would not produce serious injury. He was also shocked to learn that English schools have morning and afternoon sessions all the year round, unlike the Services' schools in Malta which switched to 'tropical routine', mornings only, during the summer months. When he joined the local Cub Pack we were warned that the cubs should not walk to meetings in uniform on their own. So we escorted Peter and in doing so met an Australian couple doing the same duty. Bruce was a lecturer in civil engineering, on sabbatical in the UK with his wife Anne. We became and remain friends, and I appreciated his support years later when I sought election as a Fellow of the Institution of Engineers, Australia.

The word 'muggings' had not yet entered out lives but occasionally a service wife would complain of being harassed in the narrow lane leading to the station and some were nervous of going out alone. There were a few thefts. And there was the RAF Hendon Sergeants' mess, just behind the fence a few yards from the backs of our houses. The inhabitants of our row of the officers' quarters had the old fashioned view that their mess parties should either end or quieten down around one AM. They seemed to think three or four more appropriate and took no heed of our complaints. There was only one easy solution. Get the Commanding Officer out of bed around two AM and invite him to come and listen.

Michael and Ros were in a damp and dismal flat in Oxford when we returned from Malta, and James often had colds and other infections. We could not make them a present of the deposit on a house so we went into partnership with them. Michael was working at Robert Maxwell's Pergamon Press and they could pay a mortgage as easily as a rent. Using our savings as a deposit we all bought a terraced house just before they were rediscovered as 'Artisan Houses', which of course were worth much more. It was a museum of gas and electrical practice, originally fitted with gas lights and then converted to three different generations of electric light and power. Michael and I reluctantly removed the beautifully jointed oak fuse boxes of the first generation electrics, rewired the house and installed central heating.

We had hardly finished the work when Michael got a new job in London and it had to be sold. I provided the advice and Ros did the footwork. An excited call to my office brought the news that she had sold it. I asked how much she had managed to get and she named a sum a thousand pounds more than I had suggested asking. Apparently she misheard my suggestion. Just as well! Another house was bought in Holloway, affordable because it was still an unfashionable area and we were willing to tackle the work, required by the Building Society, of converting the three flats back to a single family home. We rightly judged that the area would become more desirable. Ros and Michael were fairly well settled.

So what were we to do? The navy specifies dates on which officers have their last chance of promotion. In June 1977 I would be 'passed over'. It was time to make plans. My next appointment was to be back to AUWE in the spring of 1978. Systems Co-ordination was not giving me any time off for bad behaviour! For the first time in our married life we decided to move away from my work. I would commute weekly. There were many advantages. In Weymouth, Lise would be among friends, Peter would have a better school, and I would enjoy weekends in Dorset better than whole weeks in London. In the longer term, we would probably settle in Weymouth if I left the Service after being passed over.

We surprised our Weymouth friends, Bill and Marjorie. While we were with them one weekend they told us that a house a few yards from theirs was for sale. We returned half an hour later having agreed to buy it. They thought we had treated it rather like buying a loaf of bread but we were happy to move fast. We had seen some of our friends seek perfection in houses only to find that prices escalated so fast that they finished up unable to buy one at all. We didn't make that mistake and our stake began to grow again.

Married naval officers were generally popular lodgers in London. They returned home at weekends, paid their rent on time and were usually socially acceptable. I lodged in a splendid flat, full of books and treasures, which spanned the second floors of two houses in Cornwall Gardens. I hope that my landlady, Mary, would not mind being described as one third scientist, one third Scottish frugality and one third Kensington gentility. She was a lovely person, very kind to me, to Lise and to friends I introduced. She had no time for euphemisms. I got up later than usual one morning because I intended to travel by bus. She confessed to having been concerned that I might have overslept, at least until, she said, 'I passed your bathroom and smelled your scent. Then I knew you were up'. Others might have referred to 'after-shave' despite the fact that I was as always bearded. Not Mary.

Allowances made it financially easier for naval officers to live away from their families than at home, appalling but true. They even covered a pint or two in my favourite pub, sometimes enjoying the company of the sons or daughters of my friends who were now making their careers in London. I kept a straight face at the weekends if a father told me that although the permissive society was now in full swing, his daughter 'wouldn't do anything like that'. I had met their boyfriends in London and knew they certainly did but I didn't begrudge the fathers their feelings. I'm sure I would have felt the same if I had a daughter.

To balance the intake at the pub I walked the few miles to and from the office in the Strand most days, especially during the Queen's Silver Jubilee Year, 1977. There were five million extra people in London and it was the classic long hot summer into the bargain. It was not surprising that the average speed of London buses dropped below four miles an hour. The slow pace did not prevent masses of people from using them and the British queuing tradition might have broken down if it were not for the old ladies travelling by rush hour bus. They all seemed to have sharpened umbrella tips which accidently stabbed the foot of anyone who dared get out of turn. Occasionally, while striding along, my morale was boosted when I was able to overtake overweight men, often American visitors, struggling with the latest way to keep fit, jogging.

Our office in the Strand was an excellent viewing position for the Jubilee procession to St Pauls and we made reciprocal *arrangements with people whose offices overlooked the Thames so that we could see the fireworks in comfort during the evening. Lise came up to London and we invited Mary to join us. After the morning procession, Lise and I decided to take a trip along the river to Greenwich. There's a long tradition of naval officers attending the wrong wedding reception by mistake and having a splendid time. We extended the idea by walking past the man at the gangway of a launch with a cheery 'Good afternoon' only to find after the launch sailed that we had gatecrashed a company's private party. Brits often judge by appearances and we must have looked the part. The firm made us most welcome.*

Towards the end of my time a real opportunity to do some useful work came along, a one man job and I got it. The Services had five 'Petroleum, Oils and Lubricants' laboratories in the UK and two in Germany. Could they manage with less? How did Service laboratories compare with commercial practice for quality assurance of POL? I not only concluded that they could manage with less laboratories, but also discovered that the army proposed building an extra one. In addition to other possible savings, that project could be cancelled and capital expenditure of over a million pounds avoided without detriment to defence interests. A Commander's salary was about eight thousand pounds a year then. That one saving would have justified the engineering team's salaries for years, negating my argument that we should be disbanded. But it never happened. Single service thinking prevailed over defence thinking and I heard later that the army got its lab.

Our long term plan began with a 'buzz', navy-speak for a rumour. Our neighbour at Hendon, Roy, had heard that the Australian navy was short of senior officers and although protocol prevented them 'poaching' from the RN they were open to enquiries. Yes, they wanted 'pussers' like Roy and engineers. Four year commissions were available subject to examination of Admiralty records, interview, medical examination, security clearance and willingness to take Australian citizenship. At last we might get to Australia. A new adventure in a country we had admired from afar for years was infinitely better than rusticating after being 'passed over'.

I waited, 'just in case', until the final day and then posted my application to join the RAN. We began to read more about Australia, its history and its way of life. The interview gave me my first personal experience that things were often done differently by Aussies. I expected a tough interrogation by the engineer Captain at the High Commission but for half an hour all we did was chat agreeably about Australian life and my family. I tried to suggest diplomatically that we get on with the hard engineering questions. He told me quite simply that there would not be any. He had studied my records and was entirely satisfied with my engineering knowledge and experience. What mattered was whether we would all settle happily in Australia. There was no point in wasting the Aussie tazpayers' money flying us out there only to discover that we hated it. Even though we would have had to pay our own return fares, the recruitment would have been a failure. Good one, I thought.

By the beginning of December 1977 I had received a provisional offer and I asked to be allowed to retire. The Naval Secretary's approval was commendably prompt, only 22 days after my request, but retirement from the British services was not that simple. I was told I would probably have to serve for another fifteen months before retiring. No employer can promise anyone a job fifteen months down the track and an act of faith was called for. But fifteen months was not as bad as the seven years quoted at that time to a young RAF Air Traffic Controller. He really had a problem. Lise and I were not deterred, we had confidence that there was life after the RN, in Australia or elsewhere.

Most but not all reactions to the news that we were going to Australia were favourable. While in lodgings I attended an evening sculpture workshop. One response to the news there was, 'You must be a racist'. I was not expecting that but I seemed to recall that in Trevor Huddleston's 1956 book on Apartheid, 'Naught for your Comfort', he suggested that racism is entirely natural and that it is the duty of Christians, and by extension all civilised people, to overcome their natural prejudices. That gave me the answer she wasn't expecting, 'Isn't everyone?' and she didn't attack me further, contenting herself with a muttered, 'I'm not'. I read the book again recently and was surprised that I couldn't find an explicit statement of the idea, but there's no doubt that the book put the thought into my head. I still think it's a better explanation of human behaviour than a fashionable pretence that no one is racist.

My largely unproductive time in London finally ended and I rejoined AUWE team as the 'Head of Ship System Services and Minor Projects Group'. We were the odd job merchants, covering the acquisition and in-service management of echo-sounders, side-scan and other sonars for the Hydrographer of the Navy, and anything else which was not clearly some other team's work. Odd jobs they may have been but to use a modern cliche, 'someone had to do them'. They were real work and a welcome change after London. My two Special Duties List officers were among the best in the Service. They knew their subject backwards and they didn't need help from me. That was fine because I had a modest workload of my own. The three of us shared cheery clerical support. It was good to be back.

There were some managerial wrinkles which we helped iron out. AUWE had recognised the need for a system for allocating specialist support to groups such as mine. For instance, we required the part time services of a statistician. Some of the traditionalist civilian managers stood firm on the old principle that no man can serve two masters. The rest of us showed that time division was quite practical given four things. The first three were clear understandings of who was the specialist's superior, *what were the allocations of the specialist's time, and who was to settle any disputes. The final ingredient was the one least often recognised, the need for an ego free, collaborative approach by the principals seeking services. It is to AUWE's credit that such a culture existed in the area where we worked. We enjoyed working with our 0.1 of a statistician and other part-timers.*

Another interesting AUWE development was the achievement of a practical approach to working relationships between civilian and Service officers of comparable ranks. Sometimes it is very useful to have a Service officer working for a civilian or vice versa. If one is clearly of a higher grade than the other there is no problem but sometimes they will be at the generally accepted same level. In my appointment there were certain tasks on which it was appropriate for a Principal Scientific Officer to work under my direction. I believe the AUWE senior management, the scientists and their union served the navy well by accepting the Service principle of seniority. I had been a Commander for ten years, the PSO was newly promoted, he worked for me when appropriate. I was disappointed to find later that the Australian defence personnel generally worked on the older concept that there must be a rank differential. That can waste scarce effort.

There were interesting sidelines to my job. I inherited some cupboards full of World War 2 files on technical matters and my task was to separate those of historical value from those full of work-a-day trivia prior to formal sentencing by archivists. The most interesting of these was on the design philosophy for siting the electrical conversion machinery which was increasingly necessary for new equipments requiring unusual voltages or frequencies. The issue was whether to concentrate machinery in one compartment, which saved weight and complexity but made the ships vulnerable to a single 'lucky shot', or to fit a multiplicity of machines throughout the watertight compartments of ships. The latter was considered too difficult so machinery was to be concentrated. The British ships in which I did the work-up training still had the same design philosophy. The Falklands war occurred after I emigrated but I understand that the increased vulnerability of this approach remained a weakness. The German navy's distributed systems still seem preferable.

The Royal Navy allowed retiring personnel some training to prepare them for civilian life. I settled for the popular 'bricklaying course' run by the army at Aldershot. The objective was to teach the skills required to build a single story, garage-like building, on a concrete base, with glazed windows, complete with electrics and plumbing. I don't say all the students would have made a very good job of such an ambitious project but the teaching was superb and much of it has become second nature to me over the years. A bonus was that as the only naval officer on the course, I was the senior naval officer, and was invited, with the General and Air Vice Marshal, to a couple of excellent lunches kindly given by the senior officers of Aldershot.

Another course taught us about getting a job. I went to it, even though I was now almost certain to join the RAN, because there is always something to be learned. Much of the day was devoted to writing CVs but the most important lesson was undoubtedly that getting a job is a statistical business. Apply for a hundred or more if necessary, one application will come good eventually. Michael reinforced this lesson by showing me the thick file of rejection letters he had accumulated in his business circles over the years. I was grateful to both sources when, after serving with the RAN, my turn came to get a civilian job and I built up my own, equally thick, file. They had taught me not to take rejection personally.

Although the RN made my generation feel that it was privilege to be allowed to belong to the navy as an officer, it was not averse to harsh practical measures to keep us in when we wanted to leave. The long period between an officer's request to retire and his release was one. Another was the financial penalty for officers retiring between the ages of forty and fifty. We were required to sacrifice seven and a half per cent of our terminal cash grants and our pensions. Fortunately, Lise and I had learned one important philosophy from the sailors, 'Never mind, it's only money'. Ours lives might have taken a different direction if I had remained in the Service two more months to avoid that penalty. It was worth the sacrifice.

Our preparations progressed. Lise encountered another aspect of Australian life when the Immigration Service doctor at Canberra House in London immediately addressed her by her first name. It was the first of many reminders that although the British and Australian life styles appear to have so much in common, closer acquaintance reveals many differences, some fundamental, some cultural and conventional.

My own preparations included a final medical examination by a Royal Navy doctor. The risks associated with cholesterol had become well known and I thought it would be good to know what my level was as I started a new life, so I asked him to arrange the test. He asked if I was worried about my level, grudgingly agreed to the test, and shrugged off my question about whether he thought it might be a good idea to do routine tests now that the risks were known. He made no reference to the hearing loss, which fortunately was not severe, arising from my life among gunfire, Diesel engines and compressed air, nor to the early exposure to asbestos which I shared with all my generation of engineers.

My AUWE task did not include a formal brief to study and report on my group's viability but I was made aware of serious conflict between my predecessor, who wanted to expand the team, and the senior management. It would have been nice to conclude my RN career by becoming, just for once, an empire builder supporting the expansion, but our work could be done equally well with some savings in administrative resources if the *two junior officers joined a larger group and my own position was abolished. I heard after arriving in Australia that my suggestions had been adopted. So I ended my thirty one years with another hatchet job. Sad in some ways, but someone has to tell the Emperor when he's being conned. And the Christmas card from my clerical support team struck a very cheerful note, 'It's not the same without Action Man around'.*

We took to Michael and Ros' house in London all the things we wished to leave in England, furniture, souvenirs, our love letters from courtship days, some of my wooden and Maltese stone carvings, and much else, for we were only allowed to take a limited quantity of personal effects to Australia. We sold our house and were amused that after all the years when we would have loved to move into a married quarter, we could do so without difficulty in our last two months. There were many spare quarters.

Our final function in the navy was a pleasure. AUWE was invited to be represented at the launch of HMS Southampton at Vosper Thornycroft's in January 1979 and Lise and I were given the privilege. It gave us especial pleasure to see again, as Controller of the Navy, the Board member responsible for the shipbuilding program and much else, John Fieldhouse, whom we had known since his days as the Commanding Officer of HMS Dreadnought. As always, although he was a VIP player in the launch proceedings, he greeted us with his customary warmth, reminding us again what an exceptional man he was. Pleasant though the day was, we did not see the ship launched. There was an industrial dispute and we had a 'naming ceremony' instead. The ship was launched, surreptitiously, at about nine o'clock that night by the management of the yard. Another sad reflection on British life. It was definitely time to go.

On 10th February 1979, while still in London, I became a member of the Royal Australian Navy. The Australian navy takes no chances on prospective members travelling to Sydney at the tax-payers expense and then refusing to join. Lise, Peter and I said our goodbyes to Michael and Ros and our grandsons James and Jake at Heathrow. Ros pointed out that it was a topsy turvy farewell, it is usually the young who go out into the world to seek their fortune. We agreed that starting a new life just before the age of fifty was a bit late, but better late than never. And if our Australian experiment worked well they might be able to follow us, uniting the family again.

There were two footnotes to my thirty one years in the RN. The first was the Ministry of Defence letter of 31st January 1979 finally telling me that my request to be placed on the retired list had been approved. It had a fine second paragraph, 'The Secretary of State for Defence has it in command from her Majesty The Queen to convey to you, on your leaving the Active List of the Royal Navy, her thanks for your long and valuable service'. I wish someone had bothered to sign it.

The second was a personal letter of thanks and good wishes from the Chief of Naval Personnel and Second Sea Lord. It was not sent until three months after I left the RN and not received until another four months after that. They sent it sea-mail. Sad, I thought.

Chapter 22

New Beginnings

Australia scored three hits with us on our first day, Tuesday 13th February 1979. Our plane arrived early in Sydney and the Petty Officer WRAN who met us changed our bookings to get us on an earlier flight to Canberra. Good impression number one because despite a stopover in Singapore we were tired and the sooner we were settled in our motel the better. Then there was the warmth of the welcome from the friendly young Leading Seaman driver in Canberra. When he learned that we had not been to Canberra before he took us a slightly longer way to the motel so that we could see something of the beautiful city in which we were to live. Good impression number two. The third was finding that we had a suite at the motel instead of just a room. It was likely to be our home for six weeks so we appreciated the spaciousness.

Our friends from the Hendon quarters, Roy, who was now serving on an RN appointment to the RAN, and his wife Elizabeth, having been thwarted in their wish to greet us with champagne at the airport by our early arrival, appeared soon after and we celebrated. It was a happy start to our new life. But there is always a downside and we were introduced to one of the unwelcome aspects of Australian life later that day. We slept during the afternoon, then Roy took us to his house for dinner, after which we all went out onto the front balcony to have coffee. We were shocked to find the northern skyline ablaze. Bush fires were raging in the rural area at Sutton, about fourteen miles away. Some people lost everything. A day to remember!

I went to the office the next day and the warm welcome continued. My boss, the Naval Scientific Adviser, told me to take as long as I needed to get settled and said he would pick us up at the motel at four to give us an introductory tour of some areas of

Canberra where we might like to look for a house. His other assistant, a Senior Research Scientist, invited us to dinner at his home the following Friday. Could anyone ask for more? After an hour at the office, I collected Lise and Peter from the hotel. We wanted to buy a car and quickly learned that the lowest price was not to be found in Canberra, the only city in the Australian Capital Territory, but in the town of Queanbeyan, over the 'border' in New South Wales. It was our first reminder that we were now living in a Federation of six States and two Territories.

The introductory tour was a great success but we soon began to get conflicting advice on where to live from various people we met. Some thought Red Hill was the only possible place, others believed that four suburbs on the north western side of the Black Mountain were the best. Fortunately, serendipity stepped in again. An estate agent ferried us around all day on the Thursday and Friday, and we looked at dozens of houses without being drawn to any of them. Instead of more of the same on the Saturday, Elizabeth and Roy took us to the vegetable market at Fyshwick. A chance conversation with a stall holder brought the response, 'I know just the house for you'.

She did not lie. When we saw the house on a hillside in a quiet cul de sac of five houses, with views on three sides, oil fired central heating for the cold winter months, a solar heated swimming pool for the summer, and a garage which would house two cars and still have plenty of space for work benches, we threw away our financial plan and made an offer. It did not matter that it was in Fisher, an unfashionable suburb, nor that it was only of 'brick veneer' construction. We loved it and moved in six weeks after arriving in Australia. Lise's only reservation was that the occupants of the adjacent houses were said to 'keep to themselves'. That would never do and within a few months the neighbours on both sides had become, as they remain today, 'like family'.

Two days after we moved into the house, Peter joined the Scouts and brought home an invitation to the Group Committee's AGM the next night. Attendance was obviously a must. I sat at the back with another man and kept silent, appropriate behaviour for a newcomer, I thought. The retiring President persuaded people to fill every position except her own. Then she looked hard at the two of us in the back row, 'What about one of you two?' The other chap, Lou, declined. I began a litany, 'I don't know what the President of your Group is expected to do, but if you don't mind having someone who has had no contact with Scouting since the nineteen forties, arrived in Australia six weeks ago, moved into Fisher two days ago, and whose son only joined the group last night, I'll have a go'. She responded with a kindly remark, 'You will be among friends, you know'. She was right. That incident was my introduction to the reluctance of so many Australians to take a leading role. To the extent that it reflects a modest wish not to be pushy and power-hungry, it's good, but when organisations like scout groups have difficulty getting volunteers for the presidential chair, it has clearly gone too far.

There were two memorials to my time in the chair, the hall which the group built in collaboration with the local Girl Guides and a new ACT Scout Branch policy which prevents groups borrowing from the Guide movement at three and a half per cent and placing the money on the short term money market to earn eighteen and a quarter. The latter outcome gave me the most amusement. Inflation was a big enemy in funding the building project and the income from our investment helped a great deal.

My work as Assistant Naval Scientific Adviser was interesting and challenging. My boss served two masters, the Chief Defence Scientist and the Chief of the Naval Staff. We were the link between the Defence Science and Technology Organisation's laboratories and the navy. Our little branch was well organised. As a 'passed over Pommie retread' I would not have much credibility in the Navy Office, at least until I earned *some. My scientist colleague had a similar problem in the labs, 'What does he know, he only got his PhD seven years ago, and that was in astro-physics'. But if young scientist with a doctorate takes a leading role in the Navy Office and a Commander with long experience liaises with the labs, things are quite different. That way worked well.*

It was a hectic time, new country, new navy, new ways of doing things. The branch had an interest in every field of naval activity, all the specialists could come to us for help in identifying which laboratory might be able to solve their problems. There were culture shocks of course. Most meetings in UK would be arranged to start between ten and eleven in the morning to fit in with typical travel times by road or rail. On my introductory visit to the RAN Research Laboratory in Sydney the boss and I took the seven o'clock flight from Canberra and were at the lab before eight. By nine, concentrating hard on so much that was new, I was convinced it must be nearly lunchtime!

There were two other major laboratories in Melbourne and three at Salisbury, near Adelaide and I usually visited them every couple of months. Leaving classified technicalities aside, there were three major limitations on the effort available in the labs. The Chief Defence Scientist, an academic appointed to his high executive position, had underestimated the role of technical and clerical staff in supporting R and D and reduced their numbers to employ more scientists, a classic error which he regretted making. It took him years to restore the right balance.

The second problem was also a classic, the preference of scientists to 'do their own thing' instead of doing what the organisation wants. It had not been much of a problem at British establishments like AUWE, partly because of the tradition of loyalty inherited from the Royal Naval Scientific Service, and partly because scientists were judged on their classified work within the scientific civil service. The Australian defence scientific community was much smaller and tended to judge worthiness by the number of papers published in the open literature. Sometimes the pressure to publish reinforced personal inclinations to resist proposals from outside the labs. Persuasive persistence was required. We did not always win.

I was surprised how quickly I began to feel the combined effect of Australia's very limited defence science resources and, a factor new to me, the feeling of isolation. The navy required a new kind of sonar array for its Oberon Class submarines. None was available from US or UK sources. They both suggested how we could get into the new field but their proposals required resources beyond our reach. Australian Defence had to make its own way, using the small available team. I knew the magnitude of the task being attempted and soon began to wonder if we would suffer a great embarrassment. Our program involved higher risks than would be usual in the UK, and the US would never have attempted the project with such a small team. I need not have worried, the labs did us proud and within a couple of years compliments flowed from both countries. Australia's best defence scientists were as good as any I had ever met. My new country was well served by them.

There were other shocks ranging from high level national problems to the unusual behaviour of Australian colleagues. All my adult life had been lived under threat of nuclear or conventional confrontation with the USSR. I had never realised how much harder it is for a government to allocate resources to defence when there is no obvious threat. At the other end of the scale, I had to get used to the idea that the sky did not fall in if a Wing Commander walked through Canberra's central shopping area in uniform with an umbrella in one hand and a milkshake in the other. He could not return salutes. And an umbrella with uniform? I consulted a respected Aussie colleague. His simple response was, 'He could say Good Afternoon. And it was raining. What do you expect him to do, get wet?'

The Royal Navy's attitude to the wearing of uniform in public bordered on paranoia. I remember being told that if we drove to and from our work in uniform, we should not stop to buy cigarettes or petrol. Now, in Australia, it was unimportant. Many officers wore uniform and it did not matter how they travelled to work. One morning when my car was being repaired and I travelled to work by bus, a Brigadier in uniform sat next to a Private just in front of me. The conversation began with an exchange of 'Good morning' and 'Good morning Sir', then the Brigadier opened with, 'Did you watch the footie on the TV last night?' 'Yes. Who do you barrack for, Sir'. And so the conversation went on, entirely naturally. They parted with a 'Have a good day' and a 'You too Sir'. Aussies are not self conscious in the British way. There is no feeling that 'That sort of thing simply isn't done' and even less of 'Our kind of people don't do that kind of thing'. If the Secretary of a major Australian department of state wished to eat sandwiches for lunch sitting in the sun on a bench in the park, he or she would not be thought eccentric. They would just be another person doing what they wish without disturbing anyone else.

I doubt if the next example could have happened in England. While buying wine one Sunday afternoon I accidentally locked my keys in my car. A respectable fifty-something chap in open necked shirt and Royal Canberra Golf Club pullover offered to help. Although the car had modern catches designed to prevent intrusions, he opened it very quickly and I couldn't resist asking whether he did it for a living. 'I'm not allowed to', he said, 'I'm a judge'. We introduced ourselves. Such unselfconsciousness is something for the country to be proud of.

Aussies talk to one another. I only realised how natural, pleasant and rewarding that is when I experienced the traditional British frostiness in 1989. Returning to London from a holiday excursion to Malta in a 'three seats each side' aircraft, it was my turn to sit apart from Lise and our friends Aram and Marie. The couple in the two seats next to mine were well dressed, middle class Brits and I tried to exchange a few pleasantries to pass the time. Shock, horror. They didn't actually point out that we hadn't been introduced but I expected them to at any moment.

The reference to 'barracking' for a side was an introduction to the differences between Australian English and English English. Unless things have changed in Britain, 'barracking' is still verbal discouragement to an opposing side, not support of ones own. To anyone with an open mind these differences in the use of language are neither good nor bad, they just exist and have to be learned. And parting words like 'Have a good day' illustrate the large American contribution to Australian life. Fortunately, it has become, in most cases, a conventional but sincere courtesy, not the commercialised, mindless ritual often portrayed as part of the American way.

In 1979 the RAN had one class of US designed destroyers and the aircraft carrier, HMAS Melbourne, had US designed 'Tracker' anti-submarine aircraft. I needed to be acquainted with their US systems so I spent a few days in HMASs Brisbane and Melbourne, achieving a minor ambition to be catapulted off and land on a carrier in the process. There was a lovely post script to the days in HMAS Brisbane. I was landed at Jervis Bay at about five thirty one afternoon, very hot and sticky, and thought I deserved one drink at the Naval College Wardroom bar before driving back to Canberra. The scene at the bar would have done credit to Dartmouth. An elegant Commander in perfect 'whites' was chatting to an equally immaculate and elegant, blond Nursing Sister, and although these are times of equality, I'll swear she was gazing admiringly at him. Colleges are colleges are colleges seems to be the rule, but on the whole, I would rather remain part of the struggling technological navy than the rather artificial world of training establishments. I'll never be invited to the Garden Party now. Ah well.

Nothing could give anyone with any curiosity a greater sense of having a new lease of life than starting a new job in a new country with a different culture. How, for example, would the relationships between commissioned officers and ratings work in what the literature has always suggested is an egalitarian culture? Is Australia a classless society? Even finding superficial answers was, and remains, a fascinating study.

Serving and ex-Service Aussie naval ratings have taught me that one key to understanding how the rank structure works here is their expectation that the officers will know their jobs. If they do, the 'lads' will not begrudge officers the traditional marks of respect. If they don't, let them beware. An ex-Chief Petty Officer who became one of my section managers in my civilian job told me that during his twelve years in the RAN, which included the Vietnam war, he only met one officer he considered incompetent. His response was to refuse to pay him any marks of respect. Anyone who knows how armed services operate will understand that the officer could not take disciplinary action against a respected senior rating without exposing his own deficiencies. A fairly extreme case but one bit of the jigsaw of truth nevertheless.

Most, newcomers to Australia look for evidence of the existence or absence of a class structure and there are thousands of pieces in that jigsaw. Sociologists' treatises rarely make easy reading and Professor Encel's 'Equality and Authority' is no exception but his separation of the subject into 'Class, Status and Power' promotes understanding and analysis better than the vague single word 'Class'. From a homelier point of view than Encel's history and statistics, my observations contribute a couple of ideas which I did not find in his book.

With the exception of 'Ocker' Aussies clad, regardless of the social and seasonal climate, in shorts, vests, 'thongs', Australian for flip-flops, and a cold 'tinnie', it is generally less easy to identify the social and educational background of Australians and to guess their jobs, especially during their off-duty moments, than it would be in British life. The reason is simple. So much of British life appears specifically designed to permit almost instant classification of strangers. As Professor Higgins said in the 'My Fair Lady' adaptation of 'Pygmalion', 'The moment he (an Englishman that is) opens his mouth, he makes some other Englishman despise him'. Most Australians do not mind looking like and talking like other Australians. And they do not despise them. Naturally, they will seek like minded people as companions of their life and leisure, but when circumstances place them in other company they are generally friendly.

There are obviously many senses in which Australia has a class and political structure similar to any other Western country. There are men and women in the Trades Union Movement, on the right of 'Big Business', and in the Liberal/ National coalition government who seem determined to provoke divisive confrontations. Nevertheless, Australia appears to be the English speaking country with the best chance of avoiding such idiocy, with the best chance of realising, before it is too late, that there is greater benefit in collaboration that in competition. It's a hard idea to cling to at times. Greedy senior executives are just as much a menace as reactionary workers, but we have a chance.

Back on the domestic front, Lise and I found that nearly everyone we met had an investment property. It was just another way of saving. The demand for rental accommodation was strong and the law governing the relationship between landlords and tenants in the ACT was equitable. So, at the end of our first year, we scraped the bottom of the barrel, leaving ourselves only a thousand dollars in the kitty, took on another mortgage, and bought a two bedroomed 'unit', the Aussie name for a flat.

The Australian income tax policy on mortgages was the opposite of the British one. Income tax relief was not allowed on the mortgage for a family home, but interest paid on an investment property was a normal business expense and if the *total expenses exceeded the rents received, the loss could be set against the tax on other income. That enabled us to pay the mortgages on our house and on the unit. We furnished the unit as if it were our home and it paid off. We enjoyed the novel experience of being landlords, had good tenants and a high occupancy rate. And having bought when the market was at the bottom of a cycle, we sold after three years of appreciation, paid off both mortgages and had a bit left over.*

We felt some twinges at our new circumstances. Were we becoming a bit materialistic? If so, we had to admit that it didn't hurt. We had simply come to a country which, though not as rich in world terms as it used to be, felt significantly more affluent to us. And we still had to work for our benefits. During the first few months I made furniture for our lounge. We haunted the garage sales which were a rich source of cheap things, especially as we were prepared to renovate many of our purchases. Those garage sales, which are often occasions for a chat, taught us another facet of Aussie life. On learning that we were newcomers, we were always asked if we had come to stay. On hearing that we had, some small item was often produced as a present. A lovely custom but the message was clear, only those who were willing to join and identify with the country and its people would be welcome. No room for whinging Poms.

The Australian way of life exceeded our expectations. Preliminary reading in UK left the impression that there might be some residual anti-Pom feeling which might manifest itself in the response of, perhaps, taxi drivers or waiters. It never happened. There was only the good natured traditional rivalry in the mess and in similar circumstances. Adjustments had to be made though. The most obvious was the custom of sitting in the front seat of a taxi or government car and talking to the driver. Less obvious was the discovery that a taxi driver might be anyone from a recent immigrant still practicing his English to an Australian academic with a PhD, supplementing his income.

Nothing is ever perfect and we observed a few bad habits of our Aussie friends. Some, for example, were inclined to reserve the term Australian for those who were born in the country. Lise and I made a point of reminding them that we were Australians for love of the country and not by a mere accident of birth. We had become Australians on the 4th October 1979, just a few months after arriving. We felt like queue-jumpers. Many of the others at the ceremony had been in Australia for years, some more than twenty. Special rules applied to the Armed Services and dependents. The Australian government didn't want me flogging their secrets to the Russians and then seeking the protection of the British. Citizenship was the final step in assimilation.

The only sadness which accompanied that final step was the impending divorce of Michael and Ros. Leaving family and friends in UK had been a wrench but at least there was a hope that Michael and Ros would join us in Australia. Now we could not share the boyhood of our grandsons James and Jake. We had a lot of catching up to do when they left school and visited 'the Olds' on the other side of the world. Divorces are messy and Ros' father wrote that he wished to have nothing more to do with us. We shall always be pleased that Ros did not share his wish and still welcomes us warmly to the home she shares with her new husband, Steve. Pleased too, that after the dust had settled, Ros and Michael became, and remain, friends.

Before leaving the subject of nationality, it has to be said that Aussies can whinge as well as any discontented Brit. That's a relief in many ways. It exonerates the Brits from sole responsibility for whinging and as Aussies come from almost every country in the world, it suggests that humans behave much the same in the long term, regardless of racial or national origin. During the first few decades after World War 2 for example, the West Germans were as near a perfect, dedicated workforce as the world is likely to see, but when the 'economic miracle' had occurred they began to whinge with the best. The first sighs of Japanese whinging will, I hope, soon grow stronger. Whinging is healthy. Whinging is democratic.

My commission was extended for another four years. I could never understand why none of the mainstream RAN engineer officers wanted my job. Although it was an appointment to the Defence Science and Technology Organisation, working under the direction of a civilian scientist, sooner or later it involved contact with every senior officer in Navy Office. It was not a backwater and at least one of my Aussie predecessors had been promoted. Their loss was my gain. I was happy to continue in the appointment but the oldest rule in sailing ships, 'One hand for the ship and one for yourself' still applies to much more than avoiding a fatal fall from a yard-arm. The clock was ticking. At the end of my second four years in the RAN I would be fifty six and there would be little chance of a further extension. At the end of the first year of my extension, a mere boy of fifty three, Lise and I decided it was time for me to apply the lessons I had been taught in London and seek a civilian job.

I soon acquired a thick file of rejection slips and I knew why. Like others who had come late in life to Canberra, the home of the Commonwealth Government, I had been unimpressed by many of the public servants at the Assistant Secretary level. As one respected Australian colleague, Bill, put it, the demand is so great in Canberra, a city of only 300,000 people, that 'Everyone is sucked up', a neat supplement to Parkinson's, 'Given enough levels in the hierarchy, people rise to their level of incompetence'. I had decided to compete for AS level jobs but it's one thing to be unimpressed by whizz kids achieving senior positions with negligible experience and another to break into their ranks as a fifty-something. The usual pattern emerged, the young recruit their own. They do not want subordinates with longer and wider experience. I tried a more modest approach and was lucky first time. The Bureau of Mineral Resources *wanted new blood at the head of their Engineering Services Unit and after two interviews I was offered the job. The RAN had a more reasonable approach to resignations and retirements than the RN and within a month I was in my first professional job as a civilian.*

The 'BMR' was the Australian Government's principal geoscientific agency. It had strategic research commitments in the areas of petroleum, minerals, groundwater, environmental impacts and hazards. There were about three hundred scientific staff with a hundred PhDs among them, an administrative team, a Cartographic Unit and my Engineering Services Unit of sixty professional and technical staff. BMR owned two aircraft for aeromagnetic and radiological surveying, and a chartered ship, the 'Rig Seismic', was being converted to do seismic surveying offshore. The Bureau had a clear role, enthusiastic scientists, some good supporting staff, and it wasn't too big. Unlike my old Defence world, I could enter the building without a pass and leave without clearing my desk or locking the office door. It was a welcome change.

The Bureau had been reviewed and reorganised fairly recently. The Director and Division Heads all had university backgrounds and the place suffered accordingly. Some of the 'games' played at Division Head level could have come straight out of C P Snow's works. The two classic mistakes, of thinking that support staff can be reduced disproportionately and of encouraging competition for funds between divisions which should have been co-operating, were both evident. In theory I could afford to be philosophic about the mistakes I saw, but I soon became very involved. There were bits of fun though, even getting the job provided some amusing moments.

The Interview Panel included the heads of two research divisions, both academics. My case for selection rested largely on my experience of both mechanical and electrical/electronic engineering and of working with scientists over nearly thirty years. When none of the Panel's questions told me exactly what they wanted from their head of engineering, I asked them what sort of engineer they wanted and why. After enjoying their blank looks I explained that my breadth of experience had been bought at the price of depth of knowledge. If they wanted a designer, they should not hire me. If they wanted an engineering manager to recruit and train the team and deal with capital investment, finance, etc, I was their man. I ended with an apology for my interview technique, rusty because I had not had a professional interview since 1947. The younger division head's eyes rolled, he was about two years old then.

The job was mine and my geophysicist boss broke the news to the engineering team at morning coffee. Mike was not an unworldly man and I never have understood why he thought a crowd of engineering 'techo's', many of them ex-servicemen, would be pleased that he had recruited an ex-Royal Navy Commander. A dinkum Aussie ex-officer would have been bad enough, but an ex-RN'er . . . .! When I arrived, the team had been assigned naval ranks and a complete Ship's Watch Bill had been posted on a lab door. I was the Captain, the Principal Electronics Engineer the First Lieutenant and so on down to a 'bilge rat'. It was all good fun. I got the traditional Australian 'fair go' from the team and I'm happy that some who were there remain friends to this day.

The Commonwealth Public Servants of Australia are not held in high regard by the rest of the nation. The feeling is more intense than that of the British towards their Civil Service because, even after nearly a hundred years of Federation, many Australians still identify more with their home state rather than with the country. The public service is assumed, often by people who should know better, to be a homogeneous mass of identical 'bludgers'. Nothing could be further from the truth. My appointment, for instance, was part of BMR's quest for improvement and I probably took part in more public service reforms during my seven years there than had occurred during all the years since Federation in 1901. And having left a Britain which usually prized the generalist over the specialist, I was delighted to join a public service which had pay differentials in favour of Research Scientists and Engineers.

My unit's task was to design, make and maintain things for the scientists. To do so we had to buy materials, components, tools and other low value items every day, often with petty cash. The strongest complaint of my workforce on my first day was that the finance section only grudgingly authorised expenditure after my team went up from our basement and ground floor workshops to their offices on the fourth. After buying the items the cash had to be acquitted by returning to the fourth floor. Anything not covered by petty cash involved an even more cumbersome procedure. It was traditional 'safe' public practice and the finance team took no account of the significant cost of my team's non-productive time. Within seven years, I had a Finance Act delegation to spend the funds allocated to my unit, we all shared in the benefits of using Government Credit Cards, we had a cheque account for the firms who would not accept the card, and we held petty cash in my outer office.

Reform was not all fun. The biggest change was the introduction of program budgeting. When I joined, the number of staff I could employ was controlled by the administration. After the reform I was given an allocation of salary funds and could employ as many people as I could pay. The only snag was that I already had so many 'permanent' public servants on my books that my salary allocation was a quarter of a million dollars short when the financial year began. Not a fun situation. However, there were areas where work could be done just as well with less staff, thus allowing reductions as people left, and when the marine science program was able to sell its services overseas, the engineering support they needed brought in enough dollars to balance the books before I left. The economic rationalists were in the driving seat in the Department of Finance and in the administration of the Bureau, and I was reminded yet again that 'Nothing is impossible to the person who doesn't have to do it'.

Later the unit shared the Bureau's cuts when we made some staff 'redundant' and paid them off. Frankly, I was pleased to get rid of one or two of them because we had tried the normal, long winded Public Service procedures for removing inefficient staff and found them wanting. Life in the Bureau involved many struggles with members of the administration, some of whom were classic empire builders and 'turf defenders'. For instance, I enjoyed the freedom to select staff through the recruiting process, something never possible in the navy, but it irked me that only an administrator could approve the resulting appointments and promotions. My biggest regret was that I did not mount a strong campaign to get the system reversed so that the 'Human Resources' people were the advisers, and line managers like me had the authority.

We all have our failures and occasionally they come in useful. One of my team had failed to get a promotion. We were discussing his career and he dejectedly remarked, 'It's alright for you, you've been successful, you're a Class 5 Engineer and the chief of the unit'. I didn't exactly feel pleasure in failure but I enjoyed pointing out that we all have some successes and some failures, and if I had really been successful I would have been Vice Admiral Sir Geoffrey on the other side of the world.

In some ways, naval officers lead a sheltered life. While serving we have relatively little contact with trade unions and some ex-officers have difficulty adjusting to working with them. The union to which most of my unit belonged was not a doctrinaire union driven by a head office agenda. If the members could sort out their problems within the Bureau, that was the end of the matter. The Canberra Branch Secretary did not interfere and I record my appreciation here. Even when my team became involved in national disputes I was impressed by their goodwill.

Much of the Bureau's work was done 'in the field'. During one national dispute, bans had to be imposed so my team banned 'packing, loading and driving'. Those jobs were not a formal part of the duties of para-professionals, so not only was it hard to object but most of our work was unaffected. If only all unions were as sensible.

During reviews of bureau operations I formed a jaundiced view of some high priced consultants. In one, for example, private sector firms supplied the consultants with estimates of costs for work currently done in house by the Bureau. Some months later the firms were asked to tender for equivalent work. The figures they produced then were much higher, a warning to inexperienced executives not to believe all that consultants and private sector companies tell them in reviews.

Expensive management retreats to comfortable motels at the coast provided opportunities for the 'Heads of Programs' to get to know one another better. But they also revealed that some who promoted all the 'right' trends in public, didn't co-operate at all and were following their own agenda when out of the top management's view. And the Bureau always appeared to be following the trends of the moment only for appearances sake. When the chips were down, whether the topic was more open management, occupational health and safety, or whatever, there was little evidence of a real change of heart by the top management.

The Engineering Unit's was to be reviewed by a very high priced engineer from a major management consultancy. His credentials revealed that he had never actually managed an engineering organisation and at my request the Superintendent of one of the defence laboratories was co-opted to bring relevant experience to the review team. My opinion of the consultants reached a new low when they virtually asked at a formal meeting what conclusion the Bureau management would like them to reach! I had to smile though when, after I pointed out that in one matter they had reached the same conclusion as I had and no one had believed me, their leader Hugh commented, 'Geoff, you just don't charge enough!'

I had been delighted when I was offered the BMR job and enjoyed all the new experiences, new things to learn and even the struggles during my seven years there. I was pleased that I had been hired to bring new blood to a loyal and hardworking engineering unit, not to shut it down. However, I had completed most of the reforms in the first five years, and all that was left was to preside over a team which was having to make more and more cuts without corresponding cuts in commitments. There was strong pressure from the scientists to break up the unit and distribute the engineering support to their programs. I opposed this.

The scientists I've worked with over the years have often taken a short term view of what they want from their engineering support. If, for example, they happened to have analogue electronics in their instruments, they often failed to give their engineering technicians time and encouragement to learn digital techniques against the day when there would be new instruments to maintain. Some technical staff at BMR suffered from that kind of neglect before the unit was formed. They were a good team and deserved better. By 1992, I had said my piece on their behalf. I was as happy to leave the Bureau as I had been to join it.

Joining BMR had prompted me to join the Institution of Engineers, Australia. I did not join when I arrived in Australia because the Institution had a nexus between the grades of membership, military ranks and academic status. I had been a Fellow of the UK Mechanicals since 1973 and would not join the IEAust as a Member just because I was merely a Commander in the navy. Now, in 1985, I was senior enough to be eligible for election as a Fellow and becoming one would give the BMR engineering team a presence in engineering circles in Canberra which it had hitherto lacked.

There was an excellent additional reason for joining. The Institution had begun its own program of reforms. Recognising that as a single institution representing all branches of engineering it had a great advantage over the multitude of specialised engineering institutions which existed in larger countries, it was now keen to go beyond its role as a learned society and become the leading voice of the engineering profession, influencing and enjoying the confidence of the Federal, State and Territory governments. Symbols are important in marking points at which directions change. The Institution said goodbye to its last Secretary and welcomed its first Chief Executive, retired Rear Admiral Bill Rourke.

It was a good time to begin to repay the profession for the pleasure it had given me over the years. I had been a passive member of the Mechanicals, now it was time to become an activist. As usual in Australia, anyone willing to stand at the front and be shot at is welcome and I had the pleasure of becoming the Chairman of the Canberra Division only five years after joining. The haste was not intentional, just a consequence of joining so late in my working life and of a wish to make my contribution before I retired. Combining employment and service to the Institution was a good idea but a bit hectic. When the Chairmen of Divisions compared notes before a National Council meeting we agreed that it was like having an extra fifty per cent of a full time job.

It was worth the effort. My year was 1990, the first full year of self government in the ACT, the year in which the division was responsible for the annual National Engineering Conference, and the year in which Canberra became a city with engineering faculties in three universities. One of the first things I ever learned about engineering was the need to respect the draughtsmen and tradesmen, without whose skills professionals could make great blunders. An interest in the relationships between professionals and para-professionals became one of my special interests so it gave me particular pleasure to be a member of the National Council when we voted unanimously to invite 'the techo's' to join the Institution as Associates, increasing still further the usefulness of the Institution as the voice of the senior levels of Australia's engineering community.

Holding office in the Institution and representing the Division brought all kinds of pleasures and rewards. Some were professional, like the accreditation proceedings of the University of Canberra and the accreditation of courses at the Canberra College of Technical and Further Education and the Australian Maritime College in Tasmania. Some were historic ceremonies like the installation of the First Chancellor at the inauguration of the University of Canberra. Many were sheer pleasure, like the annual dinners of other professional institutions and learned societies. Perhaps the most unusual, for Lise and I, was standing at the entrance to the Great Hall of the new Parliament House with the National President and his wife welcoming the guests to the reception marking the beginning of the Institution's National Conference. After shaking about five hundred hands Lise had a good idea how the Queen feels about those who try to show their respect by excessive firmness.

However ordinary they may have been in worldly terms, those last few years of engineering gave me great pleasure. They were the last because an idea had been implanted in my mind thirty years earlier by one of my bosses at AUWE. He believed that when an engineer or scientist retired from professional work, manual labour was the best recipe for continuing health and satisfaction. He was a sailing man and a woodworker, and he went to work in a boatyard. His idea was right for me. 'Feasey Enterprises' was born just before I retired from the BMR. Some people scorn whimsy as a form of humour. I don't and Feasey Enterprises was an example. A footnote on the letterhead explained that, 'The trading name was used by Geoff Feasey for many years as a test of his public sector decisions: "Is this what I would do if this were Feasey Enterprises and I was spending my own money?"' I wasn't spending much money but I liked the name. My flier described three different activities, occupational health and safety services, sculptural woodwork, and home repairs and renovations.

The first paid well but my retirement coincided with a recession and there was little work there, the second brought modest recognition as a woodworker, modest being defined as having more than half the work offered to prestigious local galleries accepted. The third brought plenty of work and could easily have been expanded to provide a business for Peter, who was unemployed after dropping out of university some years earlier. The strategy was that people would have the confidence to give FE jobs because I would guarantee the quality of the work. Unfortunately, although Peter was a excellent workman in many fields, he was not interested in building that particular business. When he was not available, I employed casual labour and had the satisfaction of giving a few otherwise unemployed young men a few weeks of work.

The business closed after a final collection of woodwork for the 1997 Christmas market. Now, a year later, the book is nearly finished. What next? It's too late to go into politics but something is sure to turn up to supplement supporting the Institution of Engineers, using my Pommie voice, described as posh by an old friend in Hull, as a narrator for the 'Hear a Book' organisation, and 'fixing things' for friends.

And, would you believe, during my years in Australia, news reached me that not only had the Directorate of Systems Co-ordination been disbanded, but the whole Directorate General of which it was a part had gone. 'Cold comfort', said I. 'Never mind', said my informant, 'You said your piece as you thought fit'. And so I did!

Chapter 23

Sittin' and Thinkin'

People are lucky if, towards the end of a fortunate life, having had varied experiences around the world, and having done some sittin' and thinkin', they feel they have made some sense of life, the universe and everything. And if, unlike Kipling's soldier, they believe the future of the world offers more than 'Hellfires to see', they may be tempted to pass on their views. I am tempted.

Many mysteries remain. Why do we insist in increasing the world's population when starvation will be the inevitable outcome for millions? Why is there no leader of a democratic country brave enough to tell the electorate that there will never ever be full employment again unless either we squander the world's resources in a lemming-like quest for 'growth' or we learn to take more modest rewards for our labours? Why do people in this driest of continents and in many other places fail to recognise that fresh water is the resource which ultimately limits our planet's ability to support human life?

And why do so many of our fellows in the USA profess to believe the absurdity that all men are created equal when the evidence clearly indicates the variability of intellect, health and strength? Why has so much expenditure on education failed to teach everyone the probabalistic nature of both natural and civilised life? Why do we not recognise that one of the few certainties of economics is that, in the absence of sufficient intervention in a capitalist economy, wealth converges, leading first to the development of an underclass and ultimately perhaps to revolution, peaceful or violent?

Why have we found it so difficult to recognise that even if man is only an animal in 'The Human Zoo' many members of the species have moral instincts? Why have we not nurtured those

317

instincts instead of allowing religious vested interests to lead many people into ways of uncritical obedience, bigotry and even murderous hatred. Why have we failed to show those young people who turn away from the bigotry that other moral directions are possible?

Yes, it's tempting to write a few paragraphs on each of these themes and then to go on to discuss others such as the illogicality of having nine governments in a country of less than eighteen million people, the particular problems of a vast, empty, arid country with a small, very young, population, and the practical problems of supporting the central government of a vast country from a city, however beautiful, which only has a population of three hundred thousand. And to brood on contemporary social and managerial behaviour, especially as it applies to personal relationships, with its emphasis on communication to the exclusion of the old doctrine of 'Least said, soonest mended'.

As Morris West concluded in 'View from the Ridge', it is a mad world. We must make what sense of it we can, each in our own way. So just for once I shall resist the temptation to jump in.